CRISIS IN BLACK SEXUAL POLITICS

For information address:

BLACK THINK TANK
1801 Bush Street, #127
San Francisco, California 94109

ISBN: 0-9613086-2-1
Printed in the United States of America

To the memory of our parents:

Beatrice Brown Reed

Tishia Davis Hare

Will H. Reed

Seddie H. Hare

Prologue

At the moment of any historic challenge confronted by a once great people (the African Slave Trade, the Middle Passage, The Fall of Rome, the Holocaust, Hiroshima) caught in a whirlwind of physical destruction and psychological dehumanization, there is one thing that must endure across rivers and oceans of uncharted space and immeasurable time if a people are to survive -- the family.

But, when all else has failed, it is but one portion of the intelligentsia, the truly intellectual, who can bring this about, who can and must show the way to their contemporaries. For every one of these, there must be hundreds, thousands, more to foment and spotlight the relentless swarm of social contradictions such individuals of historical distinction will call out to the surface and uncover.

The distinguished contributors to this volume, among the best minds dealing with the black family today, may turn out to embody, for all we know, both levels of intellectual endeavor, one no less vital though generally less heralded and visible to the other. Like our readers, they live in a time that may prove more salient than the Industrial Revolution in its impact on human evolution, perhaps the final stage of white domination, a time of desperation and a time of the most spectacular human transformations (some potentially disastrous) that the world has ever known.

Of special relation to the African race, it is a time when the black family has crumbled more in the past two decades than the slave ship and centuries of chattel slavery could fathom. And this demise of the black or African family, in whatever degree in variegated ways, is worldwide and connected.

The essays to follow are presented here in the undying hope that the ideas they contain can, pitted together, give voice to a thunderous new dialogue, an explosive mental force of black reflection and potential sufficient to break through the intellectual blinders now permitting the systematic destruction of the most intimate and basic human relations in the black race worldwide, if not the destruction of the very earth itself.

It is in these times that the intellectuals must put aside the security of their apathy and fear and emerge once more from their soporific cocoons of political inaction and moral petrification, once and for all determined no longer to fail their roles; to every last person quivering but facing the final call of their people's unique mission. Only then can the people themselves (in the fading farmlands of the South, in the ghetto projects and skyscrapers of the inner cities) begin to speak with them; the people who would inhabit the new world, who can do this only by harking unashamedly to their past and speaking, in words unexpurgated, to their future.

Nathan Hare
San Francisco, 1988

i

Foreword

by Congressman Gus Savage

In Black communities all across the country, there have been meetings and conferences aimed at improving Black male-female relationships and building Black families that might be in disarray. Too often we tend to be overly combative toward one another, without fully examining the external forces. We live the Black experience, in many instances, on a social tight rope.

The Census reports that Black women, as opposed to white women, are more likely to be married to men who have less education than they do. The result is that professional Blacks may have a difficult time relating to, or living with, other Blacks who are not as skilled or educated.

Relatedly, a high inner city murder rate, other violent crimes, drugs, unemployment, and the prison system divert many Blacks away from normal family lives. Many find themselves struggling to survive in a racist system that will let them struggle but not survive.

The abandonment of children and wives by Black men, on the other hand, creates a hardship for many Black women who find themselves as the heads of households. The recession makes this condition worse since many of these women find the cost of living rising while their incomes are not. The extra income from another member of the household is sorely missed.

More frustration sets in. Distrust mounts. Some population experts are predicting that by the year 2000, eight out of every ten Black households in Chicago, for example, will be fatherless.

Blacks are subjected to all forms of discrimination and these realities become pressures on struggling Black families. Many Blacks, spurred by media reports praising the merits of the single life, come to the conclusion that they can go it alone.

We must strive to come together and build stronger families in the tradition of our African ancestors. We must be attuned to and resist the changing social attitudes toward marriage and quick legal proceedings which make divorce easy and painless.

We must build strong Black families to build stronger communities.

Contents

Part III: Relationships

Part IV: Solutions

PART I:

THE CRISIS

The Crisis In Black Sexual Politics

by Nathan Hare, Ph.D. and Julia Hare, Ed.D.

Although just about everybody now recognizes and concedes the existence of a crisis in the black family, few people appear to be much aware of the crisis in black sexual politics itself or in the white world's sexual-socioeconomic politics that fashion and shape the crisis in the black family. Largely unwary of these subtle forces and machinations, black leaders and intellectuals who now struggle earnestly to address and correct the black family's punishing condition (though belatedly following a two-decades decision to fall silent on the matter) today risk contributing directly, though inadvertently, to the very things that gave rise to and continue to perpetuate the black family crisis in the first place.

The black family has festered in the unisexual white feminist sun ever since the curtain came down on the patriarchy-based but gender-inclusive black consciousness movement of the late 1960s. Refusing to be denied, the black family crisis in America (subsidiary to a worldwide dimension — as we shall see later), first manifested itself in an angry, splintering black male/female rift.[1] Almost as quickly came relentless waves of devastating family decay that lashed, undaunted, against the collective denial that encased and shielded the silenced and cowering black intellectual class. The "black family crisis" exploded suddenly and undeniably in the faces of the white populace and black intellectuals and leaders alike, as they sat in the mid-1980s watching television screens flashing mass white media hype.

What zoomed into focus was a white-media defined "crisis" composed of an alleged new frenzy of black teenage pregnancy, seething bands of unemployable and socially irresponsible young males, broken marriages, never-

1

married or no-longer-married single mothers, latchkey and neglected children, growing illegitimacy, high dropout rates, difficulties in the discipline of the children in fatherless families and in inner-city public schools, chronic welfare families, and low academic and socioeconomic achievement among black youth reaching proportions which no longer could be denied, rationalized, tolerated silently, or even fully explained. Like a one-two punch, these tragic conditions were mercilessly compounded, almost at once, and complicated additionally by the cocaine and crack addiction sweeping black communities like killer forest fires, engulfing young male adults and adolescents in drive-by shooting gang warfare fomented by the lucrative drug traffic which, even as we write, continues to drag down and destroy the collective black psyche.

Ominously, the unconscionable decade and a half of black intellectual neglect of the troubled black family and, therefore, the black child (particularly the black male) in the political naivete and apathy that gripped the black intellectual class (blacked out of the media, especially book publishing and public print in all but "crossover" or white feminist-validating expressions during the 1970s decade of unisexualization) was rushing back in a hail of sociological vengeance to haunt the black intellectual class still sleeping through the artificial euphoria of the "me" generation's cult of narcissism.

In the late spring of 1984, as government and corporate policymakers were zeroing in on the welfare mothers (a minority of the poor, with chronic or perennial cases variously estimated at 15 per cent or less, and having hardly anything to do with the rising marital and family problems of the middle class black woman), projecting the welfare mother as the supposed cause of the mounting epidemic of black family decay,[2] we wrote a guest column on the editorial page of *USA Today*.[3] Among other things, we described the emergence of pulverized male/female relations no longer to be denied:

> "Increasingly, the black woman finds herself affluent without a man to satisfy, while the black man is broke with too many women. Faced with the hardships of traumatized relations, many black women give up on the desire to be loved by a man. They fall into a kind of sexual anorexia, protesting: 'I don't need a man.'

> "The black man, frequently unable to provide for his family and thus keep its respect, is impelled too often to flee the family nest — leaving the black woman with the formidable task of being mother and father to her children.

> "Where once there were pretty women and working men, there now are pretty men and working women.

"Lay it down as a sociological law: In a patriarchal society, where men are expected to provide for their families, there can be no socio-economically viable race without a socio-economically viable male.

"The bottom line is that the black woman cannot be a woman, no matter how that may be defined, any more than a black man can be admitted to full manhood privileges. To subjugate her, white society defeminizes her, just as it emasculates the black man.

"Just when the black woman is poised to gain recognition for her beauty, white society decides that beauty doesn't matter in a woman.

"Just when she is poised to gain access to the home as a housewife, to be dependent on her man (something historically denied her), she is told that it is a privilege to have to work.

"Just as she ascends the pedestal, the pedestal itself is scorned. Once again, white society has changed the rules of the game.

"This time, the goal is to turn the nonwhite poor away from marriage and childbirth. Why? Becasue white America sees the nonwhite 'population explosion' as a powderkeg of potential social unrest.

"Meanwhile, it devotes its scientific energies to ensuring that the infertile white upper middle class can reproduce itself.

"The result: more lonely black women, fewer black babies, and a generation of emasculated black men. It's not just another social problem; it's the extinction of a race."

However, black intellectuals have continued to ignore this two-pronged agenda in the systematic maintenance of white socio-eco-political dominance. In the summer of 1987, one of the authors addressed the sociological impotence of the black intellectual class more forthrightly and urgently in a "speaking out" editorial commissioned by *Ebony* for its special issue on "The New Black Middle Class," debating the national president of The Links on the designated subject, "Is the Black Middle Class Blowing It?"[4]

Saying "yes" to the question, our editorial placed a part of the problem in the political blindness middle class intellectuals experience in the awesome glare of white propaganda and mass media persuasion:

"Getting their cues from their white liberal friends, (black middle class leaders) look to white society for their definitions of reality, unwittingly lagging as many as ten or 20 years behind their white mentors. Indeed, the black middle class takes no stand on any of the

3

major issues of the day, beyond silent consent to the white liberal-moderate viewpoint.

"What is the black position on Baby M, surrogate mothering, genetics engineering, population control, AIDS testing, child abuse 'protection' modalities which too often disintegrate discipline and black families further, drug testing of athletes but not surgeons and pilots, 'voluntary' sterilization, or even abortion or 'black feminism?'

"Without a clear vision, black middle class men may too often coalesce with white females romantically, while black women too readily embrace them politically. Thus black men and women of the rainbow variety are forever chasing rainbows.

"In the late 1960s," the editorial went on to say, "when the unisexual, anti-family movement (designed to get control of the means of reproduction) was launched by the comparatively infertile white Western world, the black middle class first relegated the precipitous decline of the black family to lower class origins, then bawled that the recognition of any problem was an attack on 'the black image' or 'blaming the victim.' While black middle class persons endeavored to discover and applaud black family 'strengths' and to deny 'pathology,' the black family crumbled more in the 15 years from 1969 to 1984 than in the century or more since the end of slavery to 1969.

"However, no sooner had they recognized the black family 'crisis' than they rushed to accept solutions from the white society -- the mass employment of the black males they had rejected when proposed by Daniel Moynihan in 1965 (before millions of new jobs went to married white women), teenage pregancy, welfare mothers, and even family decay itself -- the highest forms of 'blaming the victim.' Accordingly, the black middle class is collaborating with the white world's contradictory and amoral (value-free) program of curbing the fertility of these black groups. This includes planting condoms in black high schools under the guise of a white-instigated 'sexual education.'"

The white world has already handicapped black academic/literacy education. What makes black leaders believe that a white-directed sexual education will produce any better results? The most we can expect is that black children soon will be flunking sex courses.

We have concluded that the greatest crisis in black sexual politics rests in the inability of the black intellectual class to understand and confront the problem at its sources, petrified by a crisis in comprehension, a crisis in identity,

4

and a crisis in courage. Failing to understand the true and deeper sources of the breakdown in the black family, black intellectuals unconsciously are led to collaborate inevitably with the forces of decay.

Nevertheless, we did not worry exceedingly much when black California Assemblywoman Maxine Waters boasted in *Ms.* magazine (*circa* 1984) that she had persuaded Jesse Jackson to reverse his early 1980s presidential-bid opposition to abortion in what would prove (predictably it seems to us) a futile effort to win the white feminist vote. Sterilization -- not abortion -- is the issue for the black race in America. Besides, as Pennsylvania State University sociologist, Thomas Shapiro, has noted in his *Population Control Politics,*[5] the experts already know that as abortion goes down, sterilization goes up. Especially is this so for blacks and the poor, who already suffer far higher comparative rates of sterilization.

In 1981, one year before our own independently conceived article on the subject, "Unisexualization: Blueprint for Genocide," appeared in *Black Male/Female Relationships,*[6] Angela Davis presented a thoughtful and pioneering chapter on sterilization (but one ignored by black intellectuals as a group) in the back of her book, *Women, Class and Race.* In a paperback edition of her book published in 1983, the chapter, "Racism, Birth Control and Reproductive Rights,"[7] came as a breath of clean air in a book otherwise adhering, true to black intellectual form, to a white feminist mindset and agenda: for instance, the notion that black female slaves were "locked in their roles as women." Actually, black female slaves were locked in their roles as slaves and, if anything in many ways, locked out of their roles as wives and mothers, sold apart from their children, husbands and mates, and chained to the care and feeding of the children of the white mistress and involuntary service (often sexual) to their white masters.

It is no wonder, then, that the black woman is traveling down the pike between the enforced fertility of the slavery era and the "voluntary" sterilization of today, particularly on the continent of Africa. Abortion, in the Western world and its tentacles of influence and domain, is essentially an issue for the white bourgeoisie, with white conservatives such as Ronald Reagan concerned that abortion is contributing to the white "birth dearth"[8] as the white population teeters at the waterfall of numerical decline in America and worldwide, on the brink of potential extinction -- if the trend of diminished white fertility is not reversed. In simple terms, the white race needs the babies, and it is abortion, not pregnancy, which most contributes to the black/white differences in teenage and unwed motherhood.

What the white world is doing now is amassing an armamentarium of means (seldom but sometimes openly acknowledged) to encourage white fertility while

5

simultaneously seeking to curb black fertility. For instance, although the now severely infertile European nations openly proffer maternal benefits to entice and pay their women to give birth to children ("fertility incentives"), these incentives are presented in the United States as privileges or women's rights to be fought for. Although the way in which they are formulated will mainly funnel benefits to middle class whites, they are presented as "universal" (class-free and race-free) benefits. Moreover, the contrasting approaches to white/black fertility will affect the black and white family structures differently, contributing to a white return to family and a simultaneous boomerang of black family/social decay.

It is appalling to see black intellectuals reaching out to embrace the European-style fertility incentives. The black intellectuals do this for a variety of unacknowledged reasons but expressly, incredibly, in the paradoxical hope of bringing *down* fertility among the black poor!

Among European-style fertility incentives now fostered by liberals, but endorsed in general or at least in practice by white moderates, conservatives, and the rainbow of black intellectual leaders alike, are: 1) child-centered tax benefits; 2) child care benefits; 3) maternity leave/paternity leave; and 4) guaranteed rights to the job after childbirth (but not after a furlough to start a business, cultivate a cherished hobby, tour Europe or complete a college degree). In America, such benefits will accrue disproportionately and even overhwelmingly to the middle class, that is to say, the whites and the token black bourgeoisie. While programs aimed at the poor (that is to say blacks, statistically and sociologically speaking) -- and more about this later -- are demanded of the government, programs aimed at the middle class (i.e., the whites, in predictable sociological impact) are demanded of corporate employers and insurance compaines backed only by goverment sanction through tax breaks or direct legal enforcement. (Get-tough policies on child support payments will contrarily generate more dollars from the middle class but impact more negatively on the black and the poor males who simply cannot afford to support two households).

In order to derive child-centered tax breaks from corporate employment, a person must be employed in the corporation. This obviously will sidestep the black unemployed or/and underemployed poor. The same is true of maternity leave or parental leave. You must have a corporate job to get fertility and childcare benefits (and generally a two-earner family) to be able and motivated to receive this incentive to have children. We do not begrudge childcare benefits to white mothers, let alone single mothers. But approximately 88 per cent of white children six years old or less, by last count, live in two-parent families. Many, if not most, of these white mothers (and their spouses) can pay for their own childcare. An objective or neutral approach to childcare, in any case, would be means-tested, based on a sliding scale or ability to pay. Generally, these days in America as in Europe it is proposed as "universal" on the premise that it should be and is "color-blind." The estimated two billion dollars plus a year anticipated for childcare will not be available through these means for the homeless or the otherwise more needy poor. Indeed, as Ronald Reagan has acknowledged, childcare will, on the one hand, permit or encourage the employed middle class woman (read "white," numerically speaking) to stay home sufficiently to produce and rear a child, while, contrarily, on the other hand, it will enable (or in fact, as programmed, expressly or operationally) require the low income black mother to seek alternatives in the workplace, to childbirth. Like an elevator, the same device can be programmed to go up or down; like some pills may hype up adults but calm down children. In the end, the childcare incentives will program poor black women for employment, through skills training and family-planning (in many cases employed as glorified new black nannies and childcare paraprofessionals for affluent white children while the white professional/managerial mothers seek psychological fulfillment and "identity" in the corporate world).

It is a curious development, in any case, when, as we write on this very day, we look up to see in the San Francisco *Examiner*, an article, "Parental Leave Gets Senate OK,"[9] which we now excerpt for you:

> "Bills to require companies to grant childrearing leaves of up to four months and to require group insurance plans to offer infertility coverage were passed by the Senate [state of California].
>
> "...The parental leave bill, AB2738, by Assemblywoman Gwen Moore, D-Los Angeles, was returned to the Assembly on a vote of 21-10.
> "It would make it against the law for employers of 25 or more people to refuse to grant a request by employees to take a leave of up to four months for child rearing.
>
> "...It limits child rearing leave to one month when taken in conjunction with maximum pregnancy leave of four months.
>
> "...The infertility bill, AB2787 by Assemblywoman Maxine Water, D-Los Angeles, was sent to the Assembly on a vote of 24-6. It requires group health plans and policies that are issued or renewed after Jan. 1, 1989, to offer coverage for infertility drugs treatments. The measure was amended [by the Senate, having already passed the Assembly] to exclude controversial coverage for in-vitro or 'test tube' baby fertilization."

However, we can expect that the forces of reproductive control and neo-eugenics will return to the issue of test tubes and artificial fertilization later. But,

7

for the moment, the most curious thing about these two bills (for parental leave and infertility treatment) is that they both were presented to the legislature by black women politicians -- Assemblywomen Gwen Moore and Maxine Waters. (With no Bella Abzug-type black female or male liberal in the California senate, the champion of the bills in the Senate was a white male liberal).

The pity is that the black women legislators probably believe that the bills are designed to benefit blacks. If so, in this the politicians may be following the lead of black University of Chicago sociologist William Wilson, who in 1987, in a much hyped book, *The Truly Disadvantaged*[10] (a book fast becoming the bible of white/black policymakers on the black family) echoed the white University of Houston political scientist, Harold R. Rodgers (in *Poor Women, Poor Families*[11] published the previous year, 1986) in advocating "universal" European-style fertility incentives as paradoxical means of decreasing fertility in the black "underclass" (the black poor). Wilson justifies the universal approach on grounds that race-specific or class-specific incentives would stigmatize black welfare women, damaging their self-esteem and motivation. In other words, Wilson will give the money to the white middle class that doesn't need it, and whose magnitude would bring the total bill to a staggering sum, in order to avoid stigmatizing those who need it. Except that to bring down the fertility of black welfare poor, he would give them what Europeans give their women to bring fertility up.

Wilson's book, if it continues to catch on, may have as devastating an effect on black intellectual thought in the 1980s and 1990s as Andrew Billingsley's *Black Families in White America*[12] had on black family thought in the 1970s, with its championing of the admonishments designed by white intellectuals, Talcott Parsons and Erik Erikson, urging that black intellectuals deny and turn away from black family "pathology" to emphasize black family "strengths."

On the positive side, Wilson and his collaborators at the University of Chicago presented figures confirming (and notifying most black intellectuals) that the much-hyped black teenage pregnancy explosion was a myth, that when black teenage pregnancy was hyped as a crisis in the mid-1980s, it had been going *down* for twenty years. Wilson also presented evidence, though evidence already known to demographers, suggesting that the differences in the rates of black and white illegitimacy result not so much from higher black teen pregnancy as from low or delayed marriage, from the fact that young black females, compared to white females, don't get married fast enough. Black females marry later and, when they divorce, are slower to remarry. While a pro-fertility policy might encourage black females (and males) to marry, an anti-fertility policy seeks to prevent the births instead, if not the marriages. Wilson also provided an operational validation of the impact of the much talked about "black male shortage" on the black woman's chances for marriage (called a "male-marriageable-pool" by Wilson and his collaborators).

Nevertheless, Wilson turns right around and, far from advocating black-male-augmenting remedies, focuses instead on the welfare underclass female for solutions. Not only that, his package of remedies is filled with European-style fertility incentives. Thus, while recognizing the crucial place of the broken black male patriarchy in provoking black family instability (for the middle class as well as the poor), Wilson uses the underclass black woman's plight to endorse universal fertility incentives not only for the white woman but also paradoxically as a proposal to lower the fertility of the black poor! Already, black intellectuals are jumping on Wilson's bandwagon; and these intellectuals include black nationalists and rainbow or mainstream blacks as well.

On the heels of Wilson, Marian Wright Edelman also had the perspicacity to discern the falsity of the allegedly exploding black teen pregnancy media hype which snared black intellectuals in the mid-1980s. Edelman, president of the Children's Defense Fund, doused this propaganda in her 1986 "W.E.B. DuBois Lectures" sponsored by the Ford Foundation and delivered at Harvard University, and published by Harvard the following year in her book, *Families in Peril*.[13] But Edelman did not skip a beat in her collaboration with the teenage pregnancy hoax as a black priority, diverting money and attention from more essential and in the long run consequential pursuits, including an indigenous and more effective and beneficial black-conceived and black-timed approach to teen pregnancy.

As we write, Mrs. Edelman is attempting to lead a coalition of "labor unions, Christian and Jewish groups, education and feminist organizations" to capitalize on the "election-year momentum" and pass the day-care bill. However, the church-state issue was threatening the "largely liberal coalition that has brought the measure further than appeared possible even a few months ago."[14] Although the bill, as it now stands before Congress, bars child-care organizations from engaging in "any sectarian purpose or activity," it dropped provisions "dealing with removing religious symbols" and "prohibitions against religious discrimination in employment," igniting the opposition of Jewish groups and heavily Jewish-influenced organizations -- "including the National Education Association, American Jewish Committee, Baptist Joint Committee on Public Affairs, and National Organization for women.[15]

It may be at least of passing interest to note that Edelman and Wilson are two of a handful of black intellectuals to receive the coveted MacArthur "genius" award. The MacArthur award, which cannot be solicited, is given to persons hand-picked by the foundation. Recipients receive as much as half a million dollars over a five-year period, gratis, to continue what the MacArthur Foundation believes to be good and creative work. What Wright and Wilson have in common is not so much their "genius," nor even the happy affection of fate, as their ingenious collaboration with the forces of white control of black reproduction.

In a capitalistic democracy, the ruling interests are not served or implemented exclusively by the government. Especially is this true of financial backing; private and corporate support may be expected, as expressly anticipated by the Commission on Population Growth and the American Future established by Congress in 1970 and chaired by the late John D. Rockefeller III, for the purpose of getting control of the means of reproduction in order to defuse the "power keg" of worldwide nonwhite population growth and simultaneously or sequentially to augment the waning fertility of the white race.

The *New York Times* reports this month (September 1988) that "two of the wealthiest foundations in the United States are starting multi-million-dollar programs to curb unwanted [sic] population growth in Asia, Africa and Latin America.[16] The largest donor of the two will be the MacArthur Foundation, with $23 million. The other, the David and Lucille Packard Foundation, "enriched by a $2 billion commitment from Mr. Packard, is reshaping its population undertaking, and will expand from less than $1 million a year to $10 million annually. Before the new commitments, total financing for family planning abroad by American philanthropies was $30 million to $35 million annually."

U.S. Agency for International Development, "a major supplier of contraceptives to third world counties," in a disagreement over "approach" with the International Planned Parenthood Federation and the United Nations Fund for Population Activities, has cut its family planning funds from $290 million in 1985 to $230 million. However, the United Nations Population Fund, has increased its budget from $156 milion to $176 million, with "bigger contributions from Japan and Western European governments while Planned Parenthood Federation's resources also increased ... from $61 million last year to $72 million." Further, the MacArthur Foundation will make annaual awards of $15,000 to $30,000 to "young potential leaders who can affect population policy in such countries as Mexico, Brazil, India and at least two African nations" and will also "select a group of population organizations for $100,000 to $150,000 awards."

Meanwhile, the Rockefeller Foundation, working on contraceptive development, is supporting "a number of African scientists" in "testing a male contraceptive pill, gosypol, developed in China." The Rockefeller Foundation, continuing in its major role, will spend $60 million to $75 million over the next five years, according to its director of population sciences, Dr. Shedon J. Segal. They are joined by the Mellon Foundation, the Ford Foundation, the Carnegie Foundation, the Pew Charitable Trusts and the William and Flora Hewlett Foundation. The focus will be on "self-determination" and "culturally appropriate services" promoted by indigenous leaders and organizations in "the sea change that is under way led by the big foundations." The MacArthur Foundation has called a meeting of organizations supporting reproductive control to be held this fall in an unspecified location.

All this despite the fact that the 1948 Genocide Treaty, which the United States did not sign until almost forty years later, forbids the control of the births of one population or nation by another. Self-generated population control by individuals or groups is a human right, backed by age-old wisdom; control of one's population by outside nations, not to mention oppressor nations, is genocide, without rhetoric or hyperbole.

As things now stand, we are falling into a sociological trap. For instance, Psychiatrist Frances Cress Welsing, was one of the few black intellectuals, female or male, to disdain the 1970s black intellectual defense mechanism of collective denial of the emerging problems in the black family. She also captured the black nationalist intellectual imagination in the early 1970s with her "Cress Theory of Color Confrontation," suggesting that whites fear genetic annihilation by blacks and that the terror of this fear incites in them a sociobiological imperative to suppress the rise of the black race. However, in an obviously mid-1980s article in our files, "When Birth Is a Tragedy -- Black Teenage Reproduction,"[17] carrying Welsing's byline but undated, Welsing points to correlations of teen pregnancy with alcoholism, delinquency, crime, marital decay, and other problems, then mistakenly takes teen pregnancy to be the cause of the other problems. As a matter of fact, these social problems and teenage pregnancy are similarly the product of poverty and cultural disintegration.

Understand that we are not suggesting that teen pregnancy is in anyway desirable or that it shouldn't be discouraged, especially for young girls 15 or under (less than two percent of the tenagers who get pregnant anyway). Indeed, we should not need white people to tell us that. Nor do we need white people to tell us when decreasing teen pregnancy should become our priority; especially when it serves their own interests or agenda instead of ours and has been going down for twenty years anyway. We must take care not to be deceived into misdirecting our already overwrought energies into programs which, even if successful, will not solve our problems and, in many cases, inadvertently compound them. We must look beneath the surface of things or white society will continue to send us off on all kinds of enticing and persuasive but misleading detours.

Remember, Black teenagers are not poor because they give birth; they give birth because they are poor. (Middle class teenagers get abortions when their greater access to birth control devices and strategies fail them). This is especially true of whites. Regardless of whether only affluent children can have fulfilling lives, as things now stand, most teenagers in the slums aren't likely to get very far in the socioeconomic sphere, whether they get pregnant or not. By contrast both Jesse Jackson's mother and his mother-in-law were teenage mothers. Indeed, the boys are generally regarded as worse off than the girls, psychologically and socioeconomically, and to drop out of school and the marketplace more.

11

And the boys don't get pregnant. Nor is it a proven fact that only the black children of teenagers are going astray.

Until our time, as a matter of fact, teenage was the typical age of first pregnancy all over the world. Black scholars such as Welsing who now join whites in claiming that teenage pregnancy is by nature pathological forget this centuries old fact. At best they are looking at *social* puberty instead of *biological* puberty. A case could be made that the real pathology is in the extreme length of time that society has placed between physical and social puberty. Even today, according to World Bank figures, 50 per cent of all females 15 to 17 years old in black Africa, taken as a whole, are married. In Lybia, one of the most advanced Arab nations, 70 per cent of all females 15 to 17 years old are married.[18]

Obviously, if teenage pregnancy is socially pathological, society has made it so; and society can unmake it so, just as they are doing now with motherhood and mothering for the white middle class today. Even white feminists, who once regarded motherhood (and even male/female gender differences) as oppressive, now as a group are conspicuously calling for fertility and motherhood rights, confessing that the labor force is not the haven it once appeared to be, that they may have been shortchanged or duped, that they now would like to be mothers, after all, even if it is mainly because the opinionmakers now tell them they should.

In any event, as we stated in a column, "Family Affair," in *The Final Call,* August 20, 1988.[19]

"The problem with black teenagers is not so much that they are getting pregnant as that they aren't marrying. Also, we have not setup the structures to ensure their ability and motivation to continue their education, pregnant, married or not. If the black intellectual class didn't shortsightedly agree with white rulers that there are 'too many niggers' these days (and could allow our imaginations to run free of white values [as the contributors to this volume, *Crisis in Black Sexual Politics,* have done], could begin to value once more our own children and once more to rear them for productive lives), we could even evolve or find ways -- if we set our minds creatively to the effort -- to eradicate the social pathology of teenage pregnancy that the white world itself has made."

We must begin to understand that, while the white power structure, aided and abetted by black intellectual leaders, promotes fertility incentives for the vast white middle class, it endeavors to stifle the fertility of blacks (that is, the poor, the welfare women, and the poor teens). Fertility in married black adults already has followed white patterns in the deep and longterm post-baby-boom decline; especially in the case of the black middle class. However, white opinionmakers camouflaged and manipulated this fact by computing teenage pregnancy rates as a proportion of the total. Although black teenage pregnancy had been going down for twenty years, it was deceptively made to appear to be going up (by statistically exploiting the fact that the black married adult rate was going down even faster than the teenage rate).

Those persons who suggest that only middle class people, or those best able to afford children should be allowed to produce them, are elitist at best, as most black children would never have been born. Such eugenicists should also oppose universal child care, public school education, playgrounds, other traditional support to chldren by society or persons other than their parents.

By hyping a spurious black teenage upswing, the white opinionmakers were able to kill three birds with one stone: 1) launch a stepped-up program to deneuter one of the most fertile black groups in the white neo-eugenicist determination to cutback on the population growth of the black poor (with enthusiastic support and collaboration of black intellectuals themselves); 2) blame the black teens who get pregnant for their own economic plight and, in part at least, the condition of the black race; and 3) justify setting up sex education clinics and handing out condoms in black schools. This is only a part of the process by which the white apparatus of the state is intruding deeper and deeper into the most intimate life of the black race and gaining an almost total control of the black child's mind -- again aided and abetted by well-meaning black intellectuals and leaders.

More surprising still (and Welsing has done this also and repeatedly in public lectures and tapes we have heard), is her advocacy that black persons not marry until they are about 30, not have children until they are well into their thirties, and limit their children to two. Actually, if black people should follow the first two steps of Welsing's essentially genocidal plan, they will not have to worry about limiting their children to two. It was only in recent years, in the white frenzy to increase their own fertility, that the safe age of birth for a woman was extended from 35 to 43.

Welsing's plan is genocidal in itself. It boggles the mind to see this coming from the creator of the black intellectual conceptual revelation of the fears expressed by the nineteenth century white racist theorists (Chamberlain and Gobineau)[20] and the World War I white American theorists (Madison Grant, *The Passing of the Great Race* (1916)[21] and Lothrop Stoddard's concerns with the "yellow peril," *The Rising Tide of Color* (1920)[22] that runaway nonwhite fertility and miscegenation will overwhelm and destroy the social structure of the white race, decimating them biologically and sociologically, if something isn't done to suppress the darker races. Yet, when presented with a live white program of genetics motivated by and geared directly (even expressly) to this fear of reproductive or genetic annihilation, Welsing inadvertently joins the program and, if anything, takes it a step further with the notion of postposing black marriages and childbirth, respectively, to 30 and 35 years old.

Frances Welsing is of course basing her program on the argument or motivation of improving the *quality* of the black race and black life. But all eugenicists argue quality, from Hitler and Shockley on down to stockbreeders. So also do racists, for that matter. What eugenicists, stockbreeders, and simple racists have in common is their desire to select and breed higher biological or/and social quality in the group, to improve the victims and their innate potential, instead of changing and correcting an oppressive society.

What tripped up Dr. Welsing is her tendency to emphasize a biology-based theoretics to explain social phenomena. Such "reactive"[23] theory, standing racism on its head, may be too insular to provide the needed sociological or operational implementation of its own theoretical tenets. What biology decrees cannot be altered without some biological transformation. Sociological decrees, by contrast, pull for sociological solutions. It may be no coincidence that Welsing's Cress Theory, in the first place, captured the black imagination in a time when blacks, like white reformers, were turning away from social combat with their oppression to focus on patching up themselves[24] -- through self-improvement, the power of positive thinking, "I'm okay, you're okay," "looking out for number one," "human potential," tai-chi, meditation, etc. in the age or "culture of narcissism."[25]

The insular character of Welsing's theoretics (and contemporary black nationalism generally) is apparent in the preoccupation with *melanin* (the pigmentation or color-producing element of the skin, more prominent in black or dark skin). Other than the benefits of psychological self-flagellation, the melanin preoccupation in the black movement today is limited; it is an area of experimentation for the biologist and the biochemist, not the social warriors of the movement. Even if melanin is found to contain all the mighty properties now claimed for it, we are left with the reality that we had melanin before, during and after slavery; melanin was with us regardless and impervious to our social circumstances. Melanin is something God or nature gave us, wishing no doubt that we ourselves would go on to find something we ourselves could do to help.

One of Welsing's chief recent collaborators in the cult of melaninism is Wade Nobles, who also is a leader of the clearly correct importance of incorporating African antecedents and family cultural patterns into black life and culture. Despite our criticism to follow, our own support of this strategy (insofar as it can go) is apparent in our book, *Bringing the Black Boy to Manhood: The Passage,*[26] published in 1985, when we sought to make the model of the African rites of passage a movement for our people here and now, as a prelude to the idea of returning to the African example generally, to find out what we lost in African culture that is worth saving or can serve us today, to bring Africa to America, culturally, psychologically and sociologically.

Encouraged by the impact of Maulana Karenga's Kwanzaa celebration, we sought to give practical application to the decades old pan-African nationalist expressions of the African cultural ideal. While black nationalist individuals and groups had been discussing and even administering rites of passage occasionally in one way or another for decades, we wanted to activate the idea of a rite of passage into a fullblown mass black movement and to present the idea afresh and in a way that would appeal to nationalists and non-nationalists alike, including the middle class. We have understandably been gratified by the proliferation of the idea of rites of passage which blossomed soon after the publication of the book. Indeed, Wade Nobles and Bruce Hare (no relation) have recently been at work on a rites of passage program for the National Urban League.

Building on the work of white anthropologist, Melville Herskovitz,[27] Wade Nobles has stood out generally among the "afrocentric" school of African-American scholars espousing the importance of the African family model,[28] though others, notably Janice Hale-Benson,[29] have also been considerably, and expressly, influenced by the work of Herskovitz. However, the philosophical limitations of the Afrocentrics is revealed conspicuously by Hale-Benson. Echoing Orlando Patterson's categorization of black intellectual approaches to history,[30] Hale-Benson lists three categories: "contributionists," "catastrophics," and "survivalists." Under "catastrophics," Hale-Benson, like Patterson, names three individuals: Malcolm X, E. Franklin Frazier and Nathan Hare (no doubt for the simple reason that Patterson was usurping the concept, "contributionism," which Hare had coined).

"Contributionism" refers to a popular African-American approach to history wherein history is viewed as a vehicle mainly for culling black contributions to the advancement of civilization or humanity. "Catastrophics" focus on the destruction or extreme (hence "catastrophic" to Patterson and Hale-Benson) consequences of black enslavement, subjugation and oppression in the call to resist or overturn them. "Survivalists" focus on the African carryovers or "survivals." As a matter of fact, Malcolm X and E. Franklin Frazier (despite his famous contention with Herskovitz over the extent to which African cultural patterns had actually survived the disruption of the Middle Passage, the slave plantation and the pressures of assimilation in white-dominated America), like Nathan Hare, believed in the idea of reclaiming beneficial African antecedents and the African identity long before it was popular, let alone before many of todays champion Afrocentrics came on the scene. To that extent, all three were/are "survivalists."

However, what apparently gained them the label, "catastrophics" (in the minds of Patterson and Hale-Benson) was their realization that surivival is not enough, that survival is only one level of struggle; but that another level -- and possibly a higher level -- of struggle is resistance. And here we come to a salient problem of the survivalists proper and the contemporary black intellectual class generally (including the afrocentric school). Though many of them are activists today, as a rule they (like the strength-of-black-families school they championed in the 1970s) neglect or shun the need to constantly correct ourselves and our institutional decimation here and now, not to mention the imperative to resist the destruction generated by the white agenda of domination and control.

Happily, in the natural course of dialectics, it has finally emerged that black intellectuals are attempting to some degree to combine efforts to deal with the strengths *and* the weaknesses of the black family, as advocated by one of the present authors in a 1976 article, "What Black Intellectuals Misunderstand about the Black Family," appearing in the now defunct *Black World* magazine.[31] In general, however, black intellectuals, in belatedly addressing the weaknesses of the black family today, have relied on white society's definitions of the problem and, therefore, its solutions, though often camouflaged in a cloak of Africanity.

While it is necessary to incorporate the African past and the African culture into black family life and thought, or even to fully understand the African-American family today, Africanity (Leopold Senghor's extension of the Negritude philosophy) will not be enough. The African family on the continent is itself slowly being destroyed; not only by the nature of European-induced urbanization pulling men from their families to employment in the shantytowns of Africa. Even more perilous may be the fact that the African family is presently the primary object of white Western aim, the continental target on which the neo-eugenicists are turning the guns of family/reproductive control.

Wade Nobles is correct in suggesting that you cannot have a complete theory of the black family without including the African connection;[32] but, after including the African consideration, if you do not have a complete theory of the African family in the first place, you will continue to have an incomplete theory of the black family. In fact, where you initially had one incomplete theory, you will now have two incomplete theories, doubling your quandary.

Consider, for instance, the idea of a "matriarchy," where women as a group are the rulers instead of the men. When, some twenty years ago, Daniel Patrick Moynihan,[33] echoing E. Franklin Frazier's poetic conceptualization,[34] building on W.E.B. DuBois,[35] used "matriarchy" as a metaphor to describe the broken patriarchy of the African-American family, black intellectuals jumped skyhigh. By contrast today, spurred on by the masculinity strivings of the unisexual feminist movement, black intellectuals endeavor (through a scholarship of assertion and repetition), without any tenable evidence, to reach back to ancient Africa and Egypt to concoct a matriarchy there, then.

Black intellectuals do this by exploiting the variegated looseness and past social science confusion in the usage of the word, "matriarchy," a word created in the 19th century to refer to a hypothetical form of society in which women "were the leaders and rulers."[36] The term appears to have been originated by J.J. Bachofen. Bachofen used the term "matriarch" to designate a matrilineal tracing of kinship or descent through the female and the rule of the family and control of the government by women, even the supremacy of the female deity (the moon) over the male deity (the sun). However, by the late 1940s at least, the idea of a matriarchy in actuality had been discredited for lack of evidence.

In reviving the term collaterally with white feminists, today's black intellectuals, like their European forerunners, use "matriarchy" to refer to a number of characteristics. For instance, *matrilineal* (the tracing of descent through the mother), *matrilocal* (referring to residence; e.g., a rule that the family will live with the mother's people instead of the father's), *matrifocal* or mother-centerednesss, etc. They then go on to extend it beyond the realm of the family per se, through assorted pieces of circumstantial and implausible evidence: e.g., the existence of queen wives of influence and flamboyance, the occasional reign of individual queens [reminiscent of Golda Meir of Israel, Margaret Thatcher of England, Ms. Aquino of the Phillipines, Queen Elizabeth, or even Dianne Feinstein of San Francisco or former Mayor Jane Byrne of Chicago; queen widows; queen mothers, who were nevertheless subordinate to some male king or chief; mythical queendoms such as the Amazons (myths also gave us mermaids and centaurs); and remnants of stray art objects depicting individual women in positions of authority or power]. This is not to suggest that women did not have a high place or were not treated better in ancient Africa than in ancient Europe, but that is no grounds to outwhite the white feminists in claiming to have had a matriarchy even as you reject the very thought of a matriarchy in African-America. If it's good enough for ancient Africa and our embrace of white feminist fantasy, the question arises as to why it isn't good enough for us.

Most often, black intellectuals restrict the term "matriarchy" to family characteristics but nevertheless go on to imply and sometimes to explicitly suggest the existence of a matriarchate (according to Webster's,[37] "a family, group, or state governed by a matriarchy; a *theoretical* stage or state in primtive society in which matriarchs hold the chief authority."). Except, instead of saying "matriarchate," they once more use the term "matriarchy," implying a society in which women dominate the leadership in the manner of men. Then, when someone challenges the historical and anthropological authenticity of the idea of the existence of political leadership or collective dominance on the part of women, our scholars simply retreat back into the more limited usage restricting the word matriarchy to the family situation.

Although the late Cheikh Anta Diop did not lay claim to inventing the idea of a matriarchy in ancient Africa, he appears to have launched the contemporary fad among black intellectduals,[38] aided notably by Ivan Van Sertima[39] (who repeated and magnified Diop's errors in this respect). Most other black intellectuals, in unquestioning unison, simply echo Van Sertima and Diop.

Diop built his "two cradles" theory of the history of matriarchy and patriarchy on the backs of such "universaltist" theories as espoused by Bachofen, Morgan and Engels, then branches off on a criticism of the universalist idea that matriarchy initially existed everywhere until supplanted in a later stage by patriarchy, in order to arrive at his "two cradles" theory. We do not mean to suggest that the two cradles theory is incorrect or otherwise; just that the existence of a two-cradle human cultural legacy neither requires nor proves the existence of a matriarchy (let alone a pure matriarchate). Indeed, a more nationalistic idea would hold that there was originally *one* cradle -- Africa (the European "cradle" being an aberration, derivative or divergence from the original African cradle). As a matter of fact, in other works, Diop would appear to prefer such a one-cradle theory of human history.

Although social scientists generally had decided by the 1950s to use the appropriate terms, e.g., matrilineal, matrilocal, etc. to describe phenomena in question and essentially to discard the term "matriarchy" (one reason black intellectuals of the 1960s would feel so damaged when Moynihan called the African-American family "matriarchal," referring to widespread male absence and evasion of responsibility in the family and in economic and political life), today's black intellectuals have outstripped white feminists in the frenzy and passion with which they seek to revive or resurrect the term.

Why black male intellectuals would want to do this (for males dominate the literature and oral advocacy of the idea of an ancient African matriarchy within the race) is a matter of grave curiosity and speculation, if not profound psychological and sociological analysis. Perhaps in their acute desire for racial recognition, to gain recognition from the master/mistress, they have merely seized upon an opportunity to beat white folk at their own game (as white feminists and liberals began to revive the myth). It is as if black intellectuals are getting one up on the white man (and his woman), inadvertently being once more seduced by the white woman in order to "get back at the white man" (as black male pursuers of white females used to rationalize). It also enables black intellectuals to court favor with the white liberal-moderate establishment's unisexual feminist agenda and theoretics as well as to skirt conflict which would emanate from confrontation with serious social change.

In any case, it is clear enough that the idea of an African matriarchy gives comfort to the unisexual white femnist endeavor to diminish sexual differentiation and the very idea of sexual differences (the old assimilationist fallacy of equali-

18

ty as synonymous with sameness). Aside from giving comfort to white feminism and the agenda of unisexualization (including the resultant socioeconomic shifts, policies and consequences), this implies that it is alright if not "progressive" to live at peace within a broken patriarchy as black America does today. The unisex or genderless ideal helps strip the black male (already institutionally decimated) of the social imperative or meaning of his masculinity, of a social *raison d'etre* for being a man.[40]

We pay a terrible price for the need to believe in black firstness, especially in an area so deeply antithetical to black elevation and progress, let alone an area undergoing a re-examination and revamping on the part of the white world, including leading feminist theorists, for itself.[41]

In any case, if men remain predominantly linked to authority and political and economic achievement, it hardly matters, in the pathetic effort to concoct evidence for an ancient African matriarchy if, for example.[42]

-- women could make some important decisions;

-- women were able to manipulate or charm their husbands into doing their bidding, especially if these husbands were kings;

mothers were the center or head of households;

the matrilineal method of tracing descent through the mother even though the father retained ultimate authority over the children;

-- that authority sometimes reverts to the mother's brother or the sister's son (it is still a man);

-- that women had high respect (cf. chivalry or black grandmothers in the pre-World War II rural South);

-- that feminist-style uprisings or sex strikes took place on the part of women seeking to win concessions from the males, let alone to whip recalcitrant husbands in line. In fact, seeking to have more say in a male-dominated government is not only not matriarchy, it testifies to the fact that they were endeavoring to deal with an existing male dominance;

-- that women run the home or family unit while men are elsewhere at work or at war, whatever, is in itself no proof of a matriarchy, let alone the matriarchate implied or suggested variously by black matriarchalists;

-- that society ascribes to women particular roles or tasks or specific spheres of ownership which in our society is associated with men. If men nevertheless remain the dominant occupants of political and overall economic life, there is no matriarchy.[43]

19

Finally, though black intellectuals were correct in rejecting the essentially poetic notion that black Americans of the mid-1960s had matriarchal families (in that it was not a black cultural ideal, not a culture of choice but a culture of necessity, not a culture of resistance but a culture of adaptation), a better case than the idea of an ancient African matriarchy (in terms of the rights and privileges women have and their influence within the family and their socioeconomic group) could be made for the probability that African-*Americans* live today in the most matriarchal situation that the world has ever known.

What we have here in the collective black intellectual parroting of the idea of a matriarchy is a representation of the fact that nationalists, pan-Africanists and assimilationists alike, each in their own way, are assimilating, bit by bit, to the white unisexual neo-eugenicist program. (In the manner in which liberal-moderate or assimilationist black historians become heroes for black nationalists, due to their specialized knowledge, many pan-Africanist authorities are merely "Africanists" who, like their white liberal and missionary colleagues, once specialized in the study of Africa, but now find a ready audience in pan-Africanists proper. For instance, when a late 1960s black student-faculty rebel faction called for the incorporation of Swahili into the language requirements of Howard University, the late Mark Hanna Watkins, then director of Howard's African Language Center and head of its graduate program in African Affairs, voted to fire one of the faculty members involved because, as he sought to explain privately, he "read in the Washington Post that you said the students should be able to take Swahili as their language requirement!" Frank Snowden, who was believed so "white-minded" and antithetical to black power student activism and interests the students insisted on forcing his resignation as dean of Howard's College of Liberal Arts, nevertheless, in his specialization in European "classics," had gone in the early 1960s to Greece and Rome seeking evidence for the existence of blacks in ancient Greece and ancient Rome. Snowden is the most footnoted author by the compilation of scholars in Van Sertima's *Black Women in Antiquity*.[44]

In a myriad of ways, black intellectuals of all stripes have slowly assimilated to the white unisexual neo-geneticist agenda, or at the very most, skirted the issue altogether in the few cases in which they could not find it in their consciences to make open peace with it. Many have openly made peace. For instance, Dorothy Heights, president of the National Council of Negro Women, a dominant figure with Bella Abzug in the Copenhagen International Conference of Women in 1980 and an early advocate of the white liberal program of sex education in black elementary schools as well as the recipient of funds from the Agency for International Development to aid in the U.S. reproductive control program in Africa, emerged in mid-September, 1988, as a token black member of the advisory committee of the National Institute of Health which concluded that it is morally acceptable to use human fetal tissue obtained from abortions for research and therapy.[45]

Because they have avoided the issue of reproductive control and the white neo-eugenicist agenda (except to belatedly join or parrot it, or some elements of it), we can generally make short shrift of contemporary mainstream black intellectual study of the black family. Essentially, the mainstream (liberal-moderate, assimilationist) variety of black intellectuals toss around weary platitutdes such as the effects of black male difficulties in education, employment, drug and alcohol abuse, crime and delinquency, etc. on the black family. While these factors are certainly considerable and continual in their impact, it doesn't any longer require black scholars from major universities and research centers to tell us that the black male experiences difficulties in education, employment, and other lanes on the highways of social mobility. We already know that, and have known it, even long before Moynihan restated the point in 1965.[46] But where Moynihan got into trouble, where he made his mistake, was in bruising the "black image" and the sensibilities of defensive black intellectuals, in suggesting that the family decay produced by racism and employment problems can turn around and hamper, in circular fashion, the ability of the black race to realize its full potential in the arena of employment and overall social mobility. You (racism) break my leg, but now that my leg is broken, it hampers my ability to run. Moynihan ran into a hornets nest, had the nerve as a white person to spotlight the complicated and serious dilemma of cause and effect which, as a rule, gets confused if not lost altogether.

Thus twenty-three years later today, in a book curiously hailed by mainstream and black movement intellectuals alike, *Young, Black and Male in America: An Endangered Species*,[47] black University of California, Berkeley social work professor, Jewelle Taylor Gibbs, can boldly list among the three "major factors [that] explain how these problems developed and why they have worsened in less than three decades" the "growth of families headed by females."[48] The growth of families headed by females surely had an impact, but it is itself a result in the first place. This was white Charles Murray's error in *Losing Ground*,[49] treating female-headed homes as cause instead of the result of black male socioeconomic decimation (already well documented by black sociologist Joseph Scott and his collaborator, economist James Stewart.)[50] Otherwise, Murray could not have made the sociological, if not logical, error of blaming welfare (which has been with us for decades) for the sudden plunge in black family stability in the decade of the 1970s, would not have used a constant to try to explain a change, but instead would have looked beneath the surface to see what was it that newly emerged since 1970.[51]

The growth of families headed by females is surely something to take into

21

account, but it is itself a result, in the first place. We need to explain why families headed by females emerged, before we can use this as a reason for the decline of the black male and the black family. It is in part precisely the socioeconomic destruction of the black male which has helped to produce the female-headed families.

Like most scholars, white and black but especially black, Prof. Gibbs and her contributors say nothing of the impact of the anti-family -- and at least inadvertently anti-black male -- unisexual white feminist movement of the 1970s), nothing of the anti-marriage, anti-childbirth ideals it promoted, nothing of the mass transfer of jobs and benefits to married white middle class women that might have gone to black males, nothing of the unisexual feminist neglect and smothering of the interests and needs of black male elevation. Even less is said of the impact of the neo-eugenicist forces and factors behind the unisexual movement or/and the move away from family values in the 1970s and its subsidiary policies disproportionately impacting negatively on the black male and the black family. These, you see, are sacred cows, which will get our scholars in trouble with their white liberal-moderate colleagues, mentors, friends, indeed editors and other benefactors.

Prof. Gibbs goes on to mention two other "major factors": 1) "the conservative political climate that fostered a backlash to civil rights" (with no mention of the defection of white liberals and their pushing of policies which served the interests of themselves and the white middle class generally, unconsciously the needs of post-industrial society,[52] but were antithetical to the emergence of the black male and the black race whose place white liberals, using the feminist hook, took in the center of the apple pie of reform and public sympathy); and 2) "structural and technological changes in the society [which] have shifted the economy from an agricultural and manufacturing base to a service and high-technology base...."[53]

Here we come to a diversion in the scholarship of rationalization of the status quo. The exaggeration of the impact of a shift of black males from manufacturing to service industry is apparently gaining popularity because of its grand, impersonal, no-fault character, which absolves the black intellectual of blame for the inaction and collective denial during the 1970s as well as eliminates concrete, in-the-flesh white culpitry demanding and requiring black intellectual confrontation in the present. Human beings and their policies and practices (including economic, but not exclusively) make whatever shifts that fall short of supernatural origin or metabiological or supra-human forces; and human beings can endeavor to prevent or to reverse them. If they choose to, just as the white world is now turning back toward family and childbirth for the middle class majority, that is, themselves, even as they clamp down on the pregnancy and family structure of the poor.

Although intellectuals are fond of searching for periodic "pendulum swings," the swing of the pendulum in human affairs incorporates some involvement or interference in some way, through omission or/and commission, from one or more humans. The same is true of "structural changes." People influence structural changes just as structural changes in turn influence people. By hiding behind the shield of grand results such as structural changes and imaginary pendulum swings, in unemployment, industrial shifts, or even urbanization, black intellectuals shield themselves from the fire of resistance that would follow new sparks of understanding of the perpetual and ongoing processes and developments in the clash of peoples and cultures, particularly those of the oppressor and the oppressed.

For instance, in the only chapter in Prof. Gibb's book actually devoted to employment, Tom Larson, a California State University, Los Angeles professor, at one point presents figures purporting to show this shift to the service industry and its impact on the black male.[54] Let us see how he does this. Using a favorite tool of those who wish to demonstrate a point with reference to the black male or a specific race-sex group while camouflaging a similar or greater effect for some other group, Prof. Larson presents no figures for any group other than the black male; none for the black female, nor the white female, nor the white male. Comparative figures would show the point made to be largely spurious. It is something like making a study of cowboys and concluding that cowboys eat breakfast in the morning. While that may be true of cowboys, it is also true of just about everybody else. Indeed, Larson concludes that "blacks lost jobs in all major sectors of the economy but one between 1950 and 1980 (the exception was in professional service)." Just what we would have figured.

We are bound also to suspect time periods such as 1950 to 1980 (which not only subsumes and skips over the 1960s, but more importantly in the case of black family decay, the 1970s). In other words, statisticians frequently conceal social changes and their causes and consequences in the time periods they choose. Thus, in his table of figures, when Larson does arrive at the most important decade, the 1970s, he lists no figures, content to list "NA" (not available) on each and every line. It would have been more accurate to list no column for the 1970s if there are no figures; in which case he would lay no claim to presenting any. Instead, Larson gives figures for 1950 to 1960 and 1960 to 1970, but none for 1970 to 1980, let alone post-1980. Larson might just as well have listed a column for 1990, or even 2000, or whatever, for that matter. Indeed, the figures he does present, for 1950, 1960, and 1970, contrarily show teenage black males also ever slightly but persistently leaving employment in the service industry!

Additionally, Larson restricts his figures to "male teen employment." The entire issue of teenage employment and its mid-1980s hype may have been a smokescreen related to the simple rise of carryout food and service chains and the need for mass cheap labor shrunk by the waning teenage supply. From 1980 to 1985, the fastfood chains and their need for employees rose simultaneously and approximately equal to the *decline* in the number of teenagers. The hyping of teen unemployment (as also in the case of the workfare hype) was shortcircuited or muddled only by growing white labor union apprehension and realization that their own interests would be threatened by the mass employment of teenagers and welfare women at super-cheap wages.

To begin with, teenagers ideally should be unemployed. That is, teenagers should be in school, preparing for a lifetime of employement. Besides, what teenagers need more than any employment is an employed parent, nay, two employed parents these days, now that two-earner families are the norm. Teenagers do not need to be employed in jobs at cheaper wages that might have gone to their father, or somebody else's father. White labor unions realize this, and so would black intellectuals, if their identity with white liberals did not blind them to their speical interests which go beyond, or are not merely congruent to, being included as tokens in the white package.

We were warned of this enslavement to white liberal ideology more than twenty years ago,[55] indeed fifty-six years ago,[56] at least. However, black intellectuals stubbornly persist in their chronic aping of white ideals, operating on a ''me-too,'' ''open-up-and-let-me-in,'' approach to matters economic, political and sociological, seeing their black interests as equal only to duplication of whites.

The way in which this delayed-response mimicry of whites (and a related sociopsychological need for white acceptance) affects black family/reproductive patterns and relationships and in turn the condition of the race in the pathological genesis of psychosociocultual decay -- and what we can do about it -- is the subject of this book, *Crisis in Black Sexual Politics.*

Let us turn, then, to the study and analysis of the specific nature of black male/female relationsihps and family issues as assessed and depicted by the experts and authorities contained in this volume. In the concluding chapter, we will return to take up the matter of solutions, what we can and must do, concretely, and in the end to delineate a complete theory of the black family.

The Making of the Black Male Shortage — and its Implications for the Black Family

by Nathan Hare, Ph.D. & Julia Hare, Ed.D.

Black males are at the crossroads in the United States today. They incite widespread fear and curiosity in the public mind. To some they represent crime and violence; to others, they are a source of sexual envy, resentment and sometimes admiration.

There are presently about 14 million of them (not counting those in the armed forces abroad); and, though severely outnumbered in the population at large, they reign as dominant participants and recordbreakers in the athletic and entertainment industries.

More than a few have risen to the top, even to greatness, in a panorama of other endeavors, as these avenues have been opened to them. However, as a group, Black males lag drearily in their relative socio-economic position, as well as in their ability to stay with their women and children and to provide for them.

Forty-two percent of all persons incarcerated are Black males, as often as not leaving a mate and children on the outside with diminished funds. About three out of ten Black males are counted among the unemployed (among Black youth it is 48 percent); and still others have given up the search for work altogether.

They mask their depression with hostility and acting-out behavior, and thus

25

the leading causes of death among Black youth are homicide, drug abuse, suicide and accidents.

Young Black males have a one in twenty chance of dying before they reach twenty-one; and for those between the ages of 20 and 35, homicide is the number one cause of death. Increasingly, Black males are said to be an "endangered species."

Sixty-five percent of Black children in urban areas are poor; and the dropout rate, portending ominous consequences for the future, is disastrously high—particularly among young Black males.

A study at the University of Chicago has predicted that by the year 2000, at present rates, 70 percent of Black males will be either unemployed, in jail, on dope, or dead; with obvious consequences for their women, children and for society in general.

What are the causes of the Black male's present predicament? What can be done to halt his plunge into harsher unemployment, poverty, prisons, addiction, high dropout rates and crime?

To begin with , social scientists have found that a rise of as little as one percent in unemployment precipitates a measurable and predictable increase in insanity, crime and other forms of social decay.

Since 1965, we have known that there is a correlation between the Black and White female illegitimacy rates and White and Black male unemployment.

Psychological despair and sometimes precipitous psychosis appear in husbands and fathers who become unemployed. Black males are prone to lose a sense of their self-regard and their importance in the family group; and when the going gets rough, may readily flee the family nest.

Battered and discouraged by too many years of fruitless indulgence, their women grow impatient, Unable to forgive the Black men for their failure to thrive in the marketplace, many Black women are prone to berate them in a chronic barrage of negativism, compounding feelings of incapacity.

BLACK MALE: "Baby, I think I'm going to get that job before Christmas."

BLACK FEMALE: "Yeah, I'll bet. You been saying that for years."

The next day the Black man comes home, happy and excited. "Hey, baby, I got that job!"

"Did?"

"Yeah, course it's just part-time, but the man say if I do okay in six months probation, I can go fulltime."

"You mean you took a part-time job?"

"Yeah, but—"

"I'm tired of you. I been waiting for you to get a job for seven years, then you come in with a part-time job. Momma told me ten years ago you wouldn't never amount to nothing. I'm tired. I'm leaving."

Our studies during the past fifteen years have found that while Black males tend to blame the system for their troubles, Black females come to the weary conclusion that the Black male is using "racism" for an excuse not to keep up the daily struggle and are inclined to blame the Black male for the troubles of both the Black male and the Black female, feeling that if the Black male could get himself together the Black female would do alright.

However, despite the fact that the Black female is proud of her strength and her contributions to her family (acknowledged by the Black male but too often resented), she feels that it is a strength forced upon her and one that is likely to be the death of her and her relationship with her man. Most would give their right arm to have a strong Black man to stand beside them, but find that they are too often in short supply.

It was a blow to Black females and Black males when, in the 1970s, the Black male was placed on the backburner. While everybody hyped the "population explosion," the United States was in fact undergoing a postbaby boom "bust."

Especially in those pre-immigration years, they needed a mass cheap, less rebellious labor supply. The White female became a pleasant alternative to the Black male in the twilight of the Black consciousness era.

As the white female entered the labor force, Black males were pushed out of it. Eighteen million new jobs were created during the 1970s, 70 percent given to women, the majority of them midddle class, married and White. They took that income and put it with that of their White mates, raising their standard of living while increasing the economic distance between themselves, Blacks, the single, and the poor.

Money and jobs that could have made a difference in the rise of Black males were spread among White women, without making any surstantial gains for them, relative to white males, but increasing the emotional and social isolation between the Black male and the Black female.

The solution to the White woman's problem was relatively simple. She had only to raise herself to the level of her male. But when feminism sought to unilaterally raise the Black female, the Black female looked around to find that there was no man to stand beside her. It used to be that when you walked through the Black community you encountered a lot of pretty women and a lot of working men. Now you see a lot of working women and a lot of pretty men.

The White race may have a woman problem, but the Black race has a woman problem *and* a man problem in that, unlike the White man, the Black man also is oppressed.

More damaging still, the many new programs of pseudo-liberation (false "liberations" presented or mistaken as real) in an age of unisexualization, are based on notions, theories and values which deneuter the Black male.

The White male had and retains institutional back-up, social potency (high position, wealth or prestige) to reinforce his often derided sexual masculinity with a rigid social manhood.

At the same time, the Black male is left to over-compensate; blocked from the avenues to social potency or position and complicating further his ability to play the mundane and expected: the socially acceptable role of provider or family man.

The feminist, unisexual movement condemned the very legitimacy of the quest for masculinity, only to turn around, without batting an eye, and point the finger at Black males for having now failed to attain the very social masculinity or masculine position previously berated, minimized and discredited.

Accordingly, the push for more "responsibility" on the Black males, focusing on the need to change their values, created the highest form of blaming the victims.

We can lay it down as a sociological law that in a patriarchal society there can be no viable race, psycho-socioeconomically, without a viable male. There can be no viable race without a patriarch in a patriarchal land.

The first and foremost requirement of Black leaders and intellectuals is to begin to understand more deeply the implications of policies and programs of pseudoliberation, in order to resist them and refuse to aid them in the name of false and spurious Black uplift.

We must no longer be lured into counter-productive and even self-defeating programs and directions. We must no longer blame the victim by merely treating symptoms without concern for the disease. For example, are young Black females poor because they become pregnant? Or do they become pregnant because they are poor?

Remember when it was said that there was nothing wrong with single parenting? Now single parenting (which victimized Black women disproportionately because of what society is doing to the Black male) is said to be a major Black family problem.

28

As if this is not enough, many people—White, Black, Left and Right—will, while continuing to cry about the special problems of the Black male, once ignored, nevertheless rush on relentlessly to follow dominant agendas focusing on the female. Efforts which continue to focus on the women, including welfare, will only compound and prolong the topsy-turvy balance of Black male and female relationships.

It made all good sociological sense, in a partriarchal society, as in the male-oriented Black consciousness movement of the late 1960s (frequently expressing a tenet to restore the Black male to his rightful position as protector and provider in the family group, the most basic role of the male) for a group on the rise to seek to beef up the male.

It was only in the 1960s that the Black male caught up with the Black female briefly, in college education, only to slip behind her again educationally. This leaves Black women compelled too frequently to marry beneath their station in life (with the mutual contempt and conflict characteristic of such unions) or do without a man.

Today, the Black woman is more likely to have to rear her children alone than not to. This has consequences especially for the rearing of Black boys.

Sociologists have long been aware (though not so long as our ancestors) that not only what is easy for two parents is hard for one in the way of discipline, but also that, left alone, mothers tend to do a better job of raising girls than raising boys. Without even trying, the mother can teach the girl more effectively by example and cement the girl's identity.

The Black boy, by contrast, may gain a distorted image of his role as protector and provider, rejecting the occupational world which rejects him, shunning or at least disdaining his possibilities in the marketplace and its routinized, time-clock demands. He would rather be a star, a ball player, an athlete, musician, hustler, or even a dope dealer or pimp. In his scheme of things, he has nothing to lose, and he would rather give up his minimal possibilities, with its bottom-line assurances, than to give up the dream-world of somehow making it big.

As "both mother and father" to the boy, the single mother risks unconsciously transmitting feminine ways of coping which, according to Black psychologist, Gerald Prather, are likely to be dysfunctional for the male in adulthood occupational life.

Many unknowingly compound this with an attitude of prideful humor that naughtiness in a boy is admirable or at least proof of budding manhood. "Ain't he cute? Look at him, y'all. He's going to be a heartbreaker." Some others may frequently chastise the boy with: "You're going to be no good just like your father." If the boy's father is no good, and he is just like his father, then he is no good either and all the more may just as well begin to act that way.

Accustomed to the loss of the father's presence in early childhood, and looking to their mothers for both maternal and paternal sustenance, such males may frequently reach maturity with deep and unresolved conflicts. They are doomed to live out these unconscious conflicts and maternal ambiguities in competitive struggle with their female partners.

They are the victims of a "cupboard" syndrome in which, reminiscent of their mothers, they see all women, all love objects, as extensions of their mothers and a love-hate source of nurturance, the cupboard that holds the things fed them and of course also denied them in infancy by their mothers. This is a source of much of the economic reliance of these men on their mates and their exploitation of their soul mate resources.

Such pervasive problems in the single parent arrangement may have been anticipated by African tribes as well as rural Southern Blacks who tended to accord the role of discipline to the same sex parent.

For the boy or the girl, the same sex parent not only can model the discipline employed, including unconscious features; this arrangement offsets much unresolved conflict with the opposite-sex parent. This is manifested in the fact that both males and females revealed a tendency in adult life to name the opposite-sex parent when choosing "best friend," augmenting the possibilities for harmonious male/female relationships in contrast to our own situation today.

Aside from the single parent hoax, romanticizing single parenting, fostered by the unisexual-feminist hype of the 1970s, one of the most pernicious problems in the motivation of the Black boy has been a decimation of parental authority.

At first this was pushed through an ideal of ultra-permissive childrearing. Then parents were incited to help the state take discipline from the teachers. Now, under the guise of a so-called "child abuse protection movement" (wherein child molestation and sexual deviance are lumped with punitive discipline) teachers are impelled to collaborate in stripping away parental authority.

If a boy's friend accidentally hits him with a baseball bat, that is just too bad. But if his mother accidentally hits him and the teacher sees a scratch, middle class social workers come in with the police and snatch the child from the home and place him in a foster home.

The parent may be taken to jail or endure a round of court appearances and psychotherapy before she can get her child back. Many timess the child is left confused, lonely and depressed. Thus where there was initally alleged physical abuse, we now have emotional abuse brought in by the helpers.

The net result has been the loss of authority to discipline on the part of the agents of nurturance and development (teachers and parents) to the agents of punishment and rehabilitation (police, judges, social workers, counselors and psychotherapists).

An oppressed race above all needs discipline, Lacking discipline in the home, the child may too readily grow incorrigible. Lacking discipline in the school, the teacher may be compelled to spend so much time and energy in keeping order, there is little left for teaching or anything else. In too many schools there is accordingly neither discipline nor teaching.

Educational psychologist, Janice Hale is among those who have reported that in the inner city schools, the most popular children among their peers are likely to be the mischievous ones.

In her book, *Black Children*, she sees this as related to the fact that conventional classrooms (where teachers are disproportionately female) emphasize values and patterns of behavior more compatible to girls.

During the masculine protest of latency, the boy turns away from the female-dominated home and the female-dominated school to find his mores in the streets, using his peer group as his guide.

In the mirror of the ghetto, the Black boy is likely to see in the role models reflected there a damaged "looking-glass self." There is no lack of ambition but a stark discrepancy between ambition and hope.

In a study of juvenile gangs in Chicago carried out by the University of Chicago, a question asked was: "What would you like to be doing ten years from now?" From some of the roughest gang members in the city came such things as "bank executive, medical doctor, lawyer." The next question in the study was: "What do you think you'll *actually* be doing ten years from now?" "Well, I have an uncle at the steel mill, and he says I might be able to get on out there."

It is encouraging, therefore, that some individuals and groups are concentrating on the correction of this rift between personal goals and the perception of personal possibilities.

A chapter of the Coalition of 100 Black Men on the East Coast has adopted Black boys, tutoring them and playing the role of mentor, including working out future assurances of college attendance.

When a rich alumnus of a New York school promised the sixth grade students at his inner city alma mater that he'd pay the fare of any student who later went to college, he discovered an exceedingly high number of takers.

Other programs have proved effective. A prerequisite for attendance at one school, showing considerable success, is that a child's parents participate continually in family group therapy during the entire tenure of the child.

Recently, one of the authors was a consultant to the Portland (Oregon) school system (which is working on ways to improve the academic performance of the young Black male), and with a Black male superintendent and a Black male assistant superintendent appear to hold considerable promise of doing so. Where school boards do not educate, we must educate the school boards.

However, dazzling and innovative programs are necessary but not sufficient. Nor will it be enough to correct the educational system without attention to the restoration and revitalization of the parent, the first and most continual teacher.

In the process of regaining control of our childen's minds, we must first and simultaneously regain control of our own. We must go back to the beginning, to find out what we lost in the past, what is worth saving or can be used to inform us today.

In our own manual published in 1985, *Bringing the Black Boy to Manhood*, we analyzed the African rites of passage for an understanding of their pychological, anthropological and philosophical content. Believing that a people cannot depend on the same forces that deep us down to lift us up, we wished to find the means to infuse the children with what is lost in our time without the benefits of discipline.

We need to find ways to punctuate the young Black male's psyche with commitment to family and race, community and nation, with motivation for responsibility and personal mastery.

Because we have lost control of our culture and our children's socialization, many Black youth suffer an extended adolescence.

Within the context of a decimation of Black masculinity and its social meaning, its *raison d'etre*, its very reason for being, boys reach *physical puberty* readily enough but find it exceedingly difficult to gain *social puberty*.

We sought, therefore, to find some way to begin to bring the Black boy to manhood, to highlight and sharpen the focus of the importance and significance of being a man. Otherwise, we must no longer stand perplexed when we discover that more men have confused, or failed to develop, the art and feeling of being a man.

We must now increasingly be in search of a way to give the Black boy a sense of becoming a man, a clearer sense of self and of purpose, reponsibility to his roles as father and husband, a sacredness of self and others in the context

32

of a more attentive family and community network of adult collaboration.

Black male responsibility forums are cropping up around the country, and they are to be encouraged. These include Black fathers' councils to promote the idea and the ideal of Black fatherhood, to encourage Black men to stay with their women and children, and to endeavor to provide for them and in all ways to treat them better.

Individuals, fraternities, sororities and other middle class groups and individuals can sponsor rites of passage to usher Black boys into manhood.

Two-parent families should "adopt" boys from single-parent homes and include them in normal activities to which they take or would take their son. In this way, we could begin to restore the positive virtues and the basic humanity to the idea of "surrogate" parenting.

Black ministers should work with judicial systems to devise means of sentencing first-time offenders to the laymen of their church, to offset the clutches of the hardcore criminal values awaiting them in the prisons. Each church could focus on first offenders in their own surrounding blocks.

Black women, nothers and mates of Black male convicts, should demand a renaissance in the entire prison and judicial system which captures too many of our most vibrant and promising Black males.

At the same time, Black women are in a position to become special advocates for a reclamation of parenting rights and the overall ability and authority of Black parents and the Black community to determine the proper child-rearing and the proper road to the resurrection of our Black children's minds.

Further, Black women, particularly Black female single parents, should serve as headhunters for Black male teachers in the primary, elementary and secondary schools, actively recruiting the males; drafting them for this improtant work. They must cajole school boards to offer appropriate and necessary financial incentives.

Black fraternity groups have the time and the resources to initiate weekly activities for Black male juveniles, not just the incorrigibles, but the entire spectrum. This includes their active presence and participation as well as provision of resources and structures.

We must have armies of volunteer therapists and counselors to provide free counseling, individual and group, to single parents and their boys and other families at risk. This includes attorneys, dentists, physicians, indeed all professional groups, and police officers' clubs.

Entertainers and athletes may wish to follow the example of Lou Gossett, who adopted a boy on a sort of godfather basis, or as Oprah Winfrey has done with a small group of Chicago girls. We must not forget to keep up the socialization of the girls because they can learn to have an impact on the boys before it is too late.

Black Men:
Obsolete, Single & Dangerous

by Haki Madhubuti

It was late Friday on a hot July night that the temperature rose to 101 degrees, driving mothers and fathers and children out of projects and tenements to front stoops, parks, bar stools and small backalley crap games. Anything to deal with the heat. Johnny J., T.C., and Bigfoot were throwing sevens for small change in the back of the Godfather No. 2 lounge on Chicago's west side.

At about 1 a.m., lights from two directions hit their game and they were ordered to "hug the ground" by two white male cops and one Black woman cop. One of the white cops told all three to get up and spread eagle against the wall of the Godfather lounge and ordered the Black woman cop to search all of the Black men. As the woman went up and down Bigfoot's pants legs he moved as she touched his penis and commented "ain't this a bitch." At that moment the Black woman cop, hearing only the word "bitch" and feeling his movement, fell backwards, pulling her 38 special, and proceeded with surgeon's accuracy to blow the right side of Bigfoot's head off. The Black woman cop was congratulated, promoted and decorated by her superiors and detailed to another Black community. All three Black men had records, and T.C. and Johnny J. were given three years for resisting arrest. What had been described as "justifiable homicide" was in the real world "one less nigger," murdered not by a White or Black male cop, but a Black woman cop. Few saw the significance of this act.

Bigfoot at twenty-Five was in the prime of his life and never had a chance. To die at such a young age and at the hands of a Black woman remains a mysterious irony that will plague us as we move into the 21st Century. What may be the ultimate and most profound "accomplishment" of our current situation may well be that the mothers that bring life may indeed be the mothers or daughters of mothers that remove Black men from the earth. It's a perfect situation. No voices of protest will fill the street because it is well known that "niggers with criminal records are fair game for anybody, especially if you have a license to carry a weapon."

Much of the current Black studies have focused on either the Black family, Black woman, Africa, the Black community or the Black World. Until recently, few Black scholars or activists have given serious attention to the condition of Black men. There are many reasons for this: 1) much of the published scholarly work on Black people is by Black men and they may not have seen the importance of self-analysis; 2) it is easier to get studies on Black women or the Black family published; 3) few Black male scholars wished to "wash dirty clothes" in public and the other side of that is, if the Black male situation is accurately assessed it also means for the intelligent to "clean up their own acts; 4) many of the scholars and activists are actually functioning in their personal lives contrary to the best interests of Black people (some outright traitors) and finally 5) to bring clarity and direction to the Black male situation as an integral part of the Black family/community is not popular or publishable and very, very dangerous. Too many Black scholars have looked at the Black situation in America from a European framework and in doing so their work has been instrumental in distorting reality and exists as a body of "negative ammunition" to secure faculty positions, publishing contracts and as ego grease for their warped worldview and sense of importance.

What It is

First, for the conscious observer, it should be quite obvious that this society is bent on the destruction of Black people, specially Black men, and to do it as quietly and efficiently as possible[1]. What is not talked about is that the ability of great numbers of Black men to survive America's worse conditions and their potential for revolutionary organization remains the greatest threat to white male rule. This is why most of the Euro-American systems and sub-systems are structured to systematically keep conscious Black men out. However, if Black men wish to become imitation White men, there exists within the political-industrial-military complex significant token positions[2], which are in fact used to legitimize the system and to cloud its true relationship to Black people, a relationship of slave/master and in fact the "slave" position is the major rank that Black men, regardless of title and income are allowed to occupy.

The Kerner Report, issued twenty years ago, stated that the nation was moving toward two societies -- one Black, one White -- separate and unequal and ten years after a major investigation by the New York *Times*[3] confirms the accuracy of the report. In reference to the Kerner Report, Robert Blauner in his book *Racial Oppression in America* has stated:

"Despite the Kerner Report, it is still difficult for most whites to accept the unpleasant fact that America remains a racist society. Such an awareness is further obscured by the fact that more sophisticated, subtle, and indirect forms, which might better be termed neo-racism, tend to replace the traditional, open forms that were most highly elaborated in the old South. The centrality of racism is manifest in two key characteristics of our social structure. First, the division based upon color is the single most important split within the society, the body politic, and the national psyche. Second, various processes and practices or exclusion, rejection, and subjection based on color are built into the major public institutions (labor market, education, politics, and law enforcement), with the effects of maintaning special privileges, power, and values for the benefit of the white majority."

Simply put, Black people in the United States are powerless.* As a part of the political body, Black men do not have much of any power to speak of, as a cultural unit we do not make important life-giving or life-saving decisions about general Black life on a mass level. Black men are not able on a national or mass level to protect Black women, educate Black children, employ Black youth, clothe Black families or house Black communities. Our input into a "Black" foreign policy is traitorous. Our relationship to Black women is fast approaching the point of disaster. Black economic-political clout on the world level is miniscule and our understanding of the forces that regulate our lives is embarrassing— especially since we are supposed to be the "most educated" and the most creative and talented tribe of Black men in the world.

Black Men/White Men: White on Black Crime

The concept of Black men being the first victim[5] is not to set in motion the argument of who is oppressed the greatest, Black men or Black women? Oppression is oppression, and to quibble over degrees of oppression more often than not is an accurate measure of the effectiveness of White oppression. However, there are some basic White male/Black male dynamics that need to be understood: men run the world, this is not a sexist statement but one of fact. Also, men fight men (and a few women) to maintain control of their part of the world. There may be women in leadership positions (elected and appointed) but they are there because men see such concessions as politically wise and in their best interest. White men control most of the world — economically, politically and militarily

37

— and without an ounce of doubt control all of the Western/Northern world. Other facts are: 1) White men do not now fear White women (they are concerned, yes, but fearful, no). 2) White men do not fear Black women. The White man's relationship to Black women raditionally has been one of use, sexually and otherwise[6].

3) White men do fear Black men. This fear may not be spoken and obvious to many Black people but if one understands the history of White male-Black male relationships, it is quite evident that it is a history of war, with the horrid and severe physical and psychological enslavement and elimination of Black men by White men[7]. Sterling Brown's classic words are instructive when he says of White men venturing into the Black community, "they don't come by ones, they don't come by two's, they come by ten's." "The Black-male-White male confrontation is not only racial and cultural, it is also a serious question of what group of men are going to rule the world. The concept of **shared** power has always been a major question within the White male ethos, especially if it involves the inclusion of men outside their racial or cultural grouping[8]. However, it must be understood that White men don't actually like or trust White men if they are of another cultural tribe other than their own; any serious study of European wars will validate this point. When one analyzes the war-like nature White men exhibit among each other, only the naive and severely mentally handicapped would expect White male attitudes towards Black males to be any different than they are. These attitudes are historical and cultural and therefore psychological[9] and intimate. To change such negative and "natural" attitudes would require a revolution of the most profound kind.

The Black male-White male dynamic can be best described as one of continued and unrelenting war, with Black males being constantly on the losing end of most battles.[10] One of the major problems is that most Black men in the United States are fighting the wrong war, that is, they are fighting to get a "piece of the pie," therfore not understanding the "bio-social" nature of White males, which is that of conquest, domination, self-development and not one of sharing, "power or decision-making with the vanquished. The best that any **individual** Black man can hope and work for within this society is a "job" which, indeed, has been defined by some disillusioned Blacks as "a piece of the pie."

It is true that the future of any people can be measured by their cultural sophistication and the political, economic and military success of their male population in dealing with its natural and unnatural enemies. However, when that male population can't or doesn't clearly and definitively identify the enemy, it cannot on a continuous basis develop effective means and methods of neutralizing or eliminating said enemy. If this is the case, the future of that people can only be one of doubt and continued subjugation; and subtle yet effective, elimination is all but guaranteed in any White-American "multi-racial" situation, especially when the racial minority in that culture is economically obsolete[12] and Black. When any people do not have **strong** resourceful, energetic, fearless, innovative and fighting men in a world ruled by the **force** of men, that people is in serious trouble. When a people do not have men of integrity and vision, long term and lasting development is just about impossible.

The internal direction of Black people to a large degree is destructively influenced by the on-going Black male-White male conflict. White men in the United States control everything of material value. This is true in all of the life-giving areas such as economics, politics, science, education, communication and the military. If Black men want to be a part of the Euro-American structure in an "intimate and non-superficial" way, they will have to give up the most important aspect of their being, their Blackness, and in thought and actions become white, a transformation that is ultimately impossible but tempting enough to the unconscious Black man so that millions in this country on a daily basis betray their people, themselves and the future of the Black race.

The history of Black-White interracial interaction is that even if Blacks were allowed into the White infra-structure at the important levels they still would not have access to "ultimate and decisive" information or binding decision-making powers. The reason is quite obvious. Information is power,[13] and if it is translated and used in a self-protective manner, its value is of critical importance to those who have exclusive and first use of it. Generally the information that the Black community organizes around is at best second hand and is often of minimal value, having been filtered through the White screening systems before Blacks are able to see or use it.

When any people lose their men in a world ruled by men, that people, specially if they are landless and defenseless, ceases to be a threat to anybody. Most men, individually and collectively, don't fear women. The loss of Black men between the ages of 13 and 30, which is the warrior class (Black law society) represent a danger of genocidal proportions. To destroy or neutralize Black men creates a critical void in the Black family structure and forces Black women (without men) to assume the role of women (mother) as well as men (father). More than fifty-five percent of current heads-of-house-holds in the Black community are headed by women. This unusual condition has created some obvious readjustments, mostly negative:

1) The present generation of Black children is by and large being raised by Black women and their extended family network. The strain on single parent mothers is unduly harsh and often unreal. This condition influences the mother's activities with her children as well as how she approaches future relationships with Black men.

2) Black men cease to have a major influence on the development of their children, therefore leaving the "education" of them to their mothers and outside forces.

3) It is quite obvious now, single mothers, without the proper male support, are havings serious difficulty raising sons. By the time young boys reach 13 the negative options that are available are overwhelming, especially from their peer group.

The U.S. White supremacy system works overtime to disrupt the Black family and neutralize Black men. The most prevalent tactics used are these:

1) Make Black men White in thought, actions and image, ie.e, the acculturation of a people. This produces Black men that consciously work in the best interest of their teachers. **Therefore no serious definition of Black Manhood is ever contemplated.**

2) To drive Black men out of the economic sector thereby making it impossible for them to take care of themselves and their family. A life of "crime" is the next step.

3) Supply Black men with negative options such as drugs and alcohol and unrestricted sex. The use of drugs and other stimulants has seriously affected the Black community in a negative manner.

4) Drive Black men crazy so that they turn against self and the Black community. Then the only recourse left would be: a) mental hospitals, b) suicide, c) Black on Black destruction.

5) Those who have been forced into crime are captured and put ino prison, which breeds hard non-political Black men who for the most part will return and prey on their own communities (there are exceptions.)

6) Make them into women. Whereas homosexual and bisexual activity become the norm rather than the exception. Men of other cultures do not fear the woman-like men of any race.

7) Kill them — not just mentally, but physically — and do it in a way that strikes fear into the hearts of other Black men. This fear of death and/or imprisonment has been an important part in keeping Black struggle legal and above ground.

By locking Black people (especially the men) into a legal process that by definition doesn't work for them has effectively set the Black struggle back years. **The freedom of Black people** cannot be won in the United States through legal means or **on a part time basis.** The negative politicization of Black men has effectively wiped out serious **full-time** Black male freedom fighters. Making it in America, to a great many Black men today means, **how much money they can make in the shortest amount of time,** doing the least amount of work. Family Building, Nation Building, sincere deep Black male-female partnerships, are only literary and academic verbiage for the most part among Black men. A favorite saying among Black professional men today is, "time is money." With an attitude like that, their first priority will not be **their people.**

A Definition of Black Manhood.

First let's try and give a definition of *Black manhood:* Race first. A quiet strength. The positioning of oneself so that observation comes before reaction, where study is preferred to night life, where emotion is not seen as a weakness. Love for self, family, children, and extensions of self are beyond the verbal. *Black manhood.* Making your life accessible to children in meaningful ways, able to recognize the war we are in. Doing anything to take care of family so long as it doesn't harm or negatively affect other Black people. Willing to share resources to the maximum. Willing to struggle unrelentingly against the evils of this world especially evils that directly threaten the race. *Black manhood.* To seek and be that which is just, good and correct. Properly positioning oneself in the context of our people. A listener. A student. Historian. One who develops leadership qualities and demands the same qualities of those who have been chosen to lead. See material rewards as means towards an end and not an end in themselves. Clean — mentally and physically. Protector of Black weak. One who respects Black elders. Practical idealist. Questioner of the world. Spiritually in tune with the best of the world. *Black manhood.* Direction giver. Husband. Sensitive to Black women's needs and aspirations. Realizing that it is not necessary for them to completely absorb themselves into us but that nothing separates the communication between us. A seeker of truth. A worker of the first order. Teacher. Example of what is to be. Fighter. A builder with vision. Connects land to liberation. A student of peace and war. Warrior and statesman.

One who is able to provide as well as receive. Culturally sound. Creative. A motivator and stimulator of others. *Black manhood.* A lover of life and all that is beautiful. One who is constantly growing and learns from mistakes. A challenger of the known and the unknown. The first to admit that he does not know as he seeks to find out. Able to solicit the best out of self and others. Soft. Strong. Not afraid to take the lead. Creative father. Organized and organizer. A brother to brothers. A brother to sisters. Understanding. patient. A winner. Maintainer of the I can, I must, I will attitude toward Black struggle. A builder of the necessary. *Always* and always in a process of growth and without a doubt cannot be *bought.*

That Black men affirm themselves is absolutely necessary at this time, however, *not as the opposite or superior to Black women,* but as partners and as men who are ready and able to challenge all things harmful to the development of Black people. There is a way.

1) *Brotherhoods* need to be developed in all areas of the country: these brotherhoods (small and large) must act as consciousness-raising vehicles for Black men in the areas of culture, politics, male-female relationships and self-defense and self-reliance.

2) Study — (individual family and group) serious study should be like eating. Our homes should be mind-learning institutions. A people "may" achieve liberation through sheer physical force but they cannot maintain that liberty without intelligent and wise men and women. If our children see us studying everyday they will too. *Turn the television off* — and if you watch it, do so with discretion. One of the reasons that our analysis is faulty is because our information is faulty. Study should be both practical and theoretical. However, the greater focus must be in that area that you plan to be most active. We must become "specialists" as well as men who possess a good "general knowledge" about the forces that move the world.

3) *Love* of self and people is one of our highest principles. Rather than "falling in love" —learn to love. Grow into love. Sometimes an easy process, often difficult. The *African* way is to give as well as receive. Caring beyond the normal is normal for our new direction. Be willing to share self and material possessions beyond the expected.

4) *Family Development.* First line struggle. If you and your partner cannot communicate check yourself out first. Make sure that you are aware of her needs and your own short-comings" before "jumping" into her chest. The key to family is shared values and communication. Family-making is a teaching and "being taught" proposition. The key is always "progressive compromise" around principles and values that work for us rather than against us. Open up to your woman, let her share your pain and joy, do not hide special weaknesses or special strengths that being strong is not a macho-character or expensive makeup. Strength is positive decision-making and living up to responsibilities whatever they may be.

5) *Active* in an organized manner will move us past pure theory. Struggle is not impressing others with your ability to quote revolutionaries. Struggle, in the first analysis is *work* and the ability to function productively with other Black people in an organized manner. Institution-building, party-building, nation-building, depend first on the effectiveness of Black individual building and family-building.

6) Stop crying on wives/lovers breasts about how "the man" treats you

on the job, in the streets, at school and elsewhere. It is not that we need to present a false picture of our lives, but sisters are under enough weight themselves and do not need their men's tears. That is how our women lose respect for us. They are actually waiting on us to do something about "the man" if we are going to continue to call ourselves men. If the Black women can't occasionally lean on the shoulders of the Black man, who can she lean on?

7) Fathers need to be more active in the raising of their children, especially the sons.

8) Develop a *work* attitude about the world. Nobody is giving anything of value away and if someone should give you something, they can also take it away.

9) *Search for truth* should always be our guiding force. Times and situations change. Just because something was correct in the sixties doesn't mean that it can be used in the seventies, eighties or nineties. Always be willing to question past actions as well as accept constructive criticism. Advocating Black nationalism doesn't mean being dogmatic and insensitive to other positions. Good is good no matter where it comes from.

We All Hurt

People involved in serious day to day struggle of survival are not about to get involved in political nonsense that they feel is going nowhere. It is enough just to be able to clothe, house and feed ourselves. The *personal* side of struggle is often overlooked, but mothers and fathers who maintain the family, raise their children into productive adults are to be congratulated and supported. It is clear that we cannot build and sustain a "nation" if we cannot develop families that are culturally stable, physically strong and ready to defend their people.

People endure through the power of their minds and the strength of their vision. A people's culture, if it is functioning properly, will supply the vision. Within our supreme capacity to adapt, Black people the world over, especially in America, must continue to change and grow. Whether our adaptability is in our best interest will be answered, most certainly, in the next few years. However, it is evident to those who wish to notice it, Black people are re-shaping their lives according to what they think is best and in the long run beneficial to them and their loved ones.

As Black women join White men, White women and Black men as part of the occupying force, we must certainly realize that people - all of us, *do what we have been taught to do.* Our women, just as we, move out of self-interest and self-protection. That some of them are being positioned as legal killers again speaks to the weakness of their men. If the men do not step forward to take control — the women have only one option — to do it themselves.

43

It is no accident that our leadership largely comes from the ministry. When a people have more preachers than military men in leadership positons in a world ruled by scientists, politicians, industrialists, and military men, without a doubt that people are in trouble. Contrary to popular belief, *we are not our own worst enemy.* It is that our Black male leadership has not exhibited any semblance of consistent and non-contradictory examples of Black manhood. This must be corrected, for in this world it is us (Black men and women) and them (White men and women), and we must be sure our backs are covered.

Notes:

* I mean power in terms of life-giving and life-saving decision-making, as well as having the ability (knowledge, resources and desire) to deliver on the decisions made for the best interest of the majority of Black people.

** These data were complied by Howard University Institute for Urban Affairs and published in their Urban Research Review, Vol. 6, No. 1, 1980. This entire issue of the Urban Research Review is devoted to the study of the Black male and is highly recommended, much of the work was done by Dr. Leo Hendricks.

The Black Male/Female Connection

By Maulana Karenga, Ph.D

The continuing controversy concerning the quality and future of Black male/female relationships certainly emphasizes the critical and urgent character of the question. In spite of the empty assertions of burning-bush Marxists and vulgar pragmatists, political struggle to change society has not eliminated the unavoidably need to solve personal problems as well as social ones and better our own lives as we struggle rather than after the struggle. Moreover, it is clear that the personal and political are unavoidably linked, anyhow. For it is what we do in our daily lives that defines and demonstrates our real views and values and at the same time limits or increases our human possibilities.

Male/female relationships are of fundamental and enduring concern and importance for several reasons. First, they are so fundamental because of their species-character, i.e., their indispensibility to the maintenance and development of the species. They, thus, are species-compelling, in a word, the most natural and necessary human relationships. They are so natural they don't have to be learned and they are so necessary that people without them are and feel deformed and deficient.

Secondly, male/female relationships find their fundamental relevance as a measurement of our humanity, i.e., the evolution of the human race. In other words, they reveal how far we are from the animal world, how distinct or similar we are in relation to the brutes and beasts that share our planet. Our tendency toward violence, irrationality, hoarding, alienated sex and biological reductionism in our relationships register the level of our fallen angels we might shelter of ourselves.

Thirdly, male/female relationships are at the same time important because they are a measure of the quality of social life of any given society. The treatment of women in our relationships, and by extension in society, becomes as Toure notes, "... a mirror that reflects the economic and social conditions, the level of political, cultural and moral development of a given country." Regardless of claims to the contrary, communist, socialist, or capitalist countries cannot claim a high level of social life if women are essentially reduced to bedroom and kitchen and only given selected opportunities to be ministers of culture, but no industry, of sports, but not finance and of education, but never defense.

Fourthly, male/female relationships find their fundamental relevance as a measurement and mirror of personal development and identity. We are who we are more clearly in our male/female relationships than others. The abusive, selfish, brutal man may disguise himself with his friends and larger family, but with his woman he asserts himself. Likewise, the timid, self-doubting, searcher for security, or fleshpot woman may disguise herself from her friends and larger family, but with her man, her orientation becomes embarrassingly clear.

Finally, male/female relationships are of fundamental importance because they are, in the final analysis, a measurement of a people's capacity for struggle and social construction. It is more true than trite, that the family is the conjugal family — man and woman — exploring each other and the collective posibilities they desire and discover in exchange. If there is chaos and confusion in these small circles, it will inevitably plague the nation and make it ill-equipped to define, defend and develop its interests.

One doesn't have to be as nauseatingly negative as Wallace and Shange to admit that there are substantive problems concerning Black male/female relationships. The lack of relationships, due to the scarity of men and the games one has to play to begin and sustain relationships, poses significant problems. Moreover, the quality and future of those relationships that exist are open to continuing question and challenge, given the social stress and strain with which they are daily confronted. Also, there is the obvious need for a new family form, i.e., an extended family, to correct the deficiencies of the nuclear family and lay the basis for a more proactive and mutually beneficial exchange. But who that family should include and the criteria for inclusion, as well as the moral minimum value system it should operate by for maximum mutual benefit, are still to be developed and agreed upon.

However, in discussing the problems of Black male/female relationships, it is important to keep in mind at least four fundamental facts. Black male/female relationships, like Black families, are not more problem-ridden or pathological than Jewish and Gentile families and male/female relationsips. In this regard, it might help to remember that Sigmund Freud's studies on personal and family pathology were done among Jews and Gentiles, not among Blacks or other Third World people. In other words and for whatever it's sociologically and psychologically worth, the Oedipal and Electra complexes, compulsions to slay and sleep with one's father or sleep with and slay one's mother — among other deviancies — were not discovered among Continental or Diasporan Africans.

Secondly, it is important to recognize that real life unavoidably involves problems and problem-solving. Only on "Ozzie and Harriet" did everything work out all right all the time and eventually reality ran that off the tube. The point, then, is not to be without problems, but to be resourceful in devising solutions. For it is thru boldly meeting challenges that human development and advancement reach their highest level.

Thirdly, it is important to recognize that not all Black male/female relationships are in turmoil and trouble. Certainly, there are countless relationships that not only resist attacks on their health and productivity, but succeed in developing and expanding inspite of social obstacles. However, there are enough relationships in turmoil and trouble and enough persons without relationships to make the question of Black male/female necessary for discussion.

Finally, it is of equal importance to realize that any criticism of Black male/female relationships is at the same time and in equal measure a criticism of U.S. society which has shaped us to fit and function "properly" in it. In fact, as I have argued elsewhere, "society expresses itself thru us, gives us its views and values and imposes definite forms and content on our relationships and lives". Thus, social conditions create both social consciousness and social conduct and failure to recognize this can lead one to see racial defects where social ones are more real and relevant.

It is this final contention that serves as a key point of departure for any serious analysis of Black male/female relationships. For to say we are products of our social conditions is to say the same thing about our relationships. Analyses of the major defects in Black male/female relationships clearly reveal their social rather than genetic or purely personal basis. Thus, to understand the negatives of our relationships, we must understand the negative characteristics of society which have shaped them.

These negatives of U.S. society are defined by and derived from three major structural and value systems: capitalism, racism and sexism. Capitalism is a socioeconomic system defined by private ownership of the means to satisfy needs and the ruthless and continuous pursuit of profit which turns virtually everything into a commodity, i.e., an object for sale and purchase. Racism is a system of denial and deformation of a people's history and humanity based primarily or exclusively on the specious concept of race and racial hierarchies. It expresses itself in three basic ways, i.e., as 1) historical imposition, an act of force against and appropriation of a people's history and humanity in racial terms; 2) ideology, pseudo-intellectual justifications for the imposition; and 3) institutional arrangements, structures designed to perpetuate and extend the imposition and ideology. Sexism is the social practice of using gender or sex as the key determinant in establishing, maintaining and explaining relationships and exchanges. In other words, it is a system of assumptions and acts, theories and practices which imply and impose unequal, oppressive and exploitative relationships based on gender or sex.

Capitalism, then, turns relationships and parts of relationships into commodities and utilitarian arrangements. Racism engenders self-hate, self-doubt and pathological fixation on the white paradigm. And sexism encourages artificial personal power over women as a substitute for real social power over one's destiny and daily life. The result of these three structural and value strains on Black male/female relationships expresses itself as a transformation of the relationships into what can be best described as *connections*. A connection is a short-term or tentative association whcih is utilitarian and alienated and is designed primarily for the mutual misuse of each other's body. A quality relationship on the other hand is a long-term, stable association defined by its positive sharing, its mutual investment in each other's happiness, well-being and development.

There are four basic connections which plague male/female relationships in the U.S. and by logical extension Black male/female relationships: 1) the cash connection; 2) the flesh connection; 3) the force connection; and 4) the dependency connection.

The Cash Connection

The cash connection grows out of the commodity character of society. It is informed by several capitalistic assumptions among which are: 1) everything and everyone has a price; 2) anything you can't buy ain't worth having anyhow; 3) what you invest money or material assets in is yours; and 4) money is the measure of and solution to everything. One would think, however, that these ideas which are so vulgar in conception and brutal in practice would be rejected by rational people. But, in fact, the ruling ideas in any society are the ideas of the rulers of that society and, thus, the model of what is rational in that society is the rationale of the rulers. It follows, then, that the ruling rationale is what the rulers are, i.e., capitalist, racist and sexist.

In such a context, then, it is both rational and normal for mothers to tell their daughters to look for and marry someone who can "take care" of them, as if they were disabled; for women to sell themselves to men, exchanging sex for economic security and call it marriage; for teenage men to invest in young women with a movie and Mac burger and demand their bodies in exchange; and for male idiots to claim the right to rule and ruin the lives of their wives and children on the basis of the money they bring iñ. Money and material considerations, then, form the basis for the cash connection and diminish the chances for a quality relationship which is conscious of but not ruled by material considerations.

The Flesh Connection

The flesh connection grows out of the pornographic character of society and is defined as an association based on purely or predominantly on the pursuit of sex. This connection focuses on the body and all the perverse things one can do with all or selected parts of it. Pornography, as a definite social thought and practice and as the essence and source of the flesh connection expresses itself in five basic ways. First, it is an expression of species alienation. It reflects man alienated from and oblivious of his species half, confused by the contradictory emotions toward and thoughts of her as "whore and high priestess," mother in public and sex machine in bed. In women, it is the same with confusion over the contradictory emotion towards and thoughts of men as hard penises and heroes, father and protector in public and sex freak, big Johnson and Sweet Jesus in bed.

Secondly, pornography is objectification of the species half, turning a natural partner into an object of use and disuse. It is this objificatio which leads men to say while pursuing a woman, I'm going to get "that" and to reduce women to parts of their bodies. Thirdly, then, pornography, is fragmentation of the body, hacking the body into usable pieces and rejecting the wholeness of the human personality. Thus, women and men become open vaginas and hard penises, breasts, buttocks and obscenely curved mouths. No one in a flesh connection wants a whole body, just holes in the body. After all, in a strictly utilitarian sense, it's the holes one uses; the rest is just so much extra flesh. Fourthly, pornography is brutalization, most viciously expressed in the sadomasochistic vulgarities society at its most violent and alienated level has produced. (Phillips, 1967).

Finally, pornography, as the source and essence of the flesh connection, is a sexual commodity form. Its practical expression is the selling of the body or its image. It represents the joining of the cash and flesh connection thru the packaging and peddling of the human body. Even commercials are forms of pornography where women's bodies are sold along with the product and become a part of the commodity thrust to package and sell virtually everything. Perhaps, the greatest tragedy of all this is that many women have accepted their essential "fleshness." Old women assure young women they'd better flash it while they got it, accent their best parts and shake it till they get the desired results. Whatever internal strength the best men might have, it is obviously impossible to think mother, level of mental development and life-companion when breast tips bulge thru thin blouses, puffs peer thru tight pants and buttocks outlined by flowers and arrows dare one not to notice.

The Force Connection

A third connection is the force connection which rises out of the violent and oppressive character of society. The model of manhood in U.S. society is the white conquerer who having subdued his family strikes out to conquer the world — or at least parts of it. Historically, men have used their greater physical strength to subdue women and win arguments they would otherwise lose.

Moreover, the flesh and force connection merge in the act of rape which is not so much sexual as it is psycho-cultural and physcial. For above all, it's an act of domination practiced by husbands, friends and strangers. It is man taking what he's compelled by a fantasized nature and principles of ownership to take — woman. For, in fact, the fantasy continues, she not only deserves it, she desires it. Any late nite cowboy or pirate film confirms this and cultural values inspire and validate it (Karenga, 1978a:15).

But equally damaging is the social or ideological coercion which forces women, thru censure and labelling, into traditional roles. Women are often called lesbians and matriarchs, if they dare be over-assertive in the eyes of threatened males. Moreover, they are often reduced to baby-making machines and forced to produce lumps of meat they don't even identify with and eventually abuse to prove their womanhood. In such a context men and women don't become partners, but adversaries, oppressed and oppressor and their relationship of necessity must suffer.

Finally, the force connection expresses itself in economic coercion. This operates on the principle that he who controls the means to satisfy human needs controls at the same time the humans with those needs.

The Dependency Connection

The fourth and final connection which challenges and often denies quality Black male/female relationships is the dependency connection. This connection is the logical and inevitable result of the others. After a woman has been transform-

48 b

ed into a commodity, reduced to parts of her body and physically or ideologically whipped into compliance, she can only be dependent. In such a context the dependent woman won't leave, even in the worse conditions. For she has no identity or sense of worth outside the deformation and oppression she suffers. Therefore, even if urged to leave, she will not and may even seek to justify her treatment. Like all slaves and servants, she becomes a set of reactions to her slave master, a defender of his definitions and treatment of her. Thus, interdependence, a key value in quality relationships, becomes impossible and the connection becomes the model rather than the deviance (Nobles, 1978).

III. Towards A Meaningful Solution

Although, I've argued that conditions create consciousness and conduct, it is important to stress at this point that the reverse is also true. Consciousness and the social practice that it engenders can and often does create conditions. Afterall, we would certainly be miserable creatures, if history just happened and conditions molded us into patterns we couldn't understand, oppose or direct. In fact, it's of fundamental importance that we recognize that social reality is a human construction, brought into being by what we do and do not do. Certainly, capitalism, racism and sexism shape our relationships, but they are systems created and maintained by humans and they can be changed and destroyed by humans.

But the struggle to change systems — structures and values — must begin with the struggle to change ourselves, i.e., our own views and values and the negative and non-productive ways we've organized and live our daily lives. Only then can we create the social force we need to defy and defeat our oppressor. Regardless of what dogmatists of the left and right declare, real social change will not be a product of new institutions, but new men and women to shape those new institutions in their own interests and image. This is why I argued in the 60's and continue to maintain that the key crisis in Black life is the cultural crisis, i.e., a crisis in views and values. It is a crisis further defined by our lack of a system of views and values which gives us a moral, material and meaningful interpretation of life on the seven basic levels of culture — religion (or spiritual value system), history, social, economic and political organization, creative motif and ethos.

The solution to our deficient relations, then, is rooted in our creation, acceptance and practice of a new value system. Values can be defined here as categories of commitment, priorities and possibilities. Values as categories of commitments and priorities dictate possibilities. For what we hold dear and important and what we put first in our lives decreases or increases our human possibilities. A people that has more records than books and dance their lives away have little or no human possibilities. Likewise, a people which slavishly imitates its oppressor and refuses to take its destiny and daily life in its own hands has little or no possibilities.

Kawaida, as a coherent system of critical thought and values, argues that the quality of relationships is dictated by the quality of our values. It teaches that a cultural revolution which overturns our current conception of ourselves and breaks the monopoly the oppressor has on our minds is the first step toward our full liberation. Kawaida calls for a redefinition of reality in our own interest and image, for a new definition of man and woman and the relationship they ought to have. It stresses that material security is important, but that mterial concerns and pursuits should not rule our lives.

Kawaida recognizes the value of sexual exchange, but rejects the tendency to reduce it to the physical. It is, Kwaida maintains, a part of the whole of what is shared or it is alienated, deforming and counterproductive. Kawaida outlaws force in relationships and considers a dependent woman a national liability. It advocates interdependence which expresses itself as complementarity, i.e., mutual contribution to each other's fulfillment.

Kawaida argues that a real relationship must begin with terms stated, and grows and is reinforced with common values, common aspirations and common struggle for liberation and a higher level of human life. One must begin with a **moral minimum** that cannot be compromised, a set of values which are resistent to revision because they are at the very roots of the relationship. Prohibition against violence; full, free and frank discussion; egalitarian exchange; collective decision-making; and shared responsibility in love and struggle must be a part of that moral minimum, if a relationship is to be real and mutually beneficial.

This, however, is just a beginning and outline of possibilities. The realities wil be built by those *New Africans* who dare to be other than their immediate and social conditions encourage them to be, who have seen and felt themselves in the sun and will never cuddle in the cold shadow of cavemen again.

48 d

Materialism and Chauvinism:
Black Internalization of White Values

by Na'im Akbar, Ph.D.

Many events have occurred in recent history and are still occurring in contemporary society which engender a breach between the African-American man and woman. These events have systematically undermined the conditions necessary for healthy, natural relationships between the sexes. An increased awareness of these events and their pyschological impact on African-Americans should serve as an important instrument in correcting this destructive schism.

We need not review here the devastating impact of the over 300 years of slavery on African-American identity and relationships. Though slavery was legally terminated over a hundred years ago, its persisting residuals continue to impact on present relationships. Many writers described these influences of separated families, capricious hostility, sexual assault, denigration of masculine and feminine roles, etc., which were perpetuated by the Euro-American enslavers. Connections have been demonstrated between these slavery experiences and many of the difficulties continuing to plague African-American relationships in 1980.

Similarly, there has been much discussion of the impact of racism and oppression during the neo-slavery experiences of African-Americans. Certainly, the social, political and economic expressions of such oppression have had devastating effects on African-American men and women. Particularly, identification with the white supremacist value system has resulted in serious self-esteem problems for African-Americans which have taken their toll on those relationships. Needless to say, much of the difficulty could be accounted for by analyzing slavery and oppression as many scholars have done. This discussion is intended to look at some of the more subtle values and attitudes internalized by African-Americans and how those attitudes affect our relationships and what are the prospects for reconciliation.

A problem which seriously affects African-American man/woman relations is the degree to which we have internalized many of the alien and destructive attitudes which are prevalent in Euro-American society. The two most destructive of these attitudes are materialism and sexism. These two attitudes are destructive to human relationships because they augment the already difficult social psychological ecology surrounding those relationships.

In identifying with Euro-American values, material acquisitions become a critical vehicle for affirming self-esteem for African-American men and women. The excessive materialism of the U.S.A. has resulted in the entire society's self-esteem depending upon the acquisition of material goods. The materialistic values occupy a primary focus in the family's strivings. Increasingly, potential mates are chosen primarily on the basis of their earning capacity -- true of both men and women. With such a basis for a choice, it is not surprising that relationships have brief longevity and little substance. The maintenance of the pretentious car, house, furniture, and wardrobe becomes the primary value which guides the young couple's direction. In fact, the shared goods become more highly valued than the relationship. Therefore, another wedge in the relationship. When one adds to this the stress of economics on relationships in general, this becomes yet another weight to the excessive load on African-American woman/man relations. It is not surprising that economic complaints preoccupy many troubled marriages.

Another aspect of materialism is the effect that it has on relationships in general. One consequence of increased materialism is a movement away from the intangible and inner character of things. This becomes particulary detrimental for human relationships, in which the greatest substance is unobservable and intangible. To the degree that African-Americans have internalized such values they will show a tendency to evaluate the opposite sex in accord with the value. Not only will they evaluate each other on the basis of material worth, as we have noted above, but on the basis of physical appearance, primarily. Certainly, the physical dimension remains an important aspect of human attraction within any value system. However, as people become increasingly materialistic, physical factors become more prominent as a basis for evaluating people in general. Add to this physical preoccupation, the prominence of ''white supremacy'' beauty standards and you have the ingredients for superficial and alienated African-American relationships. So the materialism which is a source of tension in Euro-American relationships becomes catastrophic in combination with the other explosive pressures on African-American relationships. We can understand how a ''white'' woman or one who looks "white" becomes more essential to choosing a mate than inner character. So the juxtaposition of materialism on the white supremacist concomitant of racism makes us ready victims to see greater beauty in skin color and hair texture, than in a host of more salient outer and inner qualities.

The issue of "sexism" has generated considerable controversy in the Euro-American community in recent years. There are pro and con arguments regarding the relevance of the political issues surrounding sexism to African-American women. The validity or *in*validity of those arguments is outside of the scope of this discussion. However, there are covert and more basic axiological questions raised from the *issue* of sexism which are relevant to the relationships of African-American women and men, at least indirectly.

One seldom considered variable is that the root of sexism in European thought resides in the basic tenets of Christianity. St. Paul makes a fundamental indictment of the feminine sex which finds consistent support throughout the Old and New Testaments. The persisting perspective is one which assumes innate danger and inferiority of women. The basis of most of the European value system rests on the assumptions of the Judeo-Christian axiology. The derisive conception of women in Euro-American society is at its basis a literal interpretation of the Genesis story which identifies woman (Eve) as being responsible for the "fall" of man (Adam). Eve's fallacy gains greater substantiation by the deceptive wiles of Jezebel, Delilah, Bathsheba, *et. als.* The entire Biblical picture of woman is derisive, negative and lays the foundation for a sexist society. A political retort is ultimately superficial in addressing this fundamental "truth" of the Judeo-Christian religions.

The active role of the Christian church in shaping the contemporary values of African-Americans brings this fact of sexism more poignantly into their relationships. An incontestable fact is that we are all affected by these values because they permeate the society. However, the degree to which people accept the entire Judeo Christian ideological system is the degree to which those values will contort their attitudes. In essence, we are urging here that to be a good Christian with a fundamentalist understanding of Christianity means that one is ideologically obligated to be a sexist. This basic distrust of women does infect African-American woman/man relationships. The tendency to view women as inferior not only affects the treatment of women by men but also women's conceptions of themselves. A frequent complaint among African-American women is the difficulty in forming close trusting relationships with other women. An hypothesis which we are putting forth here is that this is rooted in the, often unconscious, internalization of these attitudes from the religious ideology.

Of course, the depiction of the Christian deity in Caucasian flesh does much more to further the white supermacist values which we have noted above. In

51

essence, the religious institutions in this society which figure so prominently in African-American values aid and abet the cause of sexism and racism. African-Americans become predictably vulnerable to both of these influences with the consequent impact on our relationships with each other. Again, this becomes an additional source of confusion which widens the breach between African-American women and men. And we have indicated above in discussing materialism, these factors of sexism and racism affect all of the society but it becomes an overload on already overburdened relationships.

Another societal value which causes difficulty for all members of the society rains havoc on African-American relationships. This value emanates from an assumption of inevitable conflict between the sexes. This too is rooted in the Biblical descriptions of male/female relations. but finds even greater expression in Euro-American psychology. From the Freudian notion of the Oedipus/Electra complexes through Betty Friedan's "feminine mystique," there is an axiomatic presumption of the inevitability of conflict between the sexes. The concept of the proverbial "battle between the sexes" is a myth which fosters precisely those battles. This notion of perpetual conflict is fostered by the popular media and so-called experts in human relations. The result is a self-fulfilling prophecy of perpetual conflict. In societies where such assumptions are not made, it is dubious whether such conflict exists. With the assistance of the daily soap opera, American families get daily instruction on the latest twists in interpersonal conflict. Again, the assumption of the inevitability of conflict leads to an initiation and exacerbation of conflict among African-American men and women.

Reconciliation

A perusal of the above discussion would lead one falsely to conclude that the survival of African-American woman/man relations is impossible. Clearly the odds against such relationships are great, but they do survive and at much higher rates than the enumerated odds would suggest. These relationships survive not only because they are so vital and essential to human life, but because many of the above negative experiences have wrought positive outcomes which fortify relationships against many of these destructive influences.

One primary source of strength lies in the awareness of these influences. One's capacity for self-defense is, of course, improved with awareness of the dangers. To know that we still carry lingering effects of slavery in our psychological and social selves, then we must learn to avoid those circumstances which activate those conditions. For example, social and personal passivity or inactivity certainly reactivates the slavery state. African-American men and women must always take an active role in confronting their personal and social problems.

Though such passivity is a problem for human beings in general, it is particularly problematic for African-Americans with the psycho-historical experience of slavery. The attitudes which have been engendered from slavery can be mastered when people defy the tendency toward family dissolution which characterized the slavery situation.

Another source of opposition to these dissolving influences is a consciousness of the strengths which African-Americans brought into slavery. The basic respect for woman/man relations was so strong with African-American people that there were indestructible efforts to maintain those relationships. Many slave men risked their lives to reclaim forcefully separated mates. Many slave women defied threats on their lives to be reunited with their men. Clearly many of the dynamics of slave revolts, escapes and motivation to obtain freedom were generated by the strength and worth of those relationships between women and men. Consciousness of battles fought and won gives to the new troops a greater respect for their proven strength. Knowledge of our perseverance makes many of the frivolous contemporary problems dissipate within the context of African-American history.

The confusing notions of the "stud" and "breeder" among African-American men and women respectively, becomes less appealing when understood. Few men and women would willingly choose to re-enact the atrocities of slavery adaptations, if they were aware of the source of these behaviors. Consciousness of the prices paid to sustain African-American families would give them much greater value. The increased value would increase the motivation to maintain those relationships in the contemporary world.

Knowledge of the predisposition for distrust of the man's protective and provisional abilities should serve as additional incentive for the man to be an effective provider and protector. Despite the persisting economic and political oppression, one would hope that these conditions would only serve as additional incentive to take an active stance in trying to correct those economic and political ills. The African-American woman would have to work on her historically adaptive role of assuming family leadership. There must be a greater willingness to share that leadership and in some instances relinquish it. With both women and men using their historically earned strength of perseverance to deal with these historical adaptations it becomes feasible to expect solutions.

Efforts at mutual respect must be enforced in order to avoid the historically engendered disrespect. Again, knowledge of the past and active attempts to identify the emergence of disrespect in the present becomes a weapon against this killer of good relationships. Special efforts should be taken by the African-American woman to discourage disrespect by the man. She should avoid playing the role of seductress and should flatly object to being treated exclusively as a sexual object. Of course, her carriage and tolerance serve as critical stimuli in bringing about such reactions by the man. The man must pride himself in earning respect for his responsibility and his efforts to be protector and provider. These are the qualities that can begin to reverse the long-term conditioning of disrespect and a reactivation of the traditional African qualities of mutual respect between the sexes.

Ultimately, it will take extensive political action and economic planning (some even say, "revolution") to reverse the extensive racism and oppression which characterizes the treatment of African people in America. It is rather impossible to talk about improving those woman/man relationships without working to change some of the oppressive social realities. As we have discussed above, much of what affects the African-American man and woman can be directly attributable to the continuing social conditions of neo-slavery. The economic insolvency of the African-American man, the exploitation of the African-American woman, the disproportionate numbers of African-American men victimized by the penal system, the continued absence of effective political control and general control over the destiny of our communities continue to undermine the stability of male/female relations.

In the final analysis, the reconciliation of the African-American woman and man is a philosophical reconciliation. An exorcism of the deeply embedded false premises regarding materialism and sexism must occur in our thinking. We must rediscover the ancient definitions of man and woman and respect their differences and their complementarity. Ancient writers who found the origin of their wisdom on the African continent have long ago asserted that the true identity of man and woman is an inner identity. These writers suggest that we can find the prototype of the man's function in his basic role as father. Similarly, the prototype of the woman's function is in the role of mother. These ancient definitions, of course, attributed much broader meaning to motherhood and fatherhood than the biological definition of these roles.

Fatherhood was viewed as a societal function which went far beyond a male's capacity to sire off-spring. True manhood was identified in the human qualities of personal mastery and rational direction which equipped the man to be a provider and protector for the society. Motherhood was viewed as a nurturant societal function. In whatever role the woman found herself, her obligation was to nourish, cultivate, inspire and facilitate societal and human growth. Such qualities focus the developing person on her or his inner self. In order to serve these functions, the physical characteristics, material possessions, sexual roles and functions, all become secondary and incidental to the bigger definition of self.

African-American men and women must not fall victim to the expanding unisexualism so prevalent in American society. They must preserve the uniqueness of their separate, complementary roles. They must also avoid the ontological weakness which equates nurturance, dependence and supportiveness with weakness. They must also avoid the highly destructive macho notions of manhood which are feverishly trying to be realized by both men and women in their striving for a faulty liberation. We must avoid the growing individualistic mania which avows a false independence of men and women. The ancient observation that man and woman are natural mates to each other is as true today as it was 100,000 years ago. The fact that our biological evolution has not taken us beyond our reliance on each other for the purpose of reproducing ourselves is evidence sufficient that there must be some parallelled psychological interdependence which is also present.

Conclusion

African-Americans have survived the atrocities of the last 400 years because of the resilience of the relationship of women and men in their unions called "families." These families have remained the mainstay of our cultural and psychological life in the wake of the destruction of every other social support institution. Because of the endurance of these families and the flexibility of fulfilling family functions, under the imperative of collective survival, as a people we were not dehumanized. The conditions of slavery and oppression are systematic efforts of dehumanization. Destruction of human imperatives of dignity and moral responsibility is the essential vehicle of maintaining a slave. There is such a powerful drive for freedom within the human makeup that women and men would oppose slavery with every fiber of life in them so long as they have their human self-respect. Therefore, both in the days of field plantations and the consumer plantations of today, the most effective device to maintain slaves is to undermine human dignity.

Women and men together constitute the primal nexus for the crystallization of human life in its fullest potential. The unique attacks on this union experienced by African-Americans constitutes the most heinous crime in human history. The difficulty confronted by contemporary African-American men and women is fallout from the serious assaults on their relationships during their American sojourn. We have argued in this discussion that consciousness of these fragmenting experiences and destructive attitudes is initital equipment to counteract their persistent influence. There is substantial inspiration to preserve those precious relationships when one realizes the kind of opposition which they still confront. Furthermore, knowledge of the enemy forces and their effect on ones life directs ones effort towards the elimination of those influences.

This discussion has been an effort to identify some of those antagonistic psycho-historical forces and their influences, towards the end of fostering greater consciousness of the African-American self.

PART II:

THE BLACK MALE/FEMALE RIFT

The Pimp-Whore Complex
In Everyday Life

by Joseph Scott, Ph.D. & James Stewart, Ph.D.

The Crusaders have released a record called *Street Life,* Donna Summer permeates the airwaves with a piece entitled *Bad Girls,* and Linda Clifford's fame continues to grow through the impact of *Don't Give It Up.* The lyrics of these contemporary songs speak to the processes of pimping and whoring inherent in the ways Black males and females relate to one another in everyday life.

The common theme that emerges is that professional and non-professional pimping and whoring are pervasive in our community today. Evidently they are such intrusive parts of Black everyday life that the poets and the song writers feel obliged to reflect them back to us to force a critical assessment of the nature of the social forces we are allowing to destroy our girls, boys and relationships.

Many Black men and women have so scripted the pimp-whore ideology that they do not know what they are subscribing to when they mouth the comments of the following types:

"I'm going for sex; I'm going for money; if you got a car I'll take that. the first thing that I ask is, 'Do you have a job?' If you ain't working, I ain't got no time."

"If I ever find me one that is married and is gonna give me something (meaning money), here I am.... It's too bad for their wives, because nine out of ten, they got somebody else's husbands. That's the way the world go; you got my husband and I got your husband."

"I met a young man....He was 24-25....a nice looking young man. He didn't want to do nothing but lay up and wait on my welfare check....make me feel good in bed....and think that I'm gonna flip and then get out there and take care of him."

"You may be buying him a $100.00 coat every month or a $300.00 coat every month or a $400.00 diamond ring or a long Cadillac that he ain't looking for....That's where a lof of women make their mistakes. They give their man away....He wants a woman to be a woman....They don't know that a little wolf woman like me from the ghetto will take them all....I would be just the woman that would come along and get everything he's got in the world...."

In the remainder of this essay, the sociopolitico-economic context in which the pimp-whore complex, as reflected in these commentaries, emerges and the mechanisms that perpetuate the complex are examined.

Black on Black Exploitation

The content of the commentaries which were presented suggests that Black men and women are locked in a financial conflict. Women are fighting women over the available men with the available dollars and men are fighting men over the available women with the available dollars. In short, men and women are looking at one another as potential "marks" in a petty confidence game. Men and women deeply involved in the "street life" are busy setting their tender traps in order to snare those who might be sources of money. Women and men who have regular jobs become very attractive potential "marks." Even women on welfare and men on social security or disability become fair game. And why not? There is so little money available in most Black communities that those who have even a small cash reserve become "marks" in the pimping and whoring games in their many disguised forms.

Many of our expressions like, "putting the beg on," "dropping a few coins," "getting a loan from my baby," and so on, all add up to the same thing: Black men and women using their sex, their gift of gab, and their "threads" to lure someone into their webs of intrigue to establish emotional dependency over their prey so that the victims' monies may be siphoned away. "Nickel pimping and whoring" are common activities of both men and women. "Begging for some bread" and "receiving money or gifts for services rendered" are as common as fish frys on Saturday nights in most Black communities. All of us—men and women alike—expect the exploitive advances as soon as we set foot on "the street"—and there is at least one such street in every Black community.

Sometimes even on the first date a man will suggest that his escort buy him a shirt or something else of non-inconsequential financial value or a woman may suggest that her date purchase some groceries or some articles of clothing for her. Commonly, in due course—either the male or female may suggest that a "little help with the rent" is in order. In brief, the conjugal relationship soon becomes highly commercialized.

The Roots of Black Male-Female Conflict

From ongoing research, we find that the "nickel pimping and whoring" is the source of widespread conflict and mistrust in the Black community. Such behaviors are so common that men and women must always be "at the ready" lest they be "used" under the guise of being loved. Few males and females involved in the street life are willing to exchange sex for sex, time for time, dinner for dinner or companionship for companionship. One of the partners in a pair-bonded relationship generally puts a higher value on his or her own "contribution" and, consequently, feels justified in asking for further compensation in the form of financial remuneration. So, in addition to the sex, time, dinner and companionship as one lady related, "He ain't gonna lay up with me for nothing, Honey. He's going to drop some money or he's gonna go." "If she don't spend no money, I can't spend no time," one man also confided. these quotations succinctly sum up the exploitive attitudes and games which have attracted a large following.

The money "connection" between Black men and women is the root of much of the evil in their relationships. Most Black male-female conflicts revolve around money flows—how much and in what direction. Many of the hassles which continually erupt from financial abuses and uses of one another because the participants fail to appreciate the underlying dynamics.

The Factor of Racism

We suggest that the Black male-female financial conflict is generated in the Black community by White institutional racism. The small amount of income flowing into the Black community creates the motivation among Black men and women to seek whatever precious few dollars are available to Blacks. This financial deprivation is compounded by the shortage of jobs and businesses caused by institutional racism. Money makes American life go around; without it one will not be fed, be clothed, be housed, or be medically serviced. Thus the need for money is ever present and ever pressing in on us. If we can't get it from whites, from whom must we get it? From other Blacks, who have very little already as a result of the forces described below.

Three Poisons in the Pot of Life

Institutional racism attacks the life force of the Black community like a trio of poisons injected by a multi-headed viper. The first poison can be termed *institutional decimation* of Black American males. *Institutional deprivation* of gainful employment is the second toxic element while *institutional subsidization* of the single parent family, to the exclusion of public support for the two parent family is the third poison.

Institutional decimation (killing) of the Black American male has been going on for many decades. It started during slavery when masters systematically thinned out the slave population during periods in which the number of slaves constituted a threat to existing order or during economic recessions. More recently, institutional decimation has occurred through the disproportionate killing of young virile Black males in foreign wars, through death sentences imposed by the criminal justice system, "justifiable" homicides by the police, through industrial accidents and diseases, and through hypertension caused by the pressures of racism. When these reduced numbers are added to the disproportionate number of Black males who are in prison for life and those who are functionally incapacitated by drug dependency for life, the number of virile Black males available for Black females to marry is considerably depleted. This numerical shortage of Black males has created intense competition for eligible males and has created a situation where the men can "require" that their prospective lady friends have something equivalent to a "dowry" or some other financial resource before they will enter into a steady conjugal relationship. There is, therefore, pressure for women to be "financial" in order to be competitive in the marriage market and in order to be seleced early. It was submitted at the outset that the quotations which were presented clearly suggest that men, in particular, are looking at the financial worth of women in the rating, dating, and mating game.

Institutional deprivation of gainful employment (in voluntary unemployment) has been a perennial problem faced by Blacks since coming to these shores. For decades, however, high unemployment rates among Blacks have been a characteristic feature of the American economy and now the unemployment rate among Blacks is increasing at such an alarming rate that up to 50% of the young males are unemployed in most urban ghettos. Those who are not totally unemployed suffer subemployment in the forms of part-time work or low wage work. Hence, money is very scarce. the great majority of Black males find themselves subemployed at one time or other during the year, and a substantial number of the youth never work at all. Even for adult Black males, the subemployement rate has been around 20%, which means that the financial deprivation to the entire Black community resulting from structural unemployment (involuntary) runs into the billions of dollars. Coupling these facts with the recognition that adolescent and adult Black males still need food, shelter, transportation and recreation whether they are employed or not—there emerges pressure to acquire money by any means necessary. ''Hustlin'' of all types has emerged as a ghetto activity to alleviate some of this financial pressure. Pimping and whoring are just two of the ''hustles'' that ghetto residents have available to them. Some young men and women openly pimp and whore like the professional whores and pimps. Others engage in ''nickel pimping and whoring'' as part of the dating, rating and mating game and this is by far the more pervasive activity.

The money situation is so tight, that many persons in financial need are looking to others for financial help. ''First, I look at the purse,'' as often said, sums up the situation. The pursuit of money would not be an issue if it did not so perniciously demean and disrupt everyday Black male-female relationships. However, this pursuit of scarce monies leaves a path of exploitation, bitterness, and revenge. The bitterness of one relationship spills over into others and a chain reaction occurs. Men and women, looking at one another as opportunities for extracting money generates suspicion and mistrust of one another. And most of this community disorder comes from the lack of jobs available to adult men and women in the ghetto which, in effect, denies them access to necessary subsistence goods.

Institutional subsidization (welfare) is the third poison corrupting the Black community. Subsidization commonly takes the form of welfare payments to women with dependent children. With the shortage of adult men, and the shortage of gainful jobs for those Black men and women who are able and willing to work, the White power elite must somehow subsidize the Black community in order to reduce the explosive potential. The welfare system—the relief system—is an institutional device for cooling out Blacks in the depressed and oppressed ghettoes. The money is most often given to women—without a man in the house. The money given becomes an incentive for Black women to separate from their husbands and select a *White* sponsor instead. Statistical studies have shown that as the unemployment rate for Black men goes up, the enrollment on AFDC goes up. The power elite—most relatively affluent White men—knowingly keep the Black men in a debilitated state, and at the same time keep the Black women dependent upon them. This is the modern day analogue of the slave relationship between Black women and White men. Black women are being brought up to look to White men for sustenance and comfort.

With the help of TV situation comedies, and TV soap operas and TV advertisements, Black women are being programmed to look to White men for sexual satisfaction also. The process has gone almost unperceived by most Black leaders, but a critical scrutiny of commercial television programming will easily find corroborating evidence of the above assertion, i.e., the growing accommodation of Black women by White men.

The Black Male/Female Impasse*

by Harold Cruse

I am well past 50 going on 60. As such, I do not share and never have shared, many of the male/female assumptions of the younger generations. I was never legally married, but lived with a "common-law" wife for several years before splitting up. As a result of that experience, I rejected the legal married state because of the newer set of assumptions on the part of black women regarding marriage. For my part, I do not contemplate marriage until I fully retire from active duty.

The main reason, among others, that I and my "wife" separated was over career and social function. It is a rare Black woman who can live or coexist with a creative or nonconformist Black male. It was rare in my day, and even more rare today despite all the "brother-sister" talk. Of course, the reverse is usually true; the average Black male cannot coexist with a creative Black female. Which means that, generally speaking, Blacks have not been socialized to adapt what they understand as marriage with the demands of careers that do not fit into the mold of the conventional "9 to 5" workaday routine. It just so happens that we, the Black elites, who jabber among ourselves about the Black male-female conflict, do not correspond in social function or lifestyle with ordinary workaday Blacks with or without the "family." The main problem with Black females in this category is that, to them, marriage means seeking the highest "ranking" males that are available. Thus, they are after status symbols rather than genuine compatibilities in partnership. (Most of them do not even know what *that* is).

*This was a private, personal correspondence, parts of which are published by permission of the author.

63

In most cases, any Black male who attempts to conform to such expectations is asking for a marriage or an affair which is already doomed to fail. Which adds up to the inescapable conclusion that the more "successful" we become, the more "status" we achieve, the more "equality" we achieve, the more affluence we gain, the more unworkable do our concepts of marriage and personal relationships on the sexual level become. In other words, the political, social, economic and "cultural" advances that Blacks have won over the last twenty years have compounded blacks' problems of sexual and marriage relations. Black males have been challenged to give up their "male prerogatives" before they have really achieved anything resembling male *"manhood equality,"* while Black females are demanding "equal treatment" from Black males (which the men are both unable or unwilling to give) while Black females, simultaneously belittle Black males because they really have no "power" in society. One hears this attitude expressed in various ways. It comes across most flagrantly in the widespread notion among Black females who want to equally share "leadership" when there is almost totally lacking today a Black "leadership" philosophy either among males or females that really means very much. In the meantime, because of these circumstances, the Black marriages contracted are short term affairs full of conflict. I, for one, stay clear of them. But, as I said earlier, my personal role is premeditated. What I have managed to achieve was accomplished at the price of staying single and also single-minded. I make no bones about the fact that I maintain a modest number of satisfying relationships with women of both races (or better with three different races), because that is the style of life I had to adopt in order to stay personally solvent and also productive. I say all of this in order to underscore my disclaimer: Who am I to assume either the right or the obligation to attempt to solve the sexual and marriage problems of a younger generation(s) whose values I have never really shared?

Most of the women of my generation are retired or semi-retired as are most of the males. *I'm a world War Two veteran!* Consider the fact that you can hardly name an active Black male spokesman today who is of my World War Two generation. As for Black women, I find it difficult to relate to younger Black females. If it is not on a purely paternalistic basis, coupled wth a "hands-off," semi-authoritarian posture, I find it almost impossible to even establish an "intellectual" relationship. Why? because they think they *know* everything, or *understand* everything, *which they don't. And don't mention SEX*, or they'll talk about you. In fact, they'll talk about you even if you *don't* mention SEX! In my twelve years at [the University of] Michigan, it has been a rare event to find a black female student with whom one can establish an *intellectual* relationship. Their general attitude is: Well, who are you! You can't really *know* very much, that *I* don't know already! The truth is, *it is the White female students* who are the most teachable, the most dedicated, the most willing to get all they can possibly get out of you. During my last semester (Fall) at Michigan, I had the unusual experience of having a Black female medical student who was truly willing to learn from me. She even writes me letters here at Bowdoin, thanking me for the classroom experience. However, during my winter course here at Bowdoin, the most troublesome student (out of sixteen high quality Bowdoin students), the most troublesome, aggravating, contentious, petty, know-it-all, was a Black female student from...., daughter of a Black elected official. Moreover, she did the most unsatisfying work of all the women in the class. But when her father came to Bowdoin to speak on the problems in....it was then that I understood why she was what she is. How such an innocuous individual was ever elected to public office I'll never understand. But I found out that his wife (the student's mother) had put him out of the house ages ago. So I suppose this Black female was fighting her father by being petty and contentious with me. However, it was only because I was a visitor at Bowdoin that I didn't bring her up on the carpet. At Michigan, in the fall of 79, I was forced to bring two Black females up on the carpet in the Dean's office (by letter), while flunking one of them, in addition to a Black male. In the case of the male, I made him do his term paper all over again. In other words, the Black male/female thing is getting *outrageous*. Another angle that has developed is that there is a considerable number of Black females in academia who pretend to believe that African males understand the nature of the Black situation in the United States, *better* than a native born Black male, although the African just arrived the day before yesterday. However, enough of academia because academia is not the *real world*.

In the real world out there, the present Black-male/female impasse is temporarily unsolvable just so long as this "prosperity" lasts. The "closed" society has been opened just enough to allow many blacks, *both* under-privileged and upward mobile to believe they have freedom of choices, options and alternatives which are unfettered by any kind of social restraint or social authority. The only operating restraint for most Blacks is lack of money or lack of status (which, in the case of Black females seeking a man or marriage) amounts to the same thing. In the case of Black males, the main drive is sexual fulfillment and money. It is my contention that, in this regard, Black males are less hungry than Black females. Or else, the drive for status takes on other compulsions. Crime, for Black males, means the status of money. Black males usually do not "social climb" after higher-statused Black females (they already know they *can't* get them).

It is very often the White female who is most available for "status" purposes, and even here it is usually not "social" status, but *money*, either through low-level "pimping" or higher-level paramouring for materialistic gain.

Some Personal Reflections

There ought to be an informal social history of the sociology of Black male/female relationships—(minus all the self-serving clap-trap about the "defenseless" slave-woman being raped by slave masters, etc., etc.).

I have in mind here a certain Hollywood writer whose early years as an aspiring writer was spent as the paramour of a White woman of means. He didn't marry her (I don't think), but when he finally became recognized, he dropped the White woman and married Black. During my earlier years of adventuring around Manhattan, New York, I discovered that in Greenwich Village a small clique of free-lancing Black males lived by preying on young female students from Ivy League colleges vacationing in the Village for "kicks." The Black male strategy was try to marry them and then demand a big payoff from the White parents to agree to annul the marriage. One guy who I knew quite well went into a moderately successful music publishing business on money gotten this way (although he claimed he really wanted the girl).

As long as there is the Black drive for money, status and freedom," there isn't much that can be done about interracial marriage for now. Although it is increasing, it has little or no bearing on the essentials of the "group" position of Blacks generally. For these reasons, I am neither *for* nor *against* interracial marriage. To me, it is irrelevant. Speaking of the black elites, Harry Belafonte and Sidney Poitier first married Black, then married White. Why? From what I know, it was a problem of compatibility. In my view, neither of the Black females involved were able to accept the fact that *their* notions of marriage could not accommodate the free-wheeling obligations of artistic stardom on the part of their mates. Lena Horne first married "Black" but then married Lennie Hayton, White. It is assumed that her first husband could not coexist with Horne's stardom. Why this was the case, should not be any mystery. We have to understand that Blacks, for the most part, were not socialized to accept any other kind of family or marriage relationship that wasn't imposed by segregation. In my own superficial and empirical observations of the personal lives of jazz musicians, I found that 99% of them married Black women and *kept* them. When any of them carried on liaisons with White women, it was done rather semi-discreetly but *separate and away from home life.* Duke Ellington, e.g., separated from his first, legal wife, but sustained permanent "common-law" home life. However, the Broadway gossip was full of rather lurid details about his extra-marital affairs. In 1953, I had a writing appointment with Duke Ellington after a performance at the old Birdland Club. From about 1 a.m. to daybreak, there was a parade of Black women coming and going. They came to pick up their musician husbands and guard them from White women escapades. I was told by one who knew, this was the domestic strategy of most all of the Black wives of jazz musicians (on the road or at home).

In 1954, I attended a private party given for....by one of the first Black female architects, Beverly Greene. (In the late 1970's, Black females studying architecture were surprised to learn that *they* were not the first!) Beverly was also a Lesbian. ——'s husband, ——, was also at this party. It was widely known that Beverly Greene played the role of ''Mother-Confessor'' for the wives of Black musicians who were having ''domestic'' difficulties. One of these women, who was staying temporarily in Beverly's apartment, was the wife of ——, the great jazz artist. While —— was ''letting her hair down'' singing ''Lush Life'' (Billy Staryhorn's great song hit) with both Srtayhorn and Luther Henderson at the piano, the liquor was flowing, and the joint was swingin', and the food was ravishly disappearing. Everybody was wide-eyed as the Great ——, half-high, let loose. (Poor little me, who was only invited by pure accident, was shocked at the wanton behavior of —— as she dropped her lady-demure image!). Then, out of nowhere, came —— who banged on the door with loud and threatening obscenities, demanding that his wife come home. ''——, come on out of there, you bitch!'' Beverly protested, while the men tried to hold back an enraged ——. *That* broke up the party! —— beat a hasty exit before the police might arrive. (I'll expand on this significant but hilarious incident when I see you again.)

I tell this story for a number of reasons. First, there is the problem not only of Black sex and marriage, but, as you know, homosexuality and lesbianism. In the background of the Beverly Greene party affair was the suppressed problem of both male and female homsexuality—which can be a very troublesome issue. In a way, it relates to the question posed sometime ago by Robert Staples— ''Has the Sexual Revolution Passed Blacks By?'' The answer is-The Sexual Revolution has passed by the most militant Black generation-the *Sixties Generation!* In race politics, this generation was most militant, but in sexual politics they are a conservative generation, i.e., as far as the *elite class* is concerned. In my generation, and among my parents' generation, so-called sexual deviancy was known and acknowledged, if shamefacedly. During my life, both in Virginia and New York, during my formative years of the 1930's, I witnessed sexual deviancies among blacks such as: homosexuality, lesbianism, prosititution, incest, etc., among schoolteachers, church ladies, relatives, friends, male and female. Among the New York City-Harlem eilites, the sexual stories are legion. In Virginia, the favorite daughter of one of the greatest known historical scholars at Virginia State College, Petersburg, Va., (my hometown) was a wide-open, flagrant, uncontrolled nymphomaniac who slept with every ordinary soldier out of Camp Lee, Virginia from 1941 to 1945. You know the scholar, but I won't call his name bacause, tragically, the daughter died sometime after World War Two. I had a female schoolteacher, who was also a Catholic, believe it or not, who maneuvered to keep me after school over some alleged classroom infraction, but purely for sexual enticements. *Today*, this would or could hardly happen, because of the Feminist

67

movement which was inspired first of all, by the so-called *Black Revolution of the Sixties*. What I learned during the Thirties about Black sex reality was fortified by what I learned during World War Two in England, Algeria, Tunisia, Northern Ireland, Italy. Later came France, Germany and Yugoslavia. In the face of these experiences, I, as a Black male, must consider Black females of the contemporary generations as sexually conservative. As biased as this conclusion might seem, it is, nonetheless *objective*. Moreover, it is not to claim that Black males have been too instrumental in a positive counterforce against this female conservative (pseudo-liberalistic) attitudes towards Black sex and Black marriage.

In my personal view, the only way out of this Black male/female impasse is for both males and females (of the *elite* classes) to accept the unheard of principle of the ''open-marriage'' or open-cohabitational arrangement which, at any time, cannot be legally binding nor legally construed outside of the courts. However, the question of the sanctity of the (Black) family does not fall under this rather loose and libertarian attitude towards marriage. What it says is that is is not the prerogative of the black elites to be arguing about the sanctity of the ''Black family,'' since their life-styles do not approximate the needs, demands nor obligations of the workaday Black family which lives either on a 9—5 job with overtime, public welfare or the marginal welfare-crime-moonlighting mode of existence.

Once the Black elites accepted ''racial integration'' as the road to Black liberation, it is doubtful that they were fully cognizant of the consequences of what they know (i.e. hopefully). The ultimate expression of racial integration is racial intermarriage, a dubious solution to race discrimination or segregation. Thus no black can cry ''racial sellout'' at an interracial marriage. What is needed now is a reassessment of the meaning of ''integration.''

Beauty and the Beast:
The Role of Physical Attraction
in the Black Community

by Robert Staples Ph.D.

"Beauty is as beauty does" is an old folk saying in many Black communities. If folk sayings mirrored cultural practices, we would expect Blacks to subordinate physical beauty, as an important value, to more important qualities such as intelligence, honesty, sensitivity, etc. However, as in the society-at-large, beauty structures ones opportunity and life chances, especially for women, as to be the most powerful predictor of status, wealth, self-esteem—even freedom—for the Black individual. In exploring the function of beauty in Black folk, a more appropriate saying would be: "God don't like ugly." It seems that his more earthly counterparts in the Black world do not either.[1]

Only recently have social scientists studied the influence of beauty. People remain beholden to the myth that everyone is born with equal assets and equal opportunities for survival and a happy and comfortable life. In fact, after race and gender, ones physical characteristics are the most determinant of access to the society's privileges and values. This hierarchy of privilege dates back to the beginning of Homo Sapiens. According to one anthropologist, cave women who were sexually attractive enjoyed more food brought back from their men while those with less sex appeal were left to fend for themselves.[2]

In contemporary society, beauty can be a differentiating force in such diverse areas as employment, educational achievement, popularity among ones peers, dating and sexual experiences, prison sentences and the like.[3] The influence of beauty has increased in recent years due to the influence of television, which purveys a high standard of physical attractiveness as the norm on most of its programs. In urban, impersonal environments, where people are not part of a social network, physical attractiveness becomes the crucial standard by which indivduals form their first impression of each other.

As we shall see, Black Americans, particularly the elites, have become equally fascinated with physical attractiveness. However, it is ironic that a group so victimized by arbitrary standards of individual worth should succumb to the ideology that physical looks are the measure of a person's value. In a society, or world, where whites interpret the definition of beauty, those standards have always favored characteristics endemic to their group. Whiteness, ipso facto, has always been seen as more physically attractive than Blacks, Browns and Yellows. If any doubt lingers about that tendency, one need look no further than the Miss Universe beauty contest. Although non-whites constitute about 75 percent of the world's population, the winner of that contest is inevitably from some white country. Even South Africa has produced a winner, who was a fervent advocate of its racial apartheid system.

Apart from racially determined physical characteristics, standards of beauty have varied over time and in different cultures. France, for instance, has regarded feet as a sex symbol. The United States has long been obsessed with female mammary glands, an anatomical asset that would seem senseless in pre-colonial Africa where women did not wear clothing above the waist. While America currently worships the thin woman, opulent females were more highly regarded in African societies because it connoted high status and good health. Certain factors seem almost universal in determining physical attractiveness.

One is the rarity of a physical trait in its most exacting form. The more abundant a trait is, the less it tends to be highly regarded. Another is Whiteness. Even in predominantly White cultures, blondes are the preferred coloration. They are especially valued by Meditteranean whites.

As far as Blacks are concerned, lightness of skin color is the dominant criterion in determining ones beauty among women. The rhetoric about Black is beautiful notwithstanding, lightness of skin color has been the yardstick of beauty for Black women for the last four hundred years. According to Louis Villa:

> "For many decades the lighter-skinned females of the Black race were most preferred by Black men, because their color was closer to that of the White race, and the Black American had been conditioned for centuries by white Americans to believe that anything or anyone who resembled the Whites had to be better. Any Black man who had a light complected female (known in slavery as a "high yellow") possessed a status symbol of sort."[4]

70

The evidence for this cultural attitude is not forthcoming from the mouths of Blacks. In any survey of mate selection standards among Blacks, skin color is rarely mentioned. When Berkeley psychologist Juanita Papillon did a study of the effect of skin color on the emotional makeup of Blacks, she found the higher the self-esteem the darker the skin color.[5] If that study was based on self-reports, it may reflect wishful thinking rather than empirical reality. When the influence of skin color is independently verified, the prestige of lightness is apparent. A ten year Detroit area study of 250 Black couples discovered a relationship between skin color and blood pressure: those with darker skin tended to have higher blood pressure. Their conclusion was that in a color conscious society, Blacks with the darkest skins have suffered the most discrimination and therefore the greatest emotional stress. Hence, even those who live in comfortable neighborhoods show the effects of that stress in their blood pressure.[6]

It is generally conceded that white society is still more comfortable with lighter Blacks. Fairer skinned Blacks often receive preferential treatment from White employers in hiring and promotions. Some years ago Drake and Cayton reported that light skinned Blacks were the only Blacks hired for lower middle class positions such as sales clerks in Chicago.[7] Those employment practices, however, are only a variation of the general racism Blacks endured in the United States. Within the Black community, these invidious distinctions still obtain. When a group of Harvard University researchers set out to investigate the relationship between a Black male's socio-economic status and the skin color of his wife, they found out that the overwhelming majority of higher status Black males had fair-skinned wives, a proportion that could not possibly have resulted if their mates were chosen at random from the Black population.[8]

The highest status Black males continue to be medical doctors. In his classic work, *The Black Bourgeoisie,* E. Franklin Frazier made the penetrating observation that after graduation from medical school the Black doctor confirmed his status by obtaining a cadillac and a fairskinned wife.[9] How times have changed. The Black medical doctors are now driving a Mercedes Benz with a white wife sitting on the passenger's side. In some cases, both were trade-ins. Some of the biggest protests against Black men marrying white women come from lightskinned Black women who were the biggest losers in his trading up for a "better" model. Those same women had previously taken advantage of the fact that higher status Black men wanted a wife as white as possible. When the real thing (white women) became available, they rushed to them. They were rarely heard complaining when 80 percent of the Black doctors were marrying fair-skinned women and ignoring brown-skinned women.[10] It depends on whose ox is being gored.

White women continue to bear the standard of beauty in this country. It's not only whiteness but other anatomical features that are found more commonly

71

in that group that define loveliness. Again, Louis Villa recalls: "I recollect the days of my youth when the girls in the neighborhood who were the most sought after by the fellows were those who possessed the lightest complexion, thinnest lips, the straightest hair, and the biggest legs—all common traits of white women."[11] During the 1970's the interracial marriage rate of Black males more than doubled. Most of those Black males represented the top ten percent of the Black male population. White women were accused of skimming the cream of the Black crop. Moreover, Blacks give whiteness to the powerful influence of good looks in the oft heard complaint that those same Black men do not marry attractive White women. Obviously, the assumption is that men marry for beauty alone. It may be true but it forecloses the possibility that a man may marry a woman for any reason other than her physical pulchritude.

Given that many Black men prefer their women light or White, the supply of such women is limited for a number of reasons. What, then, do Black males consider in their search for a desirable mate. A couple of surveys inform us on this question. When the Roper organization asked Black and white men what qualities are most admired in a woman, the Black males ranked sex appeal fourth—White males rated it sixth.[12] When *Jet* magazine surveyed Black males in Chicago on the ten things they notice about women, they listed in this order (1)face (2)legs (3)bust (4)eyes-hair (5)personality (6) dress intelligence (7)smile (8)buttocks (9)walk (10)hands-feet-voice-conversation-sincerity.[13]

It is obvious from that ranking that a woman's primary assets are physical traits. Other sterling qualities such as personality rank 5th, intelligence 6th and ability to hold a conversation and sincerity come in dead last. Moreover, the first four physical traits are generally those most common to white women. The face should be light and keen in features, legs and bust should be big, eyes round, hair long and straight. It is a cruel twist of fate that physical traits originally designed for other functions, to allow a group to adapt effectively to its physical enviroment, have become a benchmark of beauty. More ironic is the fact that some of the desirable physical traits become liabilities over a period of time. Big legs, for instance, often reflect a retention of fluid that can later cause kidney problems. People with white or fair skin may show signs of aging prematurely. Women with large breasts may find them sagging as they grow older.

A woman's comeliness has its drawbacks for both men and women. The major problem encountered by men is that it is an ephemeral quality. The most attractive woman on a dinner date may not look as stunning the next morning sans her cosmetic accouterments. As men remain with an attractive woman over a period of time, her physical looks become routinized and subordinate to other qualities they rank as less important in their initial encounter. Beauty is also closely linked to a youthful appearance. If other qualities such as intelligence, emotional support, sensitvity are absent or weak, the male confronted with a beautiful but aging wife may feel betrayed and disillusioned in many ways and even disgusted with her reliance on charms which have faded with the passing of years.

While she is still young and attractive, her husband may be more subject to pangs of jealousy. The husbands of beautiful women are known to be paranoid over the attention of other men toward their wives. Many of them attempt to keep such wives at home lest they meet and have affairs with men they meet in the workplace. One such insecure man, who had a working wife, drove her to work in the morning, picked her up for lunch, and drove her home after work. There's no direct research evidence that indicates attractive women are more likely to engage in extra-marital affairs. Surely, they receive more propositions than less attractive women. We do know there is a positive relationship between premarital sexual activity and extra-marital intercourse for women. And, at least one study shows that good looking college women were more likely to have had premarital sexual relations than females of medium attractiveness.[14]

Beautiful women are often characterized as less inelligent than less attractive females. The evidence on this assumption is largely absent or inconclusive. A few studies have revealed that physically attractive children received higher grades in primary school. However, those studies indicate that beauty in young children may incur adult evaluations that prompt special attention. Per force, special attention may confirm a teacher's prediction of individual accomplishment. We do know that large breasts are one index of physical attractiveness. One group of researchers discovered that the smaller a woman's breast, the higher a woman's intelligence.[15] There is no reason to believe that good looking Black women are less intelligent than less attractive Black women, for reasons peculiar to that culture.

The relationship between beauty and intelligence is a complicated one. In White culture, an attractive woman does not need to cultivate her intellectual potential because she can obtain a high level of self-esteem and class mobility (through marriage) without it. The same is not entirely true of attractive Black women. Most Black families for instance, socialize all their female children to get a good education and not depend on a man for satisfying their material wants. Furthermore, in order to obtain a high status husband, most beautiful Black women have to attend a college where they can meet them. Unlike Whites, the wealthiest Blacks are generally those with the most education (even Black athletes generally attend college). Many of them will be medical doctors and dentists who attended either Howard University or Meharry Medical School. Since both Howard and Fisk University (the undergraduate school nextdoor to Meharry) have historically had high academic standards, women who wish to coast on their beauty would experience difficulty in matriculating at the schools.

While Black women need a combination of beauty and brains to attract a high status husband, it is still their looks that are the decisive factor. A sociologist did an empirical test of whether a woman's physical attractiveness was a predictor of her husband's status. He reported that if a White woman does not go to college, her attractiveness has a strong bearing on whether or not she gets a high status husband. If that same White woman goes to college, her looks bear no relationship to the status of her busband. Conversely, for the Black woman, attractiveness is influential in getting a high status husband whether or not she goes to college. But it plays a stronger role if she goes to college than if she does not.[16]

In other words, higher status Black males tend to seek beautiful wives regardless of their education. If their wife is college educated, she particularly must have a high degree of physical attractiveness. The reason for this racial differential can be found in the operational effects of institutional sexism and racism. Attractive White women often do not have to go to college in order to obtain a high status husband—Black women do. Among Whites who have graduated from college, there are a million excess men. What this means is that, historically, attractive White women were less likely to be found on college campuses and the low ratio of White men to women college graduates indicates that White males were buyers in a seller's market for comely women. On the other hand, attractive Black women find it difficult to meet high status Black males outside college because there is no comparable upper class structure in the Black community. The excess number of Black female college graduates (200,000 more women than men) suggests that higher status Black males have their choice of attractive Black women. Thus, in choosing a future wife, they can select from only the most attractive Black women among their universe. With the advent of interracial dating, they have the additional advantage of selecting from reasonably desirable White, Asian and Latino women.

Still, having found a "fox," they must cope with one of the most commonly heard complaints about pretty women: their narcissism. The eminent psychologist Karl Jung once remarked: "To me a particularly beautiful woman is a source of terror. As a rule a beautiful woman is a terrible disappointment. Beautiful bodies and beautiful personalities rarely go together."[17] One very attractive Black woman, who was quasi-psychotic, once confessed that her interaction with men was exploitative and bizarre. She did not stay in relationships long but never had trouble attracting new men. It is commonly known that men have a higher threshold of tolerance with pretty women. Hence, such women can, and do, demand all the market will bear: expensive gifts, deference, a delay of sex, etc., all things the less attractive woman can only dream about. Small wonder, then, that people with the same degree of attractiveness are more likely to stay together because a person simply feels more secure and comfortable with a mate of equal attractiveness.[18]

With all her advantages, the good-looking woman is not without problems. One disadvantage is that many desirable men will not approach her because they fear rejection. If she plays the traditionally passive role, she will only be selecting from the men who have the courage to make the initial gesture. Such men are often the playboy types who fuel their egos on the company of the best looking women in the crowd. While one of these same men will cater to a pretty woman's ego and self-indulgent needs initially, he will ultimately exhibit his own emotional immaturity, narcissism and need for dominance that drove him to her. [18] Moreover, these women realize they are trading beauty for status and generally select men with high incomes and prestigious positions. In many cases, they will probable be faced with a lot of ego and ambition, which does not leave a lot of room for pandering to their inflated ego needs. Studies reveal that attractive women have much more difficulty in their relations with men, mainly because of unrealistic expectations. [20]

As they grow older, attractive women lose almost all of their advantages when their beauty begins to fade. When a psychologist asked 513 men and women in the Chicago area how often they thought about their looks, men's responses showed less and less concern as they grew older while older women thought about their appearance as much as younger women. Other psychologists report a higher rate of depression among attractive middle aged women. [21] Another study revealed that the more attractive the woman had been in college, the less satisfied she was 25 years later. [22] There are no comparable studies that include Black women. It is reasonable to assume that they suffer a better fate when they reach middle age. They are not as likely to rely solely on beauty and it is still easier for an aging Black beauty, who is single or divorced, to find a man than her less attractive counterpart.

Not everybody in this society views beautiful women in a positive light. Whatever their character content, they are commonly perceived as self-centered, dumb, a bitch or dilettante. Other women, especially married ones, often see them as a threat to their own relationships with a man. Attractive women who achieve high positions in industry or government are pained by the realization that many people think it was her beauty, not her ability, that was responsible. Men may refuse to take her seriously because of their stereotype of the pretty doll with no brains. Comely Black women face special problems. Because beauty is synonymous with White features, many of them found they were excluded from the Black gains of the 1970s. White employers often preferred a token Black who was visibly "Black." Bernadette Swann, wife of Pittsburgh Steelers football star Lynn Swann, contends that the advantages of light-skinned Blacks is a myth. As an example she cites cases where she was turned down for modeling jobs because whe would photograph too white. [23] Of course, darker Black women might wonder

75

what their chances are of marrying a Black man who earns more then $250,000 a year.

In our discussion we have been focusing on the influence of beauty for women because the research evidence indicates it is more decisive in their life chances. When women are selecting a mate, they generally consider his level of education and income first. Since a woman is not only choosing a companion, she's determining her standard of living, his physical assets are less important. That does not mean a man's physical attributes are totally insignificant. Men over 6 feet tall are more likely to obtain high level executive positons than shorter men. Bald men suffer in employment opportunities and other areas relative to their peers with all their hair. The media has a preference for handsome men in visible positions.

Black women demonstrate a stronger preference for a physically attractive man than their White women counterparts. When the Roper organization asked Black and White women what qualities they admired most in a man, twice as many Black women listed sex appeal than did White women.[24] In a *Jet* magazine survey of Black women in Chicago, Black women ranked the ten things they notice about men in this order (1)dress/grooming (2)personality (3)eyes (4)mouth/smile (5)money (6)physique (7)thoughtfulness/walk (8)intelligence/hansomeness (9)chest and (10)buttocks.[25] Only four of the desirable attributes are non-physical ones. Unlike their male cohorts, skin color is comparatively unimportant. When they express a preference, it is for darker skinned men. Many Black women say they do not trust light-skinned men and find darker men more dependable, settled— and attractive.

Certain social forces may account for the Black female's greater interest in a male's physical appeal. Partly, it may be a function of the shortage of Black men with any tangible wealth. Given that they may not find a high status Black male in any case, they will choose one on the basis of his looks. Perhaps more important is that many Black women are not economically dependent on a man for economic support. As a result their standards for an acceptable mate have become oriented more toward the body.

Unfortunately, Black women seem to be heading in the same direction as Black men: rating a person by their physical features rather than the content of their character. It is tragic in the sense that it is similar to the racism that has victimized them as a people. When personal characteristics that are genetically influenced make such an important difference in a person's status, that is a genetic determinism that is very similar to the operation of White racism. Since the standards of physical attractiveness are set and dominated by Euro-Americans, it can only presage an increase in group self-hatred. Such a trend can only give validation to the saying: "we have met the enemy and the enemy is us."

Erroneous Assumptions
Black Women Make About Black Men

by David R. Burgest, Ph.D.
and Joanna Bowers, Ph.D.

The establishment of an authentic interpersonal relationship between Black males and Black females requires that they destroy the negative myths about Blackness and the positive myths about Whiteness. This is not to imply that every Black male or female is going to be compatible with every other Black male or female once the myths are destroyed for personal choice will continue to prevail. However, the personal choice and personal preference will not be contaminated by the prevailing myths and stereotypes perpetuated in the soicety. Therefore, the incompatibility presently existing in the Black male/Black female relationship will be lessened.

In analyzing and interpreting the literature and mass media productions, personal relationships with Black females and Black males, we have been able to compile a list of twenty assumptions, myths and stereotypes that Black females hold and twenty assumptions, myths and stereotypes that Black males hold which may facilitate or block the development of authentic interpersonal relations between Black males/Black females. It is the role of the reader to decide whether the statement read either blocks and/or facilitates the development of authentic interpersonal relations between Black males and Black females. Some of the statements refer to the Black male relationship to the White female and White society while others refer to the Black female relationship with the White male and White society. Such statements of stereotypes, myths and assumptions are necessary in that it is important to the development of authentic relations between Black males/Black females because to how they view each other are directly related to how they perceive White society and how they feel they are viewed by White society. In this paper, we will explore many of the commonly held myths, stereotypes and assumptions and demonstrate the impact of those assumptions and myths on the Black male/Black female relationship.

This self examination exercise can be an effective tool in workshops, institutes and forums with Black males and Black females. Both can exchange dialogue as to how they view the assumptions which are made thus creating an atmosphere of communication and self awareness. At the end of the self examination, there will be a discussion and analysis of each statement as well as an indication as to whether the statement either blocks or facilitates authentic interpersonal relations between Black males and Black females.

Each reader is asked to complete the self examination as they go along by choosing whether the statement indicated will either block or facilitate the development of authentic interpersonal relations between Black males and Black females.

I Am Female First And Black Second

Since the upsurge of the feminist movement of the late sixties and early seventies, many Black women adopted the notion that they needed to be liberated as "women" from the oppression of the men. For the Black women this entailed liberating herself from the oppression of Black men as well as the sexism of White men for the underlying assumption is that all men (both Black and White) are sexist and chauvinistic. Therefore, many women adopted the view that they are female first and Black second. On the other hand there were Black females who did not separate sexism from racism. They saw themselves as being oppressed because they were female and oppressed because they were Black and they were unable to separate the differences between the two. Consequently, they adopted the view of the feminist that they were female first and placed their social or ethnic identity second.

As we take a closer look, however, we will find that the dynamics involved in the White female's oppression are different from the dynamics involved in the Black female's oppression by her man and White society. First of all, the White female only debates the question of her role as a "female" in relationship to her oppression and need not be faced with the question of race. In other words, she need not delineate whether she is FEMALE FIRST or WHITE SECOND for she can look primarily at the role of oppression in direct relationship to her femininity. At the same time, the White female is only concerned about her role of oppression as it relates to the White male. This is not true for the Black female, for she must correlate the oppression she receives from a White male dominated society to both her race and her sexual identity. At the same time, the Black woman must be concerned about the oppression she experiences as a Black female with her Black man. However, the difficulties of oppression Black females experience in their relationship with Black males is minimal compared to the problems Black females face in a White male dominated society. In fact, there are, some social scientists and psychologists who hold the view that the difficulties of sexism Black females experience in relationship with Black men may be directly correlated with the oppression that both Black males and Black females experience from oppression due to their Blackness. Irrespective of the truthfulness of this theory, the fact remains that the liberation of Black females as well as the liberation of the Black males from the bondage of a White racist male dominated society are intricately tied together. A Black female cannot be liberated as a "female" before she is liberated from Black oppression.

Many Black females adopt the notion that they are female first and Black second because they identify with the way "female" is defined in White America. Historically, Black females in White America were not defined as female; rather, they were regarded as Amazons or anything other than female. White women were identified as the epitome of female while Black women were defined as less than female. Consequently, many Black women identify with myths and stereotypes of White femininity more than with Blackness because being Black and being female are considered a contradiction in White racist America. Consequently, such Black females see themselves as being female first and Black second. However, once the negative myths, assumptions and stereotypes about Blackness and Black feminity and the positive racist definitions of Whiteness and "White feminity" have been destroyed, Black females can more authentically look at themselves, Black men and Black people. This is not to minimize the effects of Black sexism and chauvinism, but such will be placed in it's proper perspective.

White Men Treat Their Women Better Than Most Black Men Treat Their Women

It is not uncommon in Black literature, novels and plays to hear Black women say "A White man treats his women better than this" or "A White man would not treat his women this way." It seems that Black females as well as Black males attempt to imitate and adopt the perceived model of White male/White female relationships as a guide for their relationships. White male and White female relationships are considered healthy while the Black male/Black female relationships are considered pathological. The truth is that most Black men and women have assimilated as positive White supremacist notions of White and Black. Consequently, many Black females end up looking for a Black man who fits the stereotypes of a White man. They may marry a Black man or engage in an intimate relationship with a Black man, but the Black man's behavioral characteristics must be what she perceives the White male model to be.

At the same time, the Black female who identifies with the perceived White male model for her husband also identifies either consciously or unconsciously with the perceived White female model for herself. This is not to suggest that Black females should not look for strengths in a Black male which are compatible with hers. However, strengths of the Black male should not be considered synonymous to the perceived White male model. By the same token, the qualities and strengths which the Black woman perceives she has must not be considered synonymous to the strengths and qualities of the White female model.

I Am Black First And Female Second

As indicated earlier, it is difficult for Black females to differentiate between the effects of racism and the effects of sexism. However, this is an issue which must be resolved between Black female/Black male relationships. The greatest impact of sexism rests in the Black female relationship with the White male dominated racist/sexist society rather than with the Black male. Consequently, it is appropriate for the first phase for the Black female to see herself as being Black first and female second.

Black Men Are Beautiful But White Men Can Be Beautiful

Most Black females express the view that they would have nothing to do with a White man on a sexual level. White men do not interest them sexually and they do not view White men as attractive. Many Black women hold the view that they are repulsed by the thought of being intimate with a White man. In other words, there are Black women who view only the Black man as beautiful even though there may be problems in the Black male/Black female relationship. The argument of most Black females is that they have been victimized by the White male for too many generations.

To be anti-White does not necessarily mean that one is pro-Black; for, even though a Black female may express negative feelings toward White men, she may not necessarily be pleased in her relationships with Black males. By the same token, many Black females may adopt a negative attitude toward White males, but may cling to perceived definitions of the White male/White female relationship model. According to some of the literature, in fact, the hostility that many Black females hold toward White males is merely an unconscious attraction to the White male. This may or may not be true.

The point here, however, is that Black females need to do away with the assumption that they must put White males down in order to build Black males up for the character and quality of the Black male stands alone. When Black females engage in such orientations, they are over-reacting to White racist America. This is not to suggest that Black females should engage in intimacy and relationships with White males as a result of liberating their view about White males; rather this is to suggest that Black females could more authentically relate to their own Black man if they remove the negativism which may exist about White men. It should be the commonality of race, culture, language, and life styles which attract Black males and females, not the anti-White male phonemenon.

It's Hard To Find A Good Black Man

A number of Black females in search of a lasting relationship with a Black man hold the view that it's hard to find a good Black man. Most women grow up with images projected onto them about what a good man is and what a bad man is. They carry with them many of the newspaper, television, radio, storybook, magazines, and other forms of the mass media. Then, there is the view Black females receive from observation of Black males in their environment and culture: the Black male professionals, pimps, preachers, their fathers, and everyday laborers. The overriding assumption of what makes a good man in this American society is somehow tied into the definition of what a White man is. Consequently, Black men are measured by White standards as in terms of what it is to be a "good Black man." That is, the Black man should have an 8 to 5 job, job security, money, weekends off, leisure time for children and wife, higher education, time for vacation, prestige in the community plus many others. Many Black men by contrast are the unemployed, underemployed, and participate in the unskilled job market, lack job security, money, lack weekends off, have little leisure time for children and wife, lack higher education, and time off for vacation. Consequently, the Black female adopts the view that a good Black man is hard to find. This, however, is not to suggest that such Black men do not exist.

On the other hand, there is a view that a great deal of Black men are on dope and in prison while a significant degree of Black men are homosexual and do not involve themselves with Black females while another group of Black men prefer relationships with White females. All of the above are real concerns and have implications for the Black male/Black female relationship. However, of the many available Black men, Black females still feel as though their choices are limited. It doesn't matter whether the Black female meets the same quality she holds for the Black male or whether she feels that she is in a different social position than most Black men; the implication remains that a good Black man is hard to find. Some of this has to do with the fact that there are fewer Black men than there are Black females, but the greatest problem rests with the definition of what is "good".

The problem doesn't appear to be one of incompatibility between Black females and Black males on an interpersonal or social level, for Black females don't seem to be as concerned about the number of Black men as they are about the quality of Black men. There are many Black females who are engaged in intimate interpersonal relationsips with Black males they would not consider a permanent relationship with because the male is perceived as not socially or economically compatible. They adopt the notion that "I am not going to take care of a man; he must take care of me." Or they hold the view that this Black male does not meet my social standards. "I am a professional and he is a mechanic." Thus, the problem isn't that there aren't enough "good males" with whom Black females may engage in the development of interpersonal relationships, but Black females must begin to re-evaluate their model of the male/female relationship. They must assess the model which is projected by White society and see if that model is adequate for Black male/Black female model. The White model of classism may be operable in a society where opportunity is available for all but not in the case where one is ostracized and discriminated against because he is Black. The essence and quality of the Black man isn't what seems to be the issue; rather the problem seems to be his position and status in society. This is similar to the age-old problem of color consciousness among Black females and males who saw the color of the person as being more significant than anything else because a light complexion was closer to that which is White.

Black Women Are Stronger Than Black Man

There are several interpretations of Black history, from slavery to the present time, which suggest that Black women are stronger than Black men. That is, Black women are dominant in the rearing of the children, supporting the family, resisting the forces of racism they face in their everyday lives, collaborating with the White bill collectors and salesmen, and making decisions in the family while the Black male sits back passively. It is not the purpose here to engage in this futile dialogue, for ultimately the man is no stronger than his woman and the woman is no stronger than her man. The two must operate as a reciprocal unit for the survival of each other, then children, and ultimately for the survival and liberation of the Black masses. It is true that Black women have played a significant role under the oppression of slavery and Whtie racism in America, and that oppression is still alive today. Some would suggest that the Black woman is more oppressed because she is faced with the double jeopardy of racism and sexism. However, the fact remains that racism still exists and neither the Black man nor the Black female as a separate or collective entity has been sucessful in alleviating racism. Consequently, it is a mute point to engage in dialogue about who is "stronger" or who is "weaker." This is similar to the fruitless dialogue of the sixties during the height of the Black liberation movement when Blacks engaged in the "Blacker-than-thou" syndrome. Thus, Blacks were competing to demonstrate who was Blacker than whom while racism/White supremacy reigned in their midst.

Skin Color And Hair Texture Should Be Unimportant In The Black Male/Black Female Relationship.

Prior to the 60's there was a dominant view in the Black community that it was better to be of a light complexion and/or have a curly head of hair. During the sixties it became popular to be of dark complexion. There were many queens on Black and White college campuses who were of dark complexion, whereas traditionally the queens were of light complexion with long straight hair. Much of the history of the status of light-complexioned Blacks stems back to slavery and following the emancipation when light complexioned blacks received preferential treatment from whites and Blacks because light-complexioned Blacks were considered closer to that which is White. White was defined as good and worthy; thereby anything which is considered near White is viewed as better than that which is Black.

According to discussions I have recently had, Black men and women are increasingly returning to the view which existed prior to the Black movement of the sixties wherein Black males/Black females seek out each other on the basis of light complexion and curly hair. This affirms the fact that the Black liberation of the sixties was not handed down to the succeeding generation. There are those who also suggest that the Black liberation movement did not have a lasting effect on the active participants of the movement. This is seen by the reversal to straightened (processed) hair, three button suits, as opposed to the dashiki, plus a move toward integration as opposed to separation.

Given the above, there needs to be a reawakening of Black identity in Black youth within Black America. However, the issue of color, texture of hair and shape of the nose would not be a determining factor in one choosing a mate or a relationship with someone of the opposite sex.

Black Men Are More Sexually Potent Than White Men

Cleaver describes this phenomenon in his book, soul on ice, as the super-masculine menial while the White male was described as the omnipotent administrator. That is, the White male, possesses a superior mind and a fragile body while the Black male posseses an inferior mind and a superior body. This myth has been perpetuated by White racist America toward protecting White womanhood and exploiting Black womanhood. More Black men have been lynched and castrated due to assumptions of Black male rape of White women than any other crime they may have supposedly committed. It is a reality that the intellectual functioning of Black men as well as Black women has been stifled by white society. On the other hand, the sexuality of the Black male is highlighted because that is the only place he appears successful in spite of the oppression and racism he faces.

There are many White females who hold the same view about Black men. Thus, during the sixties and seventies sexual revolution in America, there were many White females who placed themsleves in a position to be sexually molested by Black men. In many cases, the sexual activity between Black males and White females heightened the myth because as a result of sexual contact with Black men, the White female helped spread the rumor that the myth was true. The factors which were operating, nonetheless, were the novelty attached to the relationship and the destruction of a taboo. As for the Black female, whose sexual contact with the White man has been primarily one of coercion and rape, she has also been pretty content with the myth. By the same token, there were White females who did not believe in the myth once they had had sexual contact with Black men.

A Black Man Will Let You Down In The Crunch

There are a number of Black women who have had negative experiences with Black men and the same is true of the Black male's relationsip with Black females. Needless to say, there have been a number of negative assumptions, myths, and generalities which have been created to reflect these experiences. On the part of the Black woman, there is the assumption that a Black man will "let you down in the crunch." In other words, a Black man will put you down when the going gets tough. He will stick with you in the thick but when things get thin, the Black man will "thin out." Consequently, many Black women have difficulty developing a trusting relationship with Black men. The Black female feels as though she may be rejected or put aside at anytime.

Such assumptions are destructive of authentic relationships between Black males and Black females because they often lead to a self-fulfilling prophecy.

In other words, they create an atmosphere in the relationship wherein the Black female cannot relate authentically with a Black male because she is reserved in her feelings, emotions and desires. She cannot be as giving, genuine and loving, due to the negative assumption, and all of the behavior of the Black male becomes suspect. If he is loving and genuine, then, he is up to something. On the other hand, if he is harsh and cold, then, this is no more than can be expected.

Black females must look at Black men as individuals and vice-versa. Once this is accomplished, many of the negative myths, stereotypes and assumptions cannot interfere with the Black male/Black female relationship. This is not to say that some Black men have not jilted some Black women but to generalize this assumption to all Black men is unjustified and unwarranted. Above all, it is destructive.

He Ain't Much But He's All I Got

When such a statement is made one must question the standards being applied to Black men to say that ''he ain't much.'' He may be ''all you have'' but by what standards and criteria are being utilized to determine that ''he ain't much.'' Historically, the standards and criteria used have been those of White society. The White male is the epitome of manhood while the Black male is quite the opposite. At present, there is no counter movement existing at this time to destroy the images that the mass media, motion picture and television produce to further solidify the notion that it is better to be a White male than to be a Black male. Yes, the Black male may very well be ''all you got'' but one must truly question the assumption as to whether ''he ain't much.'' This is not to imply that Black men must be romanticized or that White men must be looked down upon; rather we are calling for an authentic look at the Black and White male devoid of all the myths, stereotypes and assumptions which suggest what they are.

All A Black Man Wants Is Your Body.

This is the point of view of many Black women who have had personal experiences with Black men. They feel that all a Black men wants is their body. The underlying assumption is that the Black male is not interested in the establishment of an interpersonal relationship with Black females, or that he is less concerned about social interaction. The primary goal of the Black male is often perceived as ''getting in the women's panties.'' The other side of the coin suggests that the Black male will stay around only as long as he is able to have your body. Consequently, there are many Black women who are cautious about engaging in a sexual relationship with Black men because they feel that this is ''all he is after.'' Within this context sexual intercourse becomes a manipulative device of the Black woman in an effort to control her man, bribe him or manipulate him. This process crops up early in the relationship and continues even within the most permanent relationships. All of this is accomplished under the assumption that "All a Black man wants is a piece of ass."

Most Black Men Prefer White Woman.

Most Black men are indoctrinated in this White racist society to believe in the myths created by White society that the White female is the epitome of womanhood, or the "effeminate elite," as Eldridge Cleaver describes it in his book *Soul on Ice*. On the other hand, the Black female is the epitome of non-femaleness or the "Amazon" as described by Cleaver. This is not to suggest, however, that most Black men prefer White women because the statistics of Black/White marriages between Black males/White females and Black/White marriages between White males/Black females do not bear this out. Nonetheless, the images that Black men possess about White femininity interferes with the Black male/Black female relationship because many Black men attempt to make "White women" out of their Black women. In other words, there are Black women who do not live up to images created by White society as to what a White woman is. Consequently, the issue is not that Black men prefer White women but they prefer the stereotypes and myths created about the role of the White female in the White society. Once these myths are exposed and exploited for what they are, then Black men will not be put in a position to impose the stereotyped images of White females onto Black women.

The "Cream Of The Crop" (Black Males) Are Married To White Women.

When one looks at the characteristics of Black males who are married to White women in the public's eye, it appears that the White female gets the "cream of the crop" of Black males. In many instances, the same may be true of Black females who are married and involved with White males. The "cream of the crop" refers to Black males who are self-supporting/economically stable with prestige and social standing in the community as well as having a profession and/or higher education. By any standards, such Black males would be considered middle class and/or upper class. In actuality, the numbers are very few but the statistics appear to be great particularly when one focuses on the Black males who are in the public view. This is not to suggest that there are not Black males who meet the characteristics of the "cream of the crop" who marry White females or that there are not Black females who meet the characteristics of the "cream of the crop" who marry White men.

There is nothing inherently wrong with Black females looking for social status and economic security in their relationships with Black males. However, the ultimate decision for marriage should rest in compatability, love, and interest of the two parties concerned. The problem is that a number of Black females view their relationship with a man as a possible means of escaping proverty (for many) while others see it as a means of increasing their economic stability and/or living the dream-life they have carried throughout childhood and adolesence. As stated earlier, the dream of the Black female as well as the male, for that matter, is tied into their perceived White World view. Consquently, the White females are not stealing the "cream of the crop," but, rather, many of them engage in relationships with Black males who fit into the stereotypes of the White male model. In the same way that Black males are indoctrinated as to what a "good Black female" is and attempt to make Black females into images of White females, the Black female attempts to make Black males into images of the White male stereotypes. This is destructive to the development of authentic interpersonal relationsips between Black males and Black females.

Erroneous Assumptions
Black Men Make About Black Women

by David R. Burgest, Ph.D. and Joanna Bower, Ph.D.

The Problem Of The Black Male/Black Female Relationship Is A Matriarchy.

There are social sicentists as well as lay persons, both Black and White, who hold the view that the problem in our relationships is simply a matriarchy; that is, the Black woman is the ruler and decision-maker in the family. At the same time as the Black woman's tryranny is presumed, the matriarchal social arrangement is considered antithetical to that of white Americans.

In reality, the problem with Black family survival in America grows out of a combination of racism, white supremacy, and exploitation by the forces of discrimination in employment and education. These combine with Black male and female assimilation of the racist myths, stereotypes and assumptions about Black people, usually negative, plus the assimilation of racist myths, stereotypes and assumptions that regard White people positively. In other words, many Black people (men and women) have been brainwashed and indoctrinated to think that the "White way" is the "right way" and the 'Black way" is the "wrong way."

I Love Black Womanhood.

There are many Black men who readily espouse the notion or idea that they love Black womanhood. It is also true that many Black females advocate a love for all Black manhood. This is dramatized in poetry, music and songs written by Black men and women. There is nothing inherently wrong with the love of Black womanhood or Black manhood, were it only genuine, but the creation of a romanticized and idealistic view of the Black woman has emerged which appears destructive. There is an old saying that one can "love humanity" but hate humans. This may also be true of the Black male who loves Black womanhood and hates Black women. The other side of the coin is that the idealistic and romantic view of Black women in general may interfere with the establishment of realistic interpersonal relations with Black women.

In other words, the Black male may be responding to the myth of Black women (whether that myth is positive or negative) and in the process is impelled to impose those myths upon the character of the Black individual female. There is absolutely nothing wrong with a Black man falling in love with an individual Black woman. But it may be destructive when he has fallen in love with Black womanhood. This sets him up to repetitive disappointments are resentments. Then there is the female who has fallen in love with Black manhood. It may be easy to love an abstraction such as "manhood" or "womanhood" but difficult to love the individual, real-life human.

The Problem With Black Women Is Black Self-Hatred.

Thre is a prevailing view in the social sciences and among lay persons, both Black and White, that all of the social ills facing Black people stem directly to the concept of Black self-hatred. This is used to explain drug abuse, marital discord, alcoholism, passivity, aggression and the breakdown in the Black family structure. Many Black men apply the same terminology to describe the difficulties they may face with Black women. Many men point to the fact that Black women press their hair, paint lips and adopt other means of facial makeup to prove that Black women are identifying with the White woman as a result of hating themselves. At the same time, Black women apply the same accusations to Black men who press their hair and attempt to buy the largest automobile as an indication of their status in identifying with White men.

First of all, all the behavior of Black people can not be equated to an identification with White people and White values or the direct result of oppression even though there are times when this may surely be true. Some behavior may be uniquely Black. The distinction of female beauty as dramatized by the female effort to dress-up, rouge her face, and wear her hair different from men is an age-old custom depicted in all cultures. The fact that the Black woman survives in a white industrialized America may be responsible for the fact of some similarities in the rouge and dress used. By the same token, owning large automobiles in this highly technological society is a symbol of status whether the White man owns one or not. In the same way that owning diamonds and gold teeth (unique Black cultural phenomena) are considered status symbols. This is not an attempt to justify the behavior and actions of Black people, rather, it is to place matters in their proper perspective. Finally, the pressing of the Black male's hair, which has often been interpreted as an identification with the White male either consciously or unconsciously, may be seen as merely a unique cultural phenomenon in the same way that many Black men wear one earring in their ear or a gold tooth in their mouth, or even a toothpick or a match stem.

Black Women Are Not Feminine Enough.

There is a view existing in this society that holds up the White woman as the epitome of femininity. In one piece of literature, she was even defined as the "ultra-femine elite," which is then characterized as being fragile, weak, helpless, delicate, dainty, tidy and neat with silk and ruffles while the Black female is defined as an Amazon characterized by dishpan hands, strong, rough and untidy. Black is defined in the American culture as deeply stained, dirty, soiled, foul, and malignant, while White is defined as purity, cleanness, clear, chaste, innocent, honorable, genuine and upright. Given the above comparisons, it is easy to see that the characterization of the White female and the Black female is no more than an extension of racism/white supremacy operating within this society. Nonetheless, for many Black men this issue is real, for they feel that the Black woman is not feminine enough.

Many Black women define femininity in the same way and submit themselves to their Black men and do not question the role of the Black man, or any misbehavior in that role (even though they may want to do so), because it will make them appear less feminine. This interaction between Black male and Black female is not authentic, and it is in the end destructive.

A White Woman Would Not Treat Her Man This Way.

This statement is similar to the statement made by Black women that "white men treat their women better than this." The Black male has bought into the negative assumptions in this society about "what Black people (women) aren't" and "what White people (women) are." It is a categorical acceptance of the negative asssumptions in this society about Black people as well as an acceptance of the positive (racist) myths, stereotypes and assumptions about White people and White soicety.

91

I Engage In Relationships With White Females Because I Don't Mix My (Black) Politics With My "Pussy."

During the early 1960s it was very popular for interracial sexual encounters to occur on college campuses and among Black males and White females who were members of the civil rights movement. When, late in the same decade, things were reversed, the Black male kept his intimate relationships with White females in the dark, though some continued to function in the open. Many Black females raised the question to their Black male: "how can you think Black and sleep White?" Often there was no open response to the Black female's question, but some Black males replied: "I don't mix my politics with my pussy." They saw it as "to the victor goes the spoils." Needless to say, many Black men were celebrating their victory a little prematurely.

However, just because a Black man dates and/or marries a Black woman or prefers Black women only is no indicator of his Black consciousness or Black identity necessarily. There are many so-called Uncle Toms who are married to Black women. By the same token, when a Black man dates and/or marries a White female, that does not necessarily suggest that such a Black man has turned his back on Black women altogether or that he has rejected the Black woman and the Black cause. It is true that, in the context of things, it may appear to amount to that. Still, it is conceivable that a Black man who marries a White woman is able to maintain his conscious identity as a Black man. This is neither to refute nor advocate the notion that such marriages or matings are antithetical to the advancement and survival of the Black race and its interests. The fact remains that one cannot separate his "politics from his pussy" in America, due to the deep entrenchment of values in this society which minimize the effectiveness of a Black man married to a White woman. In other words, who you marry carries deep political, religious as well as (sometimes) economic overtones. This is true for Black male/White female marriages, Black female/White male as well as White male/Black female and White female/Black male marriages. In this sense, marriage is as much a political institution as it is a personal institution. In any case, Blacks who establish permanent relationships with Whites tend to hamper the effectiveness of their role in Black liberation.

Black Women Are Conservative In Their Sexual Activity And White Women Are More Liberal.

There is a prevailing assumption in the Black community that White females are more liberal in their sexual activity than Black females. Often Black men point to the fact that White women as a whole are more susceptible to engage in oral sex and anal sex than the Black female. However, much of that is changing today due to the sexual revolution which has had an impact on the Black male/female sexual interaction such that oral stimulation as well as anal sex presently are more acceptable in Black sexual relations. Needless to say, many Black men have used the fact that they could get oral stimulation from a white female as a justification for engaging in sexual relationships with White females. Even though oral stimulation and anal penetration may be something a Black male may desire as a novelty in his sexual relations, the factors of rapport, sensitivity, compatibility and love are known to be more essential to satisfactory sexual interaction. Oral stimulation and anal penetration have always been a part of the interaction between homosexuals, but Black men have not sought out these interactions on the basis that the Black women are conservative in their sexual activities.

There Would Be No Problems In Black Male/Female Relationsips If I Had The Opportunities Of The White Male.

There are those who feel that the problems of Black male/female relationships will be resolved once the Black male has acquired the same opportunities in education, employment and job security as the White male. This is not necessarily true, although this is not to suggest that some of the problems Black men and women face would not be alleviated by destroying oppression. However as long as White society perpetuates the negative stereotypes and assumptions about themselves (positive) and Black people (negative), and so long as Black people continue to buy into those myths, the problems in Black male/female relationships are going to continue. There are Black males and females who are economically stable, and yet, they have difficulties because they have bought into those myths, stereotypes and assumptions we have described. Black males and females must debrainwash and decolonize their minds and in time eradicate the definitions imposed upon them by white society. This is not easy, because the brainwashing is often done very subtly. In review of television or media, we have seen commercials where the White knight always wins and the Black knight always loses. There is the Black (devil food) cake and the White (angel food) cake. In textbook, storybook, conversation and song, the notion of White superiority and Black inferiority pervades this society.

I Am Male First And Black Second.

The same factors that hold for the Black female view of herself as female first and Black second also hold true for the Black male who views himself as male first and Black second. The identification of what a ''man'' is in this society is equated with being a White male in the same way that what is considered female in this society is determined by what it is to be White female.

Such assumptions are destructive, causing too many black men to prefer to dichotomize between who they are as a race and who they are as a man. As a result of this, most Black males may feel handicapped as a Black male due to their oppression and wish to separate this from their manness. This is not to imply that Black men should see themselves as weak and powerless; rather, they should look at themselves as Black men, irrespective of the political, economical or social condition in which they find themselves.

The assumption made by many Black women that "you are not a man" does not help but rather intensifies the negative view. Many Black women either consciously and/or unconsciously hold the Black man responsible for the oppression that Black people face — if their "men" were "men" the oppression would not exist. The Black man would free the Black race once and for all.[1]

PART III:

RELATIONSHIPS

Men Who Play

by Jacqueline Johnson Jackson, Ph.D.

When the subject is black female and male relationships in the United States today, some notable omissions are common. Once such omission is the failure to describe and analyze carefully the undesirable effects on black women and children directly or indirectly attributable to the screwing of black families by black men who play or those who are dysfunctional in their roles as husbands to black women or fathers to their very own black children. They include unwed, separated, and divorced fathers who could, but who do not "pull their fair share" as economic providers for black mothers and children. This operationalized definition could be extended to include politically influential black men who generally ignore the plight of black female-headed families residing in poverty, or who support federal policies and programs likely to keep such families in poverty through successive generations.

That which follows is concerned primarily with a relatively broad overview of recent demographic trends related to black families in the United States. These trends permit some limited inferences about black men who play, and suggest some ways in which efforts may be undertaken to reduce the screwing of black families by black men who play.

Before proceeding, it should be emphasized strongly that this article is not concerned with the many black men who function effectively as husbands and fathers, nor is it concerned with those relatively few black women who may play and, thus, also screw the family. An assumption here is that the consequences of black men who play are far more detrimental on black families than are those which may be attributable to playing black women, an assumption which is, of course, open to empirical testing, over the decades and generations.

Recent Demographic Trends: Age and Sex Distribution of the Black Population

Looking back to the already completed period of the 1970's, for instance, between 1970 and 1979, the estimated size of the total black population in the United States, adjusted for the net census undercount, increased from approximately 24,574,000 to approximately 27,921,000, an increase of 14 percent. The actual numbers of black females and males under fifteen years of age decreased, while those in the remaining age groups increased over time. Thus, there was an increase in the number of black adults, and in the adult proportion within the black population.

The black sex ratio (or the number of males per every 100 females) for persons of all ages declined slightly from 96.2 in 1970, to 95.1 in 1979, as may be seen in Table 1, which also shows black sex ratios in those years by various age groupings.

Perhaps what is most significant about Table 1 is that the adjusted data differ from previously reported data by the U.S. Bureau of the Census, in that they reduce female excessiveness in the black population in the age groupings associated most often with marital and parental formations. Nevertheless, they do show female excessiveness, which means, in part, that some black women must continue to ask, "But where are the men?,"[1] or seek to expand their marital pool.

Marital Statuses of the Black Population

Table 2 shows the marital statuses of the black population, by sex and age, in 1970 and 1979, as well as the percentage changes over time. Perhaps the most striking change over time is the decrease in the proportion of black females who were married and living with their husbands. In 1970, a majority of black women between the ages of 25 and 54 years were married and living with their husbands, but, in 1979, only a minority of all black women in that age grouping were married and living with their husbands. Table 2 also shows a general decrease among black women who were married with absent husbands, a decrease in the proportion who were single or never married.

In general, the proportions of black men who were single or divorced also increased over time, while those who were married with wives present or who were separated decreased over time.

Table 2, then, shows substantial changes in the marital statuses of black women and men over the last decade, and raises critical questions about the implications of these trends for familial life, particularly for the support and socialization of minor black children.

Economic Statuses of the Black Population

Between 1959, a few years prior to concentrated federal efforts to reduce poverty among Americans, and 1978, the proportion of all black persons in poverty declined from 55.1 to 30.6 percent. But this decline was substantially greater for persons residing in male-headed families. In 1959, 50.7 percent of all persons in black male-headed families were in poverty, as compared with 15.1 percent in 1978. In contrast, 70.0 percent of all persons in black female-headed families were in poverty in 1959, and, in 1978, a majority (53.1%) remained in that condition.

The above enonomic data become particularly dramatic when they are coupled with the fact that about half of all black families are now headed by women, the vast majority of whom are younger adult women. Further, when one examines the total money incomes of black females and males in 1969 and 1978, it is found that the earnings of the former are significantly below those of the latter. For example, in both 1969 and 1978, among persons likely to have minor children, the incomes of the women were generally less than twice that of the men. But, the majority of minor black children no longer live with both parents, and, when they do not, they most often live with their mothers, the poorer of their parents.

Illegitimate Births Among Black Teenagers

Table 3 contains data about live births to unmarried black women, 15-17 and 18-19 years of age, per 1,000 unmarried women and per 1,000 total live births, between 1969 and 1977. For both age groups, the rate for live births fluctuated somewhat over time, showing a slight increase for the younger and a slight decrease for the older group. But the rate of illegitimate births increased over time for both age groups, from about 72 percent to about 90 percent for the younger group, and from about 48 percent to about 75 percent for the older group.

Unfortunately, recent data which were specific with respect to births to unmarried black women for various age groupings were not available, but for the past several years, the majority of all infants born to black women in the United States have been born to unwed mothers, a dramatic shift from patterns previously established during most of this century.

97

Demographic Summary

Overall, this brief demographic summary suggests that the black population is being characterized by shifting marital and familial trends, the most important of which are the decrease in the number of black women married and living with their husbands; an increase in the number of black female-headed families with minor offspring, a significantly large proportion of whom reside in poverty; an increase in the the proportion of illegitimate births among blacks; and a decrease in the proportion of black children who are fathered by black men who do not play.

Inferences About Black Men Who Play

Because we yet lack highly specific data useful in pinpointing the specific impacts of black men who play on black women and children, inferences about their impacts are necessary. These inferences are drawn largely from anecdotal materials, impressionistic judgments, and from available data not broken out by race.

It is fairly clear that the black population has experienced a substantial increase in the proportions of black mothers with illegitimate children and of black mothers with legitimate children who reside in households where they are bereft of husbands and fathers. Further, it seems to be the case that a substantial, large proportion of these absent husbands and fathers are not dead and are not imprisoned, and are not U.S. military personnel engaged in combat abroad. Many of these women and minor children are heavily dependent on federal, state, and local governments for their economic well-being, quite often through monies received form the AFDC program and in-kind transfers through such programs as public housing, food stamps, and Medicaid. It is true that governmental agencies seek to locate absent fathers and force them to contribute to the support of their families, but the support typically received is far below a minimum level of subsistance. Further, one must question seriously the 'manhood' of fathers who are able to, but neglect to support their offspring, or even to provide partial support unless they are forced to do so.

One of the serious problems which has emerged over the years can be seen in much of the social scientific literature concerning black families, where that literature tends to be unduly sympathetic toward black men, even holding that the effects of racial discrimination were far more severe on black men than on black women.[2] This unwarranted sympathy now should cease, because it enables many black men to screw their families unnecessarily.

A further indication of the irresponsibility of many black men (and here I recognize that some black illegitimate births were not fathered by black men, but the vast majority of them were) is seen in the rising illegitimate rates. One of the problems manifested here deals with the increasing segregation adolescents are making between 'love' and 'sex.' In earlier years, a popular way black teenagers had of referring to sexual intercourse was 'making love,' but now they more often speak of 'making out.' Certainly, this shift has been influenced by the availability of contraceptives and similar factors, but it has also been influenced heavily by the significant breakdown in ethical responsibility of parents (a responsibility which included economic support) previouly characteristic of many black communities. Again, in earlier years following slavery and for many subsequent years, norms in black communities, and among black families, did not typically condone illegitimate births; in fact, they condemned them, although they did accept them when they occurred, with varying degrees of reservation. Further, the norms held that fathers were responsible for the economic support of their offspring.

Today, there seems to be a "devil-may-care" attitude among many black men who are derelict in their economic support of women whom they have impregnated and of resulting offspring, a tendency to let "Uncle Sam" do it.

Letting "Uncle Sam" do it simply means that taxpayers, including many blacks, must help support offspring whom they did not beget, as well as a number of welfare mothers who are without the labor force and, quite important, who do not really wish to enter the labor force.

These are the kinds of men who play with the very futures of their offspring, because a disproportionately large number of them will remain severely disadvantaged, despite the plethora of federal programs presumably designed to bring about equality of results, as compared with the white population, in educational, employment, occupational, and income outcomes.

Relatively few of these men seem to realize the extreme difficulties which far too many black female-headed families, and particularly the mothers of minor children, experience in trying to socialize adequately their female and male children in a society which still favors the nuclear form of family, and, further, which still practices considerable sexism, meaning that the power of poor mothers of black chilren is generally insignificant.

Thus, I am arguing that we should still support federal programs which are effective in improving the socioeconomic statuses of all black families, and especially of those who are in poverty, but we must also encourage strongly a reduction in black men who play with their families. we must not try to excuse them, because it is inexcusable for able-bodied men to fail to support their families as much as possible in this day and age.

Stop the Screwing!

What can be done to reduce the screwing of black families by black men who play? Unfortunately, I do not have all of the answers, but certainly this is an issue which should receive high priority in future discussions of black female and male relationships. It is, I would contend, a much more potent issue than that of black males who desert black females by consorting with (and even marrying) non-black women!

Nevertheless, although I do not have the answers, let me suggest some of the ways which may be considered, or ways which at least ought be discussed:

1. Efforts to avoid unwanted pregnancies among black females should be increased, including the avaliability of abortions to poor women at extremely minimal cost. Perhaps the members of the Congressional Black Caucus could be successful in reopening this issue in the U.S. Congress, so that pregnant females who wish to abort without medical harm to themselves may do so. After all, from a cost efficiency standpoint, it is generally less costly to the taxpayers to pay for an abortion than it is to support the mother and the child over the years, and to help initiate a cycle of successive familial cohorts on welfare.

2. No matter what trends may be characteristic of white families (which means stop the racial comparisons for justificatory purposes), black families should try to socialize their daughters and their sons in ways appropriate to increasing familial stabiltiy (I shudder now when I think of the increasing numbers of black women and men in the future who will be ill-prepared for marriage and a family of procreation, primarily because they belong to the ''instant, give-me'' generation, and have not been prepared to cope adequately with problems). Most of all, they should stress the responsibilities of spouses and parents, and especially respect for women.

An option, however, is that more and more blacks should work extraordinarily hard to upgrade significantly the socioeconomic statuses of black women who are likely to be heads of families containing minor children. Here, then, I would depart from Moynihan (1965) by emphasizing not only better employment for black men, but also better employment for black women.[3]

3. Influential black male politicians and other influential blacks should work hard to obtain and enforce laws which will require that fathers of minor children (extending here through at least 22 years of age, if the children remain in school) must assist, wherever possible, with the support of their children. Far too often, black women are left with those responsibilities, and they are typically not sufficiently well-equipped financially to send their offspring through college alone. A number of their children currently enrolled in colleges throughout the country

100

perform poorly, or at least as not as well as they could, because they are also working.

    4. Influential black male politicians should consider legislative modifications which will help to increase employment opportunities for young black women and men who are in the secondary labor market, with two such suggestions -- and neither novel -- being a federal law to prohibit the employment of illegal aliens in the United States, and a reduction of the minimum wage law, a suggestion which Walter Williams, an economics professor at Temple University, has made repeatedly. In short, influential black male politicians must become increasingly concerned about what they can do to help strengthen black families, as opposed to neglecting this area.

Summary

    This article was developed to try to stimulate considerable thought in discussions of black female and male relationships in the United States today, with much of those thoughts focused on reducing the numbers of black men who play, or screw up black families by failing to support adequately their wives or mothers of their children and their children. Such discussions must be geared to what blacks themselves can do to help themselves, with an eye toward a decreasing reliance on dear ''Uncle Sam,'' who, after all, is not the father of these children.

    A broad overview of recent demographic trends related to black families was presented, as were some personal reflections on their implications.

    A final note is that, despite increased environmental concerns in our society about population control, we should never discourage blacks from bearing offspring as long as they are, at least initially, able to support them. What we should object to is the increasing tendency of many black women and men to foster offspring whom they have no intention of supporting.

Table 1

Table 1. Sex ratios* of the total black population of the total United
States, adjusted for net census
undercount, by age groupings:
1 July 1979 and 1 April 1970**

AGE GROUPINGS	1970	1979	% change
All ages	96.2	95.1	-1.2
Under 5 years	101.1	102.1	1.0
5-9 years	101.4	101.9	0.5
10-14 years	101.0	100.9	-0/01
15-19 years	100.3	101.1	0.8
20-24 years	99.4	99.9	0.5
25-29 years	98.4	98.1	-0.3
30-34 years	97.5	97.2	-0.3
35-39 years	98.2	96.4	-1.2
40-44 years	96.6	95.2	-1.4
45-49 years	94.7	95.2	0.5
50-54 years	92.1	92.2	0.1
55-59 years	88.8	88.0	-0.9
60-64 years	85.1	82.6	-2.9
65-69 years	82.3	77.7	-5.6
70-74 years	73.2	70.1	-4.2
75-79 years	65.4	63.7	-2.6
80-84 years	58.8	50.0	-14.7
85 plus years	51.2	40.9	-20.1

*Number of males/number of females x 100. **Source of raw data: U.S. Bureau of the Census,
Current Population Reports, Series P-25, No. 870, 'estimates of the Population of the United States,
by Age, Race, and Sex: 1976 to 1979,' U.S. Government Printing Office, Washington, D.C., 1980,
pp. 28-29.

Table 2. Marital Statuses of black females and males, by age, United States, 1970 and 1979*
AGE (in years)

Sex, Year, Marital Status	14+	14-17	18-19	20-24	25-29	30-34	35-39	40-44	45-54	55-64	65-74	75+
BLACK FEMALES												
% Single												
1970:	28.0	98.0	73.9	43.3	19.0	10.8	12.2	6.8	4.5	4.7	5.2	2.3
1979:	35.8	99.0	68.0	37.3	20.8	15.4	10.3	6.0	4.4	5.4	3.9	
% change, 1970-1979	27.8	0.8	21.6	57.0	96.3	92.6	26.2	51.5	33.3	6.4	3.8	69.6
% Married, spouse present,												
1970:	42.0	1.1	21.0	42.6	59.7	61.3	54.8	61.8	56.9	46.3	28.8	11.4
1979:	32.5	0.5	7.1	23.2	38.4	46.4	48.4	48.4	47.8	43.8	31.1	11.2
% change, 1970-1979	-22.6	-54.5	-66.2	-45.5	-35.7	-24.3	-11.7	-21.7	-16.0	-5.4	11.4	-1.8
% Married, spouse absent,												
1970:	12.1	0.7	5.0	12.2	15.4	20.5	17.9	15.8	16.0	15.0	4.4	5.0
1979:	10.9	0.5	3.0	7.2	15.1	16.5	15.9	19.2	17.3	10.6	7.6	2.7
% change, 1970-1979	-9.9	-28.6	-40.4	-41.0	-1.9	-11.2	21.5	8.1	-29.3	72.7	-46.0	
% Widowed												
1970:	13.5	—	—	0.4	0.3	2.0	6.6	7.9	15.4	28.5	58.0	80.3
1979:	13.0	—	—	—	1.0	1.6	5.0	5.5	15.1	32.9	49.8	78.6
% change, 1970-1979	-3.7	—	—	—	233.3	-20.0	-24.2	-30.4	-1.9	15.4	-14.1	-2.1
% Divorced												
1970:	4.5	—	0.2	1.5	5.6	5.4	8.5	7.6	7.1	5.5	3.6	1.0
1979:	7.9	—	—	1.6	8.3	14.6	15.3	16.6	13.8	8.3	5.1	3.6
% change, 1970-1979	75.6	—	—	6.7	48.2	170.4	80.0	118.4	94.4	50.9	41.7	260.0
BLACK MALES												
% Single,												
1970:	36.6	99.5	95.8	59.4	32.0	9.5	15.3	11.8	7.5	4.8	6.6	
1979:	42.2	99.8	99.2	78.3	39.4	22.4	14.1	16.7	12.4	7.5	6.8	7.5
% change, 1970-1979	15.3	0.3	3.5	31.8	23.1	135.8	-7.8	41.5	20.4	0.0	41.7	13.6
% Married, spouse present,												
1970:	48.6	0.4	3.0	35.3	57.7	75.3	62.7	66.1	67.3	76.6	64.3	39.5
1979:	40.5	—	0.8	18.4	45.3	56.6	66.4	53.4	61.8	61.9	62.9	45.7
% change, 1970-1979	-16.7	—	-73.3	-47.9	-21.5	-24.8	5.9	-19.2	-8.2	-19.2	-2.2	15.7
% Married, spouse absent,												
1970:	7.5	0.1	1.4	3.8	8.4	10.1	13.6	15.0	12.1	7.5	5.3	8.1
1979:	7.3	0.2	—	2.4	8.2	13.2	9.0	11.2	9.5	13.1	11.4	6.6
% change, 1970-1979	-2.7	100.0	—	-36.8	-2.4	30.7	-33.8	-25.3	-21.5	74.7	115.1	-18.5
% Widowed												
1970:	4.3	—	—	0.2	—	0.6	1.8	2.7	4.3	4.9	22.7	45.8
1979:	3.8	—	—	—	0.2	0.5	1.1	1.4	5.4	8.4	14.5	33.5
% change,1970-1979	-11.6	—	—	—	—	-16.7	-38.9	48.1	25.6	71.4	-36.1	-26.8
% Divorced												
1970:	2.9	—	—	1.5	1.9	4.6	6.6	4.4	5.9	3.4	2.9	—
1979:	6.1	—	—	1.0	6.8	7.3	9.5	17.3	10.9	9.2	4.3	6.7
% change, 1970-1979	110.3	—	—	-33.3	257.9	58.7	43.9	293.2	84.7	170.6	48.3	—

*Source of data: U.S. Bureau of the Census, Current Population report, Series P-20, No, 212, 'Marital Status and Family Status: March 1970,' U.S. Government Printing Office, Washington, D.C., 1971; and U.S. Bureau of the Census, Current Population Reports, Series P20, No, 349, 'Marital Status and Living Arrangements: March 1979,' U.S. Government Printing Office, Washington, D.C., 1980.

Table 3

Table 3: Illegitimate births among black women, years of age, United Staes, 1969-1977*

	Live births to unmarried black women per 1,000 unmarried-women		Live births to unmarried black women per 1,000 total live births	
YEAR	15-17 years	18-19 years	15-17 years	18-19 years
1969	72.3	129.1	720.9	482.9
1970	77.9	136.4	759.6	521.4
1971	80.9	136.3	796.3	560.3
1972	82.9	129.8	810.1	590.2
1973	81.9	123.0	825.6	603.8
1974	79.4	124.9	848.0	638.3
1975	77.7	126.8	874.0	676.0
1976	74.6	121.6	897.4	709.0
1977	74.3	125.9	904.7	746.4

*Source of data: U.S. Department of Health, Education, and Welfare. **Health United States 1979,** DHEW Publication No.(PHS) 80-1232. Washington, D.C.; U.S. Government Printing Office.

The Sociology Of
The Other Woman: Mansharing

by Joseph W. Scott, Ph.D.

There are many types of extramarital affairs and many reasons for them, but some are more consequential than others. Those affairs that are transitory do not seem to be particularly consequential in either a negative or positive sense. For example, for a man to casually visit a prostitute from time to time does not seem to be disruptive of his family life nor alienating to his emotional bond with his wife and family. But for a man to start an outside family which includes regular visitation, support and parenting obligations does seem much more disruptive and alienating. Although we seldom hear about these affairs existence, nearly every adult who has been around a significant number of married people knows about one such relationship. Thus, while these relationships are not very visible and there are no census data on the existence of such families, they do indeed exist in notable number.

Granted that they exist, some questions are: How do they come to be? What are the reasons for their existence? First, from my data, it is clear that polygamy begins with the *willingness* of single and married men and women to enter into and maintain extramarital affairs.

Before marriage, one is not only allowed but also one is encouraged to be pluralistic in one's romantic relationships. Dating and mating with more than one person during courtship is common and accepted. However, when a couple decides to marry, there is the cultural expectation that one will be loyal and faithful to the *one* person to whom one is married. In short, the cultural norms require the discontinuity of pluralistic relationships and the establishment of a monogamous marital relationships.

Discontinuity, however, is very difficult.

For many people (and the data would suggest that males more than females exhibit this pattern) a monogamous relationship is impossible. Furthermore, the trend also is that the majority of married males and females have extramarital affairs by age 40. Younger males and females are promoting it more than the older generation. One result is that more and more men and women, *without planning to*, are starting the sexual bonding process *outside* of their monogamous marital relationships. In other words, the exclusive pair bonds are declining in popularity and alternatives such as intimate friendships, nonconsensual and consensual adultery, and multilateral marriages which include three, or more persons are increasing in popularity. All of these alternative relationships involve sexual bonds with someone other than one's primary mate.

My data — from 22 in-depth interviews — suggest that extramarital families often start with a married man beginning an *outside* family with a single never-married female. Usually the single never-married female is one who has already become pregnant while still in secondary school and has been forced into single parenthood as a teenager and also forced out into the world away from her mother before the age of 20. Since welfare does not support the unwed mother well, she finds it absolutely necessary to seek other means of supplementing her income. Under ideal conditions, her choices include getting married to a responsible male with a job who is willing to take on a ready-made family. But these are not ideal times; such men are scarce: since young black men in America are perhaps the most unemployed group in the American labor force, they are generally not marriage material — if a woman is looking for a steady provider for her child and herself. This socioeconomic situation eventually forces her to look for employment for herself. But since she had interrupted her high school education, because of her school-age pregnancy and birth, she is not likely to be able to find a high-paying job. If she finds a job, it will not pay enough for her to hire a babysitter while she works. Thus, she is trapped. One recourse is for her to find a "sponsor." (A sponsor is a man who has the economic means to help support her and her child). Keeping in mind that the "sponsor" does not have to be the sole support, she often seeks a married man willing to "help" in exchange for sexual companionship. Sexual companionship is not just a "commodity" since she often seeks out such sexual satisfaction herself — without *any* exchange of money ever taking place. She too needs sexual companionship; she also needs male companionship as protection against those predatory males who seek out and exploit single never-married women whether on welfare, or with jobs of their own. In addition, she needs a good role model for her child, one who is comfortable at home rather than in the streets. Married men are said to have these qualifications and appear to be highly desirable — to the never-married single mother.

The single mothers I have interviewed seem to argue that married men are more desirable than single men because they are more generous, more stable, more family-oriented and more willing to have part-time relationships. The net result is that married men seeking to have extramarital affairs will find it relatively easy to start up relationships with single never-married mothers with children, especially those with their own independent households.

As it often happens, a young woman eventually becomes pregnant by and has a baby for her married companion. The child goes a long way toward elaborating their relationship further by adding paternal obligations to all the other commitments. As the commitments of parenting and child support become more and more operative, what was once an extramarital *affair* becomes an extramarital family. This changes the social obligations in such a way that a polygamous family is now existent.

If it were just a question of married and single never-married women setting up households together and living happily ever after, there would be no problem. But there are legal wives and their children also affected by these extramarital families. My data indicate that few wives approve of polygamous arrangements of any kind — for themselves or for their husbands. One of the reasons is that they have accepted the cultural expectations and taken them to heart. They typically desired to be married, to have children within marital relationships, and to have exclusive marital relationships. While most became pregnant before marriage, they all married before the birth of their first child. This meant that even though they were teenage mothers, motherhood came within marriage.

Their husbands seem to drift into polygamous relationships in two ways. First, some husband's never stopped seeing their other women after the marriage ceremony was performed. And over time, they became involved with single females who had babies for them and thus started outside families for them. Second, some other husbands drifted into polygamous relationships after a few years into their mutually exclusive marriages. These men felt they had gotten married while they were still "sowing his oats" and they had not completed that activity. So, they went back out into the street life, and over time they met and became involved with single never-married females who eventually became pregnant by them and had babies for them.

The wives on the other hand seem at a loss in these situations. Some maintain that as long as their husbands take care of home responsibilities they can do what they want. When they "slack up" on home responsibilities to their primary families, they have to go. (This conflict perhaps accounts for the fact that married blacks separate at a rate that is six times the rate of whites).

Other wives, especially wives whose husbands never stopped seeing their other women after the marriage ceremony, say that men are by nature "whorish" and they will always be having extramarital affairs. They say wives do not have any real choices because men will do what they want, and if wives do not like it, they can leave or accept it. Thus these wives acquiesce to mansharing. These wives do not know what it is *not* to share.

After having said all of this and after having learned how men and women, both single and married, drift into polygamous relationships, one may ask what is the bottom line of this report. My answer is that unless the decimation of black males ceases so that there is no continuing shortage of marriageable black males, and unless the employment opportunities improve so marriage-age black men can support the families they are starting, and unless black women begin to see the white man's handouts as ways to undermine black male and female relationships, the circumstances which bring black affluent married men together with struggling single never-married mothers will not be minimized.

Consensual polygamy is one thing: *extramarital polygamy* is quite another. The former is a group marriage where all parties have agreed on the group membership and the conduct of their family life. The second is a "shot gun marriage" wherein two families are forced together because of an unwanted and unplanned outside-the-marriage pregnancy. Consensual polygamy could be a partial answer to the temporary shortage of black males as well as a sexually efficacious answer to the varietal sexual needs of particular black men and women. But extramarital polygamy which is almost always forced on the legitimate wives seems rather conflictive and divisive in the black community, and if it is not checked, blacks could destroy themselves from within. We must remember that these family problems begin with the institutionalized shortage of black men, jobs, money and black female autonomy through the white man's dole.

Not Allowed To Be Friends And/Or Lovers

by Jawanza Kunjufu, Ph.D.

We are a people of the sun. We come from eastern waters, the West is not our way yet we travel into the rushing sea of acculturation. One of three marriages ends in divorce every twelve months.[1] One of every nine Black men is a homosexual, and there are twenty million homosexuals living in America. Contrary to belief at birth little Black boys outnumber little Black girls 1.03 to 1.0 but upon reaching their eighteenth birthday women, outnumber men 1.8 to 1.0[2] (This is a very conservative ratio. Many Black social scientists believe it is closer to 3-5:1.) America knows that an effective way to destroy the Black family is to destroy Black men, placing more pressure on Black women. America's success can be viewed by observing 329,000 Black men in prison, 40 percent male teenagers unemployed, suicide the second and third leading killer, mixed with drug abuse and disproportionate job loss.[3] A Black father was recently found frying his three-month old daughter in a skillet because she would not stop crying.

Cheikh Anta Diop, in *Culural Unity of Black Africa,* points out it was not always this way. "It is generally conceded in most scholarly circles, that mankind originated in Africa. This makes the African man the father and the African woman the mother of mankind. In the first African societies the woman played a major role without demeaning the man or making his role less important. The first accomplishment of the African woman in partnership with the man was the creation of a functioning family unit. This major step in human development laid the foundation for the organization of all subsequent societies and institutions.

In Africa the woman's place was not only with her family. She often ruled nations with unquestionable authority. Many African women were great militarists and on occasion led their armies in battle. The Africans had produced a civilization where men were secure enough to let women advance as far as their talent, royal lineage and prerogatives would take them."[4]

Frances Welsing, in several interviews with *Black Books Bulletin*, and in a speech delivered at the 1978 State of the Race Conference, feels it does not have to remain this way. She says, "the root of our problem is not each other but racism. The solution to our problem is in our resistance." Frances states further "that we must come to grips with ourselves. How can we build strong families without strong individuals?"[5] She advocates "we must stop fighting, lying, backstabbing, hurting and being jealous of one another. We must begin to listen, care, respect, love and reach out and touch one another."

It is difficult being moral in America. A place where receiving is valued over giving. A brother tells another brother he's in love and the brother asks why? The brother responds by saying she makes me feel good. Where is the love? It's obvious that if the sister stops making the brother feel good the love would also stop. In the collective value system, that's not love that's self-gratification. If I love you it's not because you make me feel good but because I want to make you feel good.

It's difficult being moral in a place where people view rules and codes of ethics as restrictive and confining. We have already begun living Toffler's *Future Shock* where value is placed on immediate gratification and when used simply disposed. We throw away each other like we throw away things. It has become unpopular to take positions on the use of drugs, homosexuality, interracial and extra-marital relationships and the lack of desire for children. The pendulum has swung so far to the west that the amoral has moved from once being unheard of, to the closet, to the streets, to silencing the "traditionalists." This "liberal" society has even begun to shake the roots of its foundation by asking what is moral and what is correct, knowing all the time that any answer other than their own is unacceptable.

The major reason Black people survived this raw racist oppressive society is because of each other. Man and woman relationships. We know why Moynihan, Shange, Wallace (and there will be others) are promoted and allowed to indict these relationships. America knows, if we don't, that all we have left in our defense is each other. Black men and women are extremely lonely. It is a rare blessing to possess a friend of either sex who will share with you both the beauty and the pitfalls of life.

Many sisters have been able to enjoy an open honest relationship with one another. Others choose "associates" who do not provide them with competition securing a man or with whom they cancel plans when a man calls with an alternative. Most brothers have been able to capture a friendship with one brother. Due to America's strong attempt to destroy Black men, there are fewer men available for friendship, or it's confined to prison and war terrain. It's confined to prison and war terrain. Remaining brothers and sisters usually spend most waking hours just trying to "make it." What little time remains is spent with their lover rather than "just a friend." Friendships between brothers and sisters are essential and I proposed the continuance of brotherhood and sisterhood.

In our attempt to be happy we look for lovers before securing friends. We place value on the external rather than the internal. A brother knows two women, one is his lady who looks very good and the other is "just" his friend who does not look quite as well but provides more companionship. The brother valuing the external will choose his lady for marriage. Approximately eighteen months later he begins to have problems with his lady and discusses it with his friend. This set of events repeats itself with the friend providing emotional security but never moving up to the "lady" position. The cycle stops when the friend gets frustrated and proposes an all or nothing relationship to which the brother refuses because his external values won't allow it.

Other examples of friendships between men and women are when one or both of them are married. The institution of marriage is in jeopardy. It faces the effect of racism and the lack of traditional values, but more importantly marriage is faced with the heavy burden of providing all of the spouse's needs. I feel the assumption is highly improbable and verging on arrogance. Recently my sister saw an old female friend of mine I had been trying to reach. During their conversation, the friend asked of my whereabouts. My sister responded and also mentioned that I was married. The friend then said "that's alright." You would have thought I had a disease with the only cure being divorce.

It should also be made clear there are other needs exclusive of sex even in a heavy sex-oriented society. Due to the prevailing sexual attitude, most people assume that friendship involving the opposite sex intended and leads to sexual activity. The people who suffer most from this are those who had "moral intentions" but have to lie about their whereabouts because few would believe them when they say "nothing happened we're just friends." This projection of immoral behavior on moral people sounds so similar to Jomo Kenyatta's *Facing Mt. Kenya*, where he describes how Europeans viewed their culture. The Gikuyu had stages of sexual involvement that required discipline that Europeans either did not have or did not want therefore. What you do not understand or appreciate, if insecure you abolish.

In conclusion, I feel our major problem is racism. We must become honest and respect one another with communication at the highest level. This forum should not be excluded to one-on-one relationships but should include sisterhoods, brotherhoods and kupendas. (The Swahili word for love.) This session (Kupenda) developed by Nathan and Julia Hare is more of a collective sensitivity session. It speaks to three major weaknesses in our current educational system. Previously we were taught how to read, write and count, but seldom have we been taught how to choose a mate, how to keep a relationship together and how to rear children.

Poly-nuclear structures, while an alternative for some, does not eradicate Black male destruction. Poly-nuclear structures do not speak to the real issues of male destruction. Second, and more importantly, polygamy does not automatically increase the quality of the relationship. If monagamous relationships lacked respect and communication, why should we assume that increasing the numbers will improve the quality?

We must return to our traditional values. Stability is a result of rules and codes of ethics. We must resume valuing the internal and longterm happiness versus the external and short-term pretty faces in dark bedrooms. Men and women can be friends, when they choose to value friendship; and collectively discuss a non-sexual relationship.

Woman-To-Woman Marriages In Africa & Afroamerica

by Bamidele Ade Agbasegbe, Ph.D.

In a recent issue of *Black Male/Female Relationships,* Akilimali Funua Olade[1] remarks: "if you examine most African cultures, you will find relationships between persons of the same sex are given a natural, unlimited range in development, but at *no* time did the African get such a relationship confused with a physical male-female relationship." This observation on Africa stands in contrast to other remarks she makes regarding eroticized same-sex relationships among Afroamericans.[2] To amplify some of Olade's observations, this paper examines the form and function of same sex marriage in African and Afroamerican societies. Such an examination seems particularly warranted in view of the recent confusion exhibited by the well known poet/professor Audre Lorde[3] in her essay, "Scratching the Surface: Some Notes on Barriers to Women and Loving," which appeared in *The Black Scholar's* issue devoted to *Blacks and the Sexual Revolution.* Decrying the "anti-lesbian hysteria" in today's Afroamerican community, Lorde reaches back to Africa to demonstrate and buttress her argument that among Afroamericans, homophobia is a form of human blindness. The plethora of half-truths, unsubstantiated assertions, and inaccurate statements in her article could very well impede our understanding of African traditions and how these traditions are or are not related to Afroamerican behavior. The spurious points made in Lorde's paper are more closely examined below.

Bonding

According to Lorde,[4] the attack on the Afroamerican lesbian, particularly by Afroamerican women, is one indication that "we have been encouraged to view each other with suspicion, as eternal competitors, or as the visible face of our self rejection." Lorde therefore reminds us that Afroamerican women have a tradition of supporting each other against seemingly insurmountable odds. As evidence of this supportive bonding, Lorde[5] cites complex, involved, and cooperative relationships. Lorde[6] states: "In all these cases, the women involved are recognized parts of their communities, evaluated not by their sexuality but by their respective places within the community." Eagerly advancing her notion even further, Lorde[7] queries why "the recent hysterical rejection of lesbians in the black (American) community is based solely upon an aversion to the idea of sexual contact between members of the same sex (a contact existing for ages in most of the female compounds across the African continent, from reports)".

For ages *social* contact between persons of the same sex has existed in Africa. For example, often the sexual division of labor facilitated social contact between members of the same sex. Initiation training for adulthood very definitely bifurcated along lines of sex. And many voluntary associations (whether economic, social, or political in nature) also demarcated on the basis of sex. *There is no reason to assume that such social contact was a sexual contact.* Lorde indicated that the "sexual contact" existed in most female headed compounds. However, she does not cite her sources except to say that her data are "from reports" Besides, what "female compounds" are being referred to: female headed compounds, female initiation-training compounds, family compounds with a numerical preponderance of females, or some other type of female compounds? We however are not told.

Knowledgeable in African cultural traditions. the East African savant John S. Mbiti[8] in his book, *Love and Marriages in Africa*, remarks: "though no proper studies of the problem have been in traditional African societies, homosexual practices seem to be rare or only confined to boys and girls before marriage." Furthermore, Mbiti[9] continues by noting that: "Even when people of the one sex remain together for a while, for example during initiation rites, hunting expeditions or raids, the reason bringing them together occupies them to such an extent that there is little or no opportunity for them to develop homosexual relations."

Lorde[10] is inaccurate when she claims that sexuality is not a basis for societal evaluation of a person in Africa. A survey of the ethnographics in the Human Relations Area Files would reveal that females (and males too) are expected to adhere to the norms governing sexual behavior in their societies. None of the ethnographic data demonstrate that African societies provide for the cultrual endorsement of homosexual relations between women, including cases of women-to-women marriages. Women (and men) are indeed evaluated by their sexual behavior.

Speaking to Afroamerican women, Lorde[11] pleads: "most of all as black women we have a right to recognize each other without fear and to love where we choose, for both homosexual and heterosexual black women today share a history of bonding and strength that our particular sexual preferences should not blind us to." It is important to recapitulate however, that the bonding that developed on the African continent was not imbued with the eroticism that Lorde leads us to believe was/is the case.

Marriage

Reading Lorde's paper, one could easily assume that female homosexuality was an accepted way of life, even to the extent of being celebrated in marriages between women. Lorde[12] tells us virtually nothing about the form, function, and development of same sex marriages in Africa except to note that: they "occur throughout Africa"; "some are homosexual relationships"; and they "are arranged to provide heirs for women of means who wish to remain 'free'".

That women have been allowed (and even encouraged) to contract marriages to other women in traditional African societies seems to be a well accepted notion by anthropologists. Although the ethnographic data are often scanty, anecdotal, and hapharzardly gathered, one may attempt to construct an ideal type, designated here as *woman-to-woman marriage*.[13] The purpose here is to sketch its most salient cross-cultural features as found occuring on the African continent.

Woman-to-woman marriages appear to occur only in those societies that have patrilineal descent systems (i.e. "blood" kinship traced through a line of fathers). Moreover women who are most likely to become female husbands are elderly women who have one or more of the following characteristics: barrenness, wealthy status, royal status, and occupancy of a significant religious or high political position. Some reports suggest that the women who become female husbands are regarded in some respects as men in their societies. And there are other studies which argue that the female husband is not to be interpreted as a woman adopting a man's role. Rather, the role — husband — is open to those that meet the societally determined criteria, irrespective of sex.

The potential female husband, not unlike her male counterpart, has a major concern for procreating descendants for her patrilineage. Thus, like a husband she is expected to make a bride-gift (i.e. bridewealth, brideprice) presentation to the kinsfolk of her bride-to-be. As in all African nuptial arrangements, the bride-gift is a significant feature of the marital contract. In societies with patrilineal kinship, the bride-gift establishes both the husband's legal paternity and the paternal lineage affiliation of any resultant children from the union. The wife of the female husband is impregnated by a genitor who may be mutually selected by either the female husband and the wife. (And in some cases the genitor may be selected by either the female husband or the wife.) The literature also reports that because the female husband is the legal spouse, she may also sue those males who take sexual liberties with her wife without her expressed permission. Some female husbands even become polygynists and establish large compounds with a number of wives and children.

A major point to be gleaned from the data is that woman-to-woman marriages are overwhelmingly concerned with the procreation of descendants. Of course it should be mentioned that in no society in which woman-to-woman marriages occur is there a sexual relationship between the women concerned. This seems not to have been understood by each social scientist observing the phenomenon. For example, Charles K. Meek[14] expressed the gross opinion that: "The custom may have had its origin in sexual perversity." Melville J. Herskovits[15] followed with an equally pernicious conjecture: "it is not to be doubtful that occasionally homosexual women who have inherited wealth have utilized this relationship to women they 'marry' to satisfy themselves." And complementing these erroneous speculations was the Human Relations Area Files[16] relegating the woman-to-woman marital arragement to file "no. 588: Irregular Unions" But to whom was this arrangement irregular: the athropologists or the Africans?

Woman-to-woman marriages appear to occur among the Nuer of East Africa, the Lovedu of southern Africa, and the Fon, Igbo, and Yoruba of West Africa[17]. As an illustrative case study, we may go to the northerly region of Yorubaland in Nigeria, West Africa. Although the case study, excerpted from *African Progress,* is concerned with problems the woman-to-woman marriage institution faces in a changing society, one should still be able to discern the major features of the institution as operative among the Yagba Yoruba. The story centers around the female husband-father, Madam Onisango, who is a priestess of the Yoruba God of thunder. Moreover, Madam Onisamgo, who is a cultivator who lives and works on a thirty acre farm.

> Mr. Bruaimoh Are instituted a civil suit against . . . Madam Fatimoh Onisango claiming ownership of two children born to him by another woman, Madam Musili. In addition, Mr. Are claimed the return and legal custody of Madam Musili as wife. The defendant Madam Fatimoh Onisango in her counter-affidavit, equally claimed to be the legal 'husband' of children in the association between the plantiff, (Mr. Are) and Musilli.

116

The lower court hearing this case

> awarded the child to the plaintiff on the grounds that it was foreign
> for a woman to marry another woman. The court told the defendant,
> Madam Fatimoh, that all she could be entitled to was the refund of
> the *L*5 dowry (i.e. bride-gift) she claimed to have paid for Musili.[18]

Appealing to a higher court against this judgement, Madam Onisango said
that the judge of the lower court erred in law by: allowing the woman for whom
she presented a bride-gift to leave her by force; granting the woman for whom
she presented a bride-gift to another person without the consent of the woman
in dispute; and setting aside the customary legal traditions of the Yagba Yoruba
which allows a childless and/or wealthy woman to marry another woman as wife.[19]
In an interview with a journalist, Madam Musili, the wife said:

> 'I have given the two children to Are as ordered by the court; one
> day the children will return to me because anyone who paid dowry
> for a woman is the legitimate husband. In my own case, my parents
> collected dowry from Madam Onisango and not from Buraimoh Are.
> I only recognize Buraimoh Are because Madam Onisango arranged
> with him to have affairs with me as laid down by our customs,[20].

Although Madam Musili has refused to leave her husband, Madam
Onisango, this is only a partially won battle (if it can be called that). The prejudice against the woman-to-woman marriage institution is mounting in modern
Nigeria. One journalist spoke with a "third-class" chief in Kwara State who "confirmed the existence of the custom among the Yagbas and joined in the call for
the complete eradication of the custom, which he described as outmoded and out-
dated."[21]

To recapitulate, woman-to-woman marriages are sanctioned in some
African societies having patrilineal descent groups. Such being the case, these
marriages, not unlike man-to-woman marriages, are to a great measure concerned with the perpetuity of the husbands' consanguineal kin groups. In marriages
contracted between woman, the parties are expected to assume the roles, husband and wife, with all the rights and duties attached to those roles. This is exclusive of course of sexual bonding. The phenomenon in which aged, barren,
and/or high status women marry younger women, although rooted in the jural
tenets of the traditional societies is now being confronted with a relatively new
superimposed jural order.

Since Herskovits'[22] imputation of homosexuality to the woman-to-woman
marriage phenomenon, all recent writers on this institution have had to take some
time to expunge this unwarranted conjecture.[23] But Lorde, who is neither an

117

Africanist nor a cultural anthropologist, sees fit to cite this portion of Herskovits' work which is in reality a piece of bad psuedoscientific anthropology. Unfortunately, non-Africanists and non-anthropologists reading Lorde's article would find it difficult to resist questioning if the woman-to-woman marriage institution in traditional Africa is at the base of the woman-to-woman marriage institution among the Afroamerican population. It is therefore important to compare, or more correctly to contrast, woman-to-woman marriages in Africa with those among Afroamericans.

Unlike African woman-to-woman marriages governed by traditional laws, Afroamerican woman-to-woman marriges[24] are not lawful unions according to the tenets of the state. In Africa, the women in same sex marriages do assume the spouse roles, husband and wife, such that the senior woman is the husband and the junior woman is the wife. Because the husband role is not a *priori* identified as masculine, one can not assume that a female husband in Africa takes on the role or social identity of a man. (This point is currently being debated in the literature.) In Afroamerica, while husband/wife-masculine/feminine role playing is not necessarily a correlate of same sex unions, Ethel Sawyer's[25] study of Afroamerican lesbians does indicate the presence of gender specific dyadic roles: "fish" (feminine role) and "stud" (masculine role). The "stud" role is said to have the higher status of the two roles and is the ultimate in female homosexuality.

One case study which is suggestive of some of the features of same sex unions among female Afroamericans can be gleaned from Bob Lucas,[26] story which appeared in *Jet.* Based on an interview with the wife we are told that Denease "Denny" Conley met, wooed, and eventually married Sherry "Dimples" Richardson in a non-legally binding "holy union" at Metropolitan Community Church. The bifurcation of roles in their marriage seems to mirror what occurs in contemporary American conjugal families. Thus, Denny, the husband, is a member of the Navy; and Dimples, the wife, is a cosemtologist aspiring to a career in modeling. Denny, like other American husbands, appears very much to be involved in the "public domain." Moreover she promised to provide the financial wherewithal (i.e. instrumental functioning) to meet her wife's career objectives. Dimples, on the other hand, appears to have brought expressive functioning to the relationship. In the role of wife, she commented on her relegation to the "domestic domain": "I couldn't leave the house. All I had to do was stay home, look pretty, cook meals, and have sex"[27].

From the data examined, we can say that woman-to-woman marriages among Afroamericans are conjugal bondings in which spouses derive sexual fulfillment from each other. No doubt this facilitates (in some cases) the emergence of a sexualized masculine stud role in Afroamerica which stands in contrast to a non-sexaulized, non-masculinized female husband role in Africa. Woman-to-woman marriages in Africa are not homosexal unions.

Because same sex marriages are oriented toward fulfillment of personal affective needs in Afroamerica, it would appear that these unions are not geared toward procreation. Of course this does not rule out the possibility of one or both female spouses having children. The African data are contrastive. While the monogamous or plural marriage of a female husband may reflect and reinforce that senior woman's prestige and status in an African community, woman-to-woman marriages are not aimed at mere self aggrandizement. As with virtually all marriages in Africa, the procreation of descendants for the expansion and intergenerational continuation of compounds, extended families and lineages is of paramount concern in woman-to-woman marriages.

Concluding Remarks

Audre Lorde[28] has raised a number of issues in her essay on ''barriers to women and loving'' which demand serious re-examination. Her attempts to get Afroamericans to see the wrongness or ''human blindness'' of homophobia rests on a questionable interpretation of same sex bonding in traditional African societies. Furthermore, the contrastive examination of same sex marriages among females in African and Afroamerican societies throws into relief Lorde's misunderstanding of African sexual behavior and marital traditions. Thus any linkage (implied by Lorde or perceived by her readers) between the African heritage and Afroamerican female homosexuality is shown to be a spurious relationship.

Studies of woman-to-woman marriages both in Africa and among Afroamericans should be continued. Indeed, studies of these marital forms, although different from each other and different in various respects from man-to-woman marriages, may yield interesting comparative and contrastive data for understanding sex roles, gender and identity, sexual stratification, friendship, marriage, dominance in the conjugal union, family organization, and so forth. Certainly some of these are the very areas that those who are concerned with strengthening Afroamerican male/female relationships have pin-pointed for special attention.

Finally, the objective of this paper has not been to buttress the ''anti-lesbian hysteria'' that Lorde[29] sees as rampant in the Afroamerican community today. Rather the purpose has been merely to elaborate, clarify, and/or put in broader perspective some of her questionable formulations.

Woman's Place In African Antiquity

by Prof. John Henrik Clarke

In Africa [before its invasion by the Europeans], the woman's "place" was not only with her family; she ofen ruled nations with unquestionable authority. Many African women were great militarists, and on occasion led their armies in battle. The Africans had produced a civilization where men were secure enough to let women advance as far as their talent, royal lineage and prerogatives would take them.

Dr. Cheikh Anta Diop writes that, during the entire history of Pharaonic Egypt, African women enjoyed complete freedom, as opposed to the condition of the segregated Indo-European woman of the classical periods. whether she was Greek or Roman. he further informs us that

> "no evidence can be found either in literature or in historical records—Egyptian or otherwise—relating to the systematic ill-treatment of Egyptian women by their men. They were respected and went about freely and unveiled, unlike certain Asian women. Affection for one's mother, and especially the respect with which it was necessary to surround her, were the most sacred of duties."

In Chapter Two of his book *[The Cultural Unity of Black Africa: the Domains of Patriarchy and of Matriarchy in Classical Antiquity]* devoted to "Criticism of the Classical Theory of a Universal Matriarchy," he calls attention to societies, such as the so-called aborigines of Australia, where the two social systems, the matriarchy and the patriarchy, peacefully merged. When these societies in Africa and in the South Seas are compared with early Europe, we

121

find that the European women had no basic rights. Dr. Diop observes that

"the husband was able to sell his wife or select an eventual husband for her, in anticipation of his own death (...) Eunuchs were made to watch over the women."

By contrast, the women of ancient Ethiopia had rights equal to that of men, and equal power. Ethiopia was the first country in the world to have been ruled by a Queen. Although Makeda, known as the Queen of Sheba, is the most remembered by historians, mainly because of her romance with King Solomon, she was not the greatest queen of Ancient Ethiopia. The line of queens who took the name Candace were some of the most able female rulers of all time. The value of this book and of Dr. Diop's study of "The Domains of Patriarchy and of Matriarchy in Classical Antiquity" is that it is also the study in essence of the African woman in power and of how that power developed.

It is generally conceded, in most scholarly circles, that mankind originated in Africa. This makes the African man the father and the African woman the mother of mankind. In the first African societies, the women played a major role without demeaning the man or making his role less important. The first accomplishment of the African woman, in partnership with the man, was the creation of a functioning family unit. This major step in human development laid the foundation for the organization of all subsequent societies and institutions.

During the rise of the great dynasties in Egypt, Kush and Ethiopia, the African women made impressive strides; some became heads of State. The appearance of Queen Hatshepsut, about 1,500 years before the birth of Christ, launched the beginning of their historical prominence in the affairs of State. Hatsheput's reign was one of the brightest in Egyptian history, proving that a woman can be a strong and effective ruler. She was, according to the Egyptologist James Henry Breasted, "the first great woman in history of whom we are informed."

The Black Coed
Growing Into Womanhood

by Nathan Hare, Ph.D.

The Black coed, poised on the threshold of Black womanhood, must be prepared for the most exciting and, simultaneously, most provocative emotional stage of her life. As she leaves adolescence and faces the psychoanalytic dilemma involved in finding true love (intimacy versus isolation), she encounters a number of special conflicts, owing chiefly to the emerging shortage of Black males shunted into prison and related places instead of college and commerical firms. Thus, sometimes she will be moved to marry beneath her station in life and otherwise inherit the added burden of the necessity for massaging and managing a frustrated male ago.

The Double Whammy

However, the young Black woman's problems are not due merely, as many too quickly grow to believe, to the Black male and his frustrations. She must also cope with problems of her own self esteem and may also experience an acute sense of deprivation in her most feminine striving — the longing to be desired and desirable. Understand that Afro-Americans, unlike Jews, for instance, are rejected in their corporeality, their physical features, in the color of their bodies, the literal embodiment of the self. Thus racism hits the Black female in the heart of her femininity, her Black female beauty, which moreover is denied and denegrated and only grudgingly acknowledged to this day. What is more, she is likely to internalize white society's resentment of her deep strength and beauty, so that she may not even fully recognize her own desirability. This is the true, most hurting, double whammy of the Black woman. The young Black woman must know the beauty of the Black woman in the deepest way, believe down in her bones that she most personally is a "natural fox."

"So many negative reinforcements for the young Black woman exists," says Dorethia DuVal, a counselor for the Multi-Service Center in Marin City, California, "that she has a hard time liking it (Black womanhood). If you feel like you're not beautiful, or don't feel positive about yourself, you may let your mate move into your space and take advantage of you." Ms. DuVal believes moreover that while the Black woman may appear to be aggressive, often out of sheer necessity, she also must be wary of the passive side of her nature. These feelings merely represent two contradictory sides of the coin of the female connection with masculinity.

The Black Male And Female Relationship

The Black coed, however, accumulated the advantages of her know-how and cognitive skills in understanding and manipulating the masculine ego. For instance, she may find that many Black men, blocked from the routine avenues to social power and position, may overcompensate with extreme sexual interests. The young Black woman must be able to see the socio-psychological side of these distorted tendencies and to handle them with class and calm discretion while neglecting to take them personally. At the same time, she must not permit neurotic males unwarranted privileges, nor place consideration from them above her own. She must, nevertheless, be prepared to cope with the sometimes agonizing and subtle nuisances of male-female relationsips. One crucial area is the mutual displacement of rage onto each other too often exhibited by the Black woman and the Black man. She may unconsciously seek to undercut or condemn his masculine prowess while he combats and resents her virtues and capacities as a woman.

Someone To Depend On

The Afro-American woman, moreover, has historically been denied the basic dependence on her man enjoyed comparatively by the white woman. Women's liberation protests to the contrary notwithstanding. At the same time, as the young Black woman begins to reap some benefits deriving from the token gains of the Black middle class (even as the lower class slips further back), she will now experience ambivalence and confusion in the face of novel and often alien male-female values extolled by vocal white feminists. She typically longs for a strong Black man to stand beside her, yet finds him, she complains, in tragically short supply. She may further discover that the Black male, whose patriarchy has been broken, is inclined to both idealize and resent her necessary strength.

Hence, the Black coed must practice avoiding the displaced power struggle. She must never become a door mat for anybody or indulge her man's too ready inclinations to fall or falter when the going gets rough. She is the nurturant one, the backbone and ultimate expert in family relationships. She may even encounter unfulfilled needs for nurturance in her mate. The warrior is the primal role of the male, whose primary function of protecting and providing for the family in the case of the Black nation now under captivity has been thwarted and suppressed.

The young Black woman will do well to be supportive of her man while remaining firm in her rights, understanding while not necessarily condoning her mate's hesitation in the face of unfair adversity. Rather than chastise her man, however, for his mediocre occupation, she might better find something good to say while remaining alert to signs of simmering ambition on his part as a basis for further encouragement on hers. In addition, she might strategically let him overhear her praising some quality of his in telephone conversations with her female friends.

The Formidable Task

Clearly, on the shoulders of the young Black woman rests a formidable task. For she will be the value-setter, the model of strength and virtue and beauty for the young Black girl, for her daughter or some other, at the same time as she massages and molds the self esteem of her, as yet, unwary Black son.

However, the Black coed is fortunate in at least one important area of her family role. She combines expertise in communication skills with the special orientation toward personal independence an oppressive experience has taught her. She must overcome the Black male's too frequent reluctance to communicate routinely about the cares of a given day, the Black male who, hearing her complain of occupational insults suffered at the hands of a white employer, feels still powerless to do anything about it and does not wish to hear her (would rather take a walk).

In His Absence

Should it fall the young Black woman's lot to become both mother and father to her children, to have to play both parts, how will she fight understandable yet crippling bitterness and rage? How will she hold in her hurt sufficiently to protect the budding egos of her innocent young children without damaging her perhaps already battered self esteem? How will she retain her ancient and inexorable femininity yet take on the job of helping her man protect and provide for the family, or in his absence, to provide alone? How will she lure him, in or out of the home, into extending a stronger and more ready helping hand?

Beyond these, there are many questions whose answers cannot be found in textbooks. She must nevertheless begin to seek. For instance, what will she tell her chidren about the snares of racism, about Black consciousness? How will she infuse them with a sense of pride in race and racial awareness without simultaneously destroying their sense of personal competence, without bestowing on them the handicap of undying feelings of overwhelming control from the outside?

The Pillar Of Strength

In the end, according to Adama Sanders, a community mental health worker in San Francisco, the young Black coed may need to discard old and obsolescent motives of dependence and security to be sought in her choice of a mate. She must learn to be totally comfortable and serene in her own emerging strength. "The Black family often doesn't have the economic base or the money to sit her down, so lacking a sufficient financial stake, she must begin to feel a sense of her own efficacy, to feel that she can make it in the world on her own, whether financially or otherwise."

This concern with being her own woman and achieving individualization from the male is echoed by Jackie Fletcher, an Oakland marriage and family counselor. She sees the young Black woman of today moving away from total preoccupation with pleasing the man to satisfying herself, as well. "You can't be supportive at your own expense. You have to be aware of your own needs and what they are then and there, although of course they may change. If you don't it'll just rage totally out of control and you'll find yourself playing catchup later on."

In the process, says Pamela McCoy, Director of the Booker T. Washington Center in San Francisco, you become more tolerant and understanding of life's situations and of your man. "You learn to accept hurt and you also do some hurting — it's a two-way street. but don't grow bitter and close off new experiences. Sometimes you won't think so, but there's always somebody to love. You just have to have a little patience. When you're young you think things are supposed to happen right now, just like that — make a big salary, going to get married — but you may find it'll take you ten whole years. But, believe me, there are joys and reinforcements along the way, enough to keep up your faith in the natural order of things."

To Be Black, Gifted, and Alone

by Bebe Moore Campbell

By the time Leanita McClain was 32, the Black journalist had won the Peter Lisagor Award from the Headline Club (the Chicago Chapter of Sigma Delta Chi, the national journalism honorary fraternity); the 1983 Kizzy Award for outstanding black women role models; and top honors from the Chicago Association of Black Journalists for commentary. She was also the first Black to become a member of the *Chicago Tribune's* editorial board in that newspaper's 137-year history; a prestigious position that carried with it a salary of approximately $50,000 and the opportunity to influence the attitudes of millions of people. In March 1984, McClain was selected by *Glamour* magazine as one of the ten most outstanding working women in America.

Two months later, on the evening of May 29, 1984—Memorial Day—McClain killed herself.

To many observers, McClain's accomplishments seemed even more astounding because she had grown up in a housing project in Chicago's predominantly Black south side, an area known for gang warfare, poverty, and despair. her success had netted her a posh address in the city's predominantly white, gentrified north side, but McClain wasn't entirely comfortable in her new setting. In October 1980, in *Newsweek's* "My Turn" column, she wrote, "It is impossible for me to forget where I came from as long as I am prey to the jive hustler who does not hesitate to exploit my childhood friendship. I am reminded, too, when I go back to the old neighborhood in fear—and have my purse snatched—and when I sit down to a business lunch and have an old classmate wait on my table. I recall the girl I played dolls with who now rears five children on welfare,

127

the boy from church who is in prison for murder, the pal found dead of a drug overdose in the alley where we once played tag....Sometimes when I wait at the bus stop with my attache case, I meet my aunt getting off the bus with other cleaning ladies on their way to do my neighbors' floors.''

McClain realized that she couldn't go home again. Yet, despite her fair skin and sandy hair, despite her credentials and awards, she didn't have full access to her new world either. ''I....have fulfilled the entry requirements of the American middle class, yet I am left, at times, feeling unwelcomed and stereotyped,'' she wrote.

She confided to a friend that she feared being a token on her job, and she worked at a frenzied pace to prove her competence.

Her dress-for-success uniform belied the fact that her emotional underpinnings had been created on the other side of town. ''She got thrown into a white world and was expected to act the part,'' says a friend. ''She was often fighting and grappling with her real self. She couldn't even write what she wanted. She had to bottle up her rage.''

While McClain the journalist scaled corporate heights, her private life was conflicted, and her personal problems were exacerbated by her rapid professional rise. ''She was sort of guilty about her success,'' says Monroe Anderson, a columnist and reporter for the *Chicago Tribune* and a close friend of McClain's. ''Her parents still lived in the ghetto. Their problems were her problems.''

But she had problems of her own as well. Her eight-year marriage to Clarence Page ended in 1982. Page, a journalist who has since been named to replace McClain on the *Tribune's* editorial board, says the divorce was McClain's idea. ''She began to express dissatisfaction with the marriage; she wanted love to come and hit her out of the blue. I told her, 'You're looking for something that's not there.'''

McClain found that her success could be intimidating. Her new-world expectations demanded that a mate match or better her salary and status. She dated a younger man, Keenan Michael Coleman, a computer salesman; their affair was stormy, yet McClain, desiring marriage, held on. She purchased an expensive house in Chicago's Hyde Park section, only to put it back on the market 24 hours later when her relationship dissolved.

As her personal desires eluded her and the values of her old and new worlds collided, close friends witnessed spells of hysterical crying, brooding silence, and mounting depression. She began stockpiling the potent antidepressant amitriptyline prescribed by her physician. For all of her accoutrements of professional success, McClain was as full of despair as any ghetto dweller.

On the night of what would have been her tenth wedding anniversary, McClain swallowed a huge overdose of amitriptyline and left both worlds behind.

It is rare for a black woman to ascend to the professional heights that McClain attained. Black women in corporate America are still scarce: according to the Bureau of Labor Statistic's report for 1984, among the classification "executive, administrative, managerial, and professional specialty," there were only 1,474,000 Black women, 5.9% of the total, as opposed to 22,250,000 white women, 91% of the total number of working women in this category. Understandably, then, the loss of McClain's influence, power, and her ability to be role model is perceived by some Blacks as a group loss. "It hurt me to see a Black woman who's achieved so much take it all away from us," says Paulette, a 38-year-old television producer in Los Angeles. Paulette is one of a small random sampling of Black female executives—most working in upper middle management positions for large corporations and earning between $40,000 and $80,000 annually—who agreed to talk to me under a cloak of anonymity. These women admit that a Black woman's climb to corporate power is at lease as arduous as survival in the ghetto: They see a part of themselves in Leanita McClain's life, if not in her death.

Stress is the common experience these women all share. Not the Alka Seltzer stress of fighting deadlines and office politics while maintaining homes and families, this stress is from the oppressive combination of racism, sexism, and professional competition that separates Black women not only from their white colleagues, but also insidiously pits them against their Black male professional counterparts. The overload on Black executive women often results in their pulling away from a cultural identity that includes family and old friends. Corporate racism, they expected. What was unexpected was the various degrees of culture shock, isolation, and alienation that Black women experience as they attempt to acclimate professionally and to assimilate their culturally distinct selves into organizations that reward uniformity.

"I met Leanita a month or so before she died," says the director of a large, midwestern state agency. "We were both receiving the same award. When she sat down, I took one look at her and said to myself, 'The sister has problems.' I noticed it because I've been there before....It was hard for me to believe that she committed suicide just because of job stress. When you're down there competing with white folks, you go through any number of changes. We've been brought up to expect that."

No one ever imagined the time when Blacks would be insiders. Although Martin Luther King dreamed aloud of that day and thousands of Blacks and whites marched, fought, and died to prevent or bring the moment closer, no one fully understood what overcoming the barriers of discrimination would mean for people who had been outsiders for centuries. Freedom, yes. But freedom to do what? To be whom?

When Leanita McClain began working for the *Chicago Tribune* in 1973, she was part of the first generation of corporate Blacks that affirmative action helped to create. Although it may have appeared that McClain easily glided from one world into another, her transition, like that of other black female executives, was far from smooth.

"I was very uneasy around whites when I first entered the corporation," says Yolanda, 35, a human resource manager for a large hair-care firm in New York City. "I come from a middle class family. My father is a lawyer, and my mother is a teacher. My grandparents went to college. We were far from poor, yet I still grew up in a Black world. My childhood was spent in a middle-class section of Los Angeles. I went to all-Black schools from elementary school through college.

In 1970, Yolanda began her career as one of two Blacks out of 40 people in a Sears management training program in Los Angeles. "Coming into big business, I had culture shock, but I didn't know it," Yolanda explains. "The sixties had just ended," she recalls,"and I was wearing my hair in a six-inch Afro. My consciousness was as high as my hair. One evening, my manager, a white man, took me aside and told me to wear jeans and a T-shirt to work the next day, because I'd be on the loading docks. Now I realize that working there was standard procedure, but I can remember wondering then if he was going to give me menial work to do because I'm Black."

What some people would term Yolanda's "hypersensitivity" is a cultural orientation that most American Blacks share and find difficult to shed: a tendency to be preoccupied with race and racism.

"Preoccupation with race can be very debilitating," says Ron Brown, Ph.D., a psychologist whose firm, Banks and Brown, counsels white and black managers from Fortune 500 companies on racial attitudes. "Back in the late sixties, it was obvious that Black managers were having difficulty adjusting to the cues and norms of the corporate environment. Some of them were starting from ground zero. Blacks are trying to learn an ingrown system without coaching and mentoring. They can do it, but it takes longer. And some are paying a heavy price in stress."

Even after ten successful years in the corporate world, Yolanda still struggles with some degree of cultural unease. "I'm still uncomfortable around Whites in social situations," she says. "If I have to go to cocktail parties with Whites,

I don't feel completely at ease. We're all uncomfortable. When we're away from the job, the differences between us appear greater.''

Many Black executive women claim that in addition to the usual conformity that is required of all corporate professionals, if they want to succeed, they must make the Whites around them feel comfortable, a difficult feat. Black women consciously choose their speech, their laughter, their walk, their mode of dress and car. They trim and straighten their hair, lest kinky curls or corn-rows set them apart. At work, they try not to congregate in groups of more than two, so that White colleagues will not suspect a "plot."

McClain, fair and freckled as she was, couldn't blend in with her White co-workers even by changing her style. In *Newsweek* she declared, "I am painfully aware, that even with my off-white trappings, I am prejudged by my color...." Although White women may chafe under corporate dress codes, behavioral constraints, and sexism, they don't have the additional burden of compromising their cultural selves. If Black women, however, truly relinquish their cultural selves, they are unable to function in the old world that still claims them. They learn to wear a mask.

"Each day, when I get into my car, I always begin the ride to work by turning on a Black radio station so that it blares," say Karen, 35, a Harvard MBA who works for an Atlanta-based telecommunications corporation. "I boogey all the way down the highway. A few blocks from my job, I turn the music down and stop shaking my shoulders. When my building comes into view, I turn the music off, because I know the curtain is about to go up."

"I try hard not to be what they expect," says Estelle, 31, a fair-skinned Black woman who is the vice president of the business division of a large bank in Los Angeles. "I don't misconjugate verbs. I don't wear a natural....it probably helps that I'm not real dark-skinned. That's sad, but I know that kind of thing influences them."

Regardless of how Black executive women may want to express themselves—and not all feel a conflict—they are pragmatic. Karen concludes, "The choice to enter the corporation is a choice to conform. Loudness, street talking, afros, flashy cars—that's not what White folks buy into. I've given up some self-expression. The trade-off for the salary is to play by the rules."

McClain knew the rules well. She came to work dressed for success and she wore her light brown hair in a straightened style. She lunched with White co-workers. She was articulate and pleasant. "Most Whites thought Leanita was wonderful," says Monroe Anderson. "She was an actress around them."

As Black executive women move up, they become isolated from those in their old world. McClain's parents and her two sisters were unaware of the pressures she was under. "Her sisters had no idea what bad shape she was in," one co-worker said. "She wasn't confiding in them." Many Black executive women have few people to confide in. As they move up the corporate ladder they also become isolated from other Blacks who work in lower positions in the same company.

"Not long ago, my division laid off several hundred people," says the 36-year-old director of career devopement for minorities at a New York television network. "Two of my closest friends were let go. There was nothing that I could have done to prevent it. I was hurting with them. Once they left, they told the other Blacks in the company not to talk to me because I was management. I was very, very hurt. Blacks began to stay away from me. What could I do? I couldn't go to my boss about it. I felt as though I'd been ripped apart."

Some accept the isolation as par for the course. "The higher up you move, the more you'll be isolated," says the Los Angeles banker matter-of-factly. "I have less in common with those of the same class or income, be they Black or White."

If some Black women are pragmatic about assimilation, many are pained by the thought of "losing their blackness" and strive to maintain cultural ties. For Linda, a human resources manager for a fast-food chain headquartered outside of Chicago, the decision to remain in the Black south side brings turmoil. "I firmly believe, although it's being chipped away, that if Blacks don't live in the Black community, there will be no role models for inner-city kids."

But Linda's voice is weary as she talks about the disadvantages. "I have a 35-mile one-way commute. Obviously, property values are much lower. And two company cars have been stolen from in front of my house. One was right in the driveway.

"I've been to the homes of Whites I work with who live in the suburbs; I haven't invited them to mine."

Leanita McClain had felt guilty about moving away from her old friends; she felt awkward about fitting the militant Blacks' stereotype of a "sell out." "I am not comfortably middle class,' she wrote. "I am uncomfortably middle class."

Not assimilating into the corporate mold, which includes an acceptable lifestyle away from the job, isn't overlooked by companies. "Eventually, when upper management considers someone who maintains a visibly Black lifestyle for increased responsibility, she might be ruled out as not being a 'good fit,'" says Ron Brown.

If being alienated from Blacks brings stress, at the same time there are new pressures from those in the old world who view the executive woman as having made it. Black organizations demand time and money, as do friends and family. Some Black executives find themselves alternately being used and abused as they are made to pay for their success. "I am a member of the Black middle class who has had it with being patted on the head by White hands and slapped in the face by Black hands," wrote McClain.

Isolated from Blacks, Black executive women often are alienated from the Whites with whom they are supposed to assimilate. "When I was placed in a fast-track development program, I was really estranged from my white co-workers," says Cora, 33, who manages 105 people in a Chicago communications company. "I felt that they were all watching me. They had all worked their way up to management. I came in off the street into a management position. They knew I'd been tapped to move up. They were waiting for me to fall on my face. They resented me because I was black, female, young, and headed to be a company executive."

"I have to interpret what my white managers are saying two and a half times," says Yolanda, the hair-care manager. "They filter out infomation because I'm a Black woman."

McClain clearly questioned the ties that bound her to some of her white peers. She wrote, "Some of my 'liberal' White acquaintances hint that I am a freak, that my success is less a matter of talent than of luck and affirmative action. I may live among them, but it is difficult to live with them."

For some Blacks, the mask they wear begins to crack under the pressure as their rage bubbles to the surface. When the late Chicago Mayor Harold Washington, a black man, was running for office, Chicago became a hate-filled city. In a series of columns, McClain vented her feelings of anger and disillusionment, but it was in *The Washington Post* that her article, "How Chicago Taught Me to Hate Whites," potently articulated the rage that she felt as the mayoral campaign progressed to what she called "a race war." Her anger was directed toward Whites who spoke disparagingly of "the Blacks." "'The Blacks,'" McClain wrote. "It would make me feel like machine-gunning every white face on the bus."

McClain could powerfully externalize her fury, but most black women lack that access to public confrontation. They turn their rage inward. Nearly all of the women interviewed by me show a series of disturbing symptoms: hair loss, nervous exhaustion, chronic stomach pains, insomnia, and depression. "I thought I had high blood pressure," says the Los Angeles television producer. "My heart was beating fast and I had shortness of breath. I had migraines. The physician couldn't find anything wrong. Finally I went to a therapist and we discussed my negative feelings about my job and career. That gave me some relief." "I see a high rate of alcoholism and cocaine and marijuana abuse. Lots of tranquilizers," says Audrey B. Chapman, a therapist and human relations trainer in Washington, D.C., who specializes in stress management seminars for female professionals. "The women exhibit a lot of psychosomatic pain in their backs and necks. They have severe menstrual cramps. The pain isn't so much physical as it is mental," says Chapman. "The stress leads to the real killers of Black women—hypertension, diabetes, and strokes."

As prevalent as racism is, many Black executive women declare that, at times, they are aware of discrimination because of gender even more than of race.

According to findings from Black Values in the American Workplace, a conference held in March 1984, funded by the Xerox Corporation and organized by John L. Jones, that company's director of affirmative action, sexism is a major problem for Black executive women.

"I was in the hall talking with one of the big bosses, an older White guy," says the Los Angeles television producer. "As I turned to leave, he swatted me on my behind with a rolled-up newspaper. I was in a state of shock. If anybody ever does that to me again, I swear, I'll grab him by his collar and throw him up against a wall."

Although White males see them as fair game, Black women complain that Black males are most often the perpetrators of chauvinistic behavior. "Most of my trouble came from Black men," says the agency head from Illinois. "They had problems because I was a firm manager. I fired all of them eventually because they did a poor job. One of the men I let go came to me and said, 'Your problem is that you're just evil.' I told him, 'Evil is what your girlfriend or woman may be. I'm efficient. And your ass is gone.' He couldn't believe that a woman would let him go."

If a Black woman's managerial status is threatening to the Black men with whom she works, so it is that her success may inhibit or spoil her personal relationships. No other group is as likely to be divorced—over twice the rate as for White women. The divorce rate for Black women is 10% higher for those with college degrees, 15% higher with one year of graduate school, and 19% higher for those with two years of graduate school.

Among the never-married, the search for a "suitable" mate is frustrating. According to Census figures, there are nearly 1.5 million more Black females than males: the largest difference in male/female ratio of any racial group in the country. And, for many years, there have been more college-educated Black females than males. According to Joyce Payne, director, Office for the Advancement of Public Black Colleges, the number of Black women awarded professional degrees increased by 71%; there was a 12% decline for black males. The single women interviewed all told stories of failed relationships with professional Black males. These women claim that the male/female ratio allows men to "romp"; they add that Black professional men are intimidated by the success of the women.

"I've had long-term relationships that have ended, and the next thing I knew, my ex-boyfriend was dating a secretary," says the midwestern agency director. "I think that Black professional women must be too honest. I was going with a man who headed a local agency and who was trying to go into business for himself. He had some good ideas, but he had some dumb ones, too. Maybe I should have just pretended that everything he said was wonderful. Also, he had this irritating habit. Whenever he'd come to my office, he'd close the door, sit in my chair, put his feet up on my desk, and say, 'Now, if I were the boss, this is how I'd run this agency.'"

"In the old days, Black women who were professionals married pullman porters and postal workers, the only jobs most Black men could get," says Chapman. "What today's women expect is less available." Still the hunt for the elusive Black male professional continues.

Toward the end of her life, Leanita McClain's loneliness was perhaps a heavier burden than her professional struggles. The combination was, for her, unbearable.

"It wasn't a question of either her professional problems or her personal ones causing her the most difficulty," says Monroe Anderson, the *Tribune* reporter. "Her focus was on her personal life. What happened was that with her rapid success and her still not being happy, the personal came into focus. It's difficult for a Black woman to make it without a personal relationship. Black women have to battle racism and sexism and then come home to loneliness, or again do battle. For the majority of professional Black women, it's not good."

Yet, most Black executive women admit that their brothers' quest for professional ascendancy is far more frustrating than their own. "Black men have a harder time," says one executive Black woman, echoing most others, "because White males are intimidated by them."

The progress of Black men is tied to the progress of Black women. Black women cannot contribute the best of their talents to the corporation if they are placed in the position of being an affirmative action buffer zone, fulfilling federal government standards at the expense of professional opportunity for Black men. Until Black women develop strategies to overcome many of their own self-inflicted

135

problems, they will be ensnared by their own success, forging ahead while straining under a staggering emotional load.

Leanita McClain finally laid her burden down and escaped the narrow alley located between pain and desire to another place. Her unanswered question continues to haunt her sisters.

"I have made it, but where?"

Reprinted with permission from *Savvy*.

Sexual Anorexia

by Nathan Hare, Ph.D. and Julia Hare, Ed.D.

Sexual anorexia, now increasingly visited upon the black woman in our time, in epidemic proportions, is a term we coined in 1975[1] to categorize those women who suffer a period of emotional exhaustion in the endeavor to locate and endure a suitable mate, then give up for a period of six months or more on the hope of making a satisfactory love adjustment.

"Honey, I don't need no man." "These n---- men ain't no good." "all the best ones are either already taken or gay." " Deliver me from these no good n---- men."

Unlike amoraphobia (an acute inner fear of loving that is more characteristic of the male and a syndrome we will take up in detail later), sexual anorexia is mainly a reactive malady. It is more likely to strike the woman in her 30s and 40s, as she approaches or enters middle age and has felt in too many cases that she has had Prince Charming by the heartstrings only to discover that she had the devil by the tail.

Although her plight or experience has been often due in part to a personal problem in mate selection, she hides behind a defense mechanism of denial and projection of blame on such factors as "the black male shortage." Following a seemingly relentless series of false starts in matters romantic, rather than have her heart broken every day, she wraps herself in an emotional armor of animosity, dragging between the job and lonely routines made necessary all the more, in her mind, by a waning feeling of physical and sexual energy.

In this regard, she is victim of the fact that unlike men, who store up sexual energy and crave sex more the less they indulge, many women are prone over prolonged periods without sex, to grow accustomed too readily to a sex-free existence, adopting a "take-it-or-leave-it" attitude. This is especially so if their sexual partners immediately preceding the period of abstinence or elective celibacy have been essentially unfulfilling, but it is born more so of a woman's inclination to value the nonsexual aspects of a relationship, wanting something more than raw or uncaring sex (after which she may suffer both feelings of guilt and of having been used).

Her efforts to break out of this inclination, spurred on by the rhetoric of feminism and unisexualism today, may only expose her all the more frequently and precipitously, over and over again, to making still another false choice of a mate, once more playing out a compulsion or tendency to focus her hopes on a fickle, ineligible or otherwise unavailable male, repeating the old pathology instead of breaking free of it.

Some, on the other hand, have been known to declare a vow of celibacy, or temporary celibacy, but for the majority of women, celibacy's powers of purification may have been greatly exaggerated.[2] After an understandable period of recuperation and relative social exclusion, it is healthy for a woman to pick herself up and get back in the race. Rather than using her false choices or uneven fate as justification for giving up on "these n--- men," unconsciously accommodating to the black male shortage instead of organizing to help halt it, she will struggle to learn from her unfortunate experiences and to use this knowledge and resolve to guide her as she goes along.

Indeed, there are so many subtle factors predisposing a person to fall in love, sometimes it is quite a tumble. In the face of the reproductive challenge, women have needed, throughout the millenia, to be careful or selective in the choice of a mate. However, a woman may nevertheless be thwarted by powerful social forces as well as worrisome psychological motivations more complicated, if not more devastating, than the males more primitive sexual passions. Needing someone to hold them and help them, particularly during the vulnerable months of pregnancy, to protect them, "to fight [off] the bear" in the once inhabited wilds (even in the economic perils of "sexually liberated" today), women have evolved a deeply imbedded attraction to the most adaptive male.

Despite all the contemporary talk to the contrary, women as a group appear in large part still to be guided by the longing for security and male protection. They are characteristically drawn to a man's social potency (his high social position, wealth, prestige, power, intelligence) not merely his personal and physical charms. Paunchy old men with riches, power or fame, can emerge as widely coveted sex objects while dashing male paramours without visible employment or at least a convincing desire for same will ceremoniously be pitched out into the street, despite the black male shortage.

In the case of the black woman, this feminine attraction to the adaptive male complicates an already difficult situation. For one thing, there are differences in what constitutes an adaptive male at different stages of a black woman's life. Early in puberty, within the adolescent subculture of the ghetto, she encounters the most adaptive male in the form of the jive cat, walking-tall-looking-mean-talking-clean "Superfly" character type. He knows he can dance and romance young women with enough rapping and cultivated pimpish mannerisms and maneuvers. The adolescent female is inclined to be attracted to his very self assurance as well as his adaptability within the constraints of the adolescent social world, to be drawn precisely to his ability to relate well to and manipulate females sexually and romantically.

As a young or maturing woman seeking to mold a satisfactory love life (with Superfly still dancing in the streets, hanging out in bleak poolrooms, or iced away in prison), the young black woman growing older tends to turn her attention to the once inept Booker T. Shy and withdrawn in adolescence, Booker T. had been inclined to spend inordinate amounts of time in the library or even the church house or in other pastimes remote from the arena of adolesent courtship.

But now Booker T. has become Mr. Booker T., Esq. Unlike the undisciplined Superfly, he now has a good, steady job. For all practical purposes, he may still be a square, but he suddenly seems sweet enough just talking like a banker and wearing a coat and tie and starched white shirt on a regular basis in broad daylight. Thus many women may be impelled to live out their lives in an undying struggle to negotiate the duality of desiring Superfly and Booker T. both.

Meanwhile, the Booker T.'s of the world, for their part, may remain perennially embittered by early female rejection. Seeking to save their injured adolescent egos, they may wrap themselves as adult men in a frenzied endeavor to makeup for lost sexual time, coldly exploiting the middle class black male shortage and their own newfound appeal to the female multitudes now jilted by Superfly but liberated enough to pursue the adult world's most adaptive males. The Booker T.'s thus join the Superflys and an even more deadly variety of males which the Superflys may mimic, the amoraphobics and the appollomaniacs.

Women who have felt that there are men who suffer an acute fear of loving or even an abhorence of the situation of serious emotional involvement, have been entangled with a kind of man psychologists might call amoraphobics. While amoraphobics are by no means restricted to or characteristic of black males, it is understandable that black males encountering the emotional traumas of racial and socioeconomic oppression produce their share of amoraphobics.

Apprehensive about getting too close, amoraphobic men experience considerable difficulty in keeping their commitments. They flit from woman to woman (and sometimes man to man). but, unlike the male variation of the nymphomaniac (the appollomaniac), who seeks sexual fulfillment as a physical and concrete alternatives or decoys in the compensatory quest for an elusive feeling of emotional satisfaction, amoraphobics are not so much engaged in a futile attempt to find sex in a love they cannot feel as caught in the grips of anxious avoidance of what they view as inherently antagonistic or potentially perilous.

However, like the appollomaniac, who may seek out a multitude of women in the search for sexual intimacy as a simple compensation for a feeling of emotional estrangement, looking for his mother in every woman, the amoraphobic is hooked on an emotional dilemma in his approach to love: an acute form of the tension between the desire for sexual variety and the need for psychological and social stability which confronts men in general.[3] Like the pimp, which he sometimes becomes (or, more likely endeavors to -- for his fear of intimacy may interfere with the facile efficiency essential to the pimp), he rejects those whom he fears may eventually reject him. Unlike the pimp, who is turning the tables on society and the woman, reversing the soical-sexual roles he feels rejects him.[4] The amoraphobic is turning his back on the women he fears may exploit him emotionally if he allows them to get too close or if he weakens enough to take a chance on love. Masking their depression with hostility, many amoraphobics may focus periodically on one woman but shatter stability with chronic fits of jealousy and stormy conflict.

It may be more than a platitude to say that too many black men as children lose their fathers (not infrequently amoraphobics themselves), or lose and miss the emotional and social availability of the father as a disciplinary and companionate model of manly deportment, even when the uninvolved or unapproachable father is in the home. To fill the void, the mother, the opposite-sex parent, must take his place as father and mother psychologically camouflaged in one. Out of this ambiguity can emerge an aucte ambivalence in the boy, and a resentment born of resistance to the mother's double-duty disciplinary role which he may not be able to shake in his adulthood encounters with the female extensions of the mother with whom he must endeavor to mate.

Homicide Among Black Men and Women: Fatal Black Attractions

by Morris F.X. Jeff, Jr., Ph.D.

The poet proclaims: we are the children of the ones they could not kill. And yet there is a horror transpiring in most urban communities that threatens Black people's very existence. This threat of our lives is not by the direct hands of White America (at least, it is not obvious to the eyes of its victims). More insidiously, this threat comes from certain members of the Black community. We are children of the ones White folks could not kill; but will there be children of those who are now being killed by Black folks? Yes, we have survived. By the grace of the collective love, unity and spirit of Black people, we have survived. We do survive. The existential question is will we survive the autodestruction of the Black-on-Black homicide syndrome that is now accelerating in most urban communities?

What madness of malady, what neurosis is this that we would dare set off an epidemic of killing our own kind? Given the epochal residue of our historical experience as targets of death at the hands of White America, and given our rightful, historical fear of being killed, wiped out, by White America, how do we account for this pattern of internecine killing of ourselves?

After persistent inquiry into the phenomenon of homicides in the United States, for five consecutive decades dating back to 1920, through 1979, there emerges a profile which contains a set of uniform patterns. It is now evident, for example, that murders are not committed for the most part by strangers. Murder symbolizes the complete renunciation of the common notion that it is

141

the marauding stranger who poses the greatest threat to a person's life. To the contrary, a person is more likely to be a victim of murder at the hands of a friend, relative, acquaintance or lover.

Through the centuries, males, both White and Black, have been the perpetrators and the victims of homicide. Males between the ages of 15 and 44 are most vulnerable of all. Those between the ages of 20 to 24 are more susceptible within that group precisely. This is particularly true if they live in the Southern region of the country, in a metropolitan center where the economic levels are low, the schools are of poor quality, and the housing is sub-standard. These age and ecological factors linked to a male's social pattern of intimate involvement with a woman frequenting taverns, bars and restaurants on weekends between 8:00 o'clock p.m. on Friday and midnight on Sunday, heighten the chances of falling victim to homicide.

If by circumstance, the male is Black and fits the above criteria, his life chances are immediately reduced, since his homicide rate is five to ten times higher than his White counterpart. As a victim, he is likely to be killed by another Black male who is three to four years younger, the weapon used is primarily a gun, or sometimes a knife, depending on geographic and spatial location of the incident. His White counterpart will most likely be killed by a fellow White male with a gun or less likely beaten to death. In most cases, homicides are intra-racial and primarily between males. However, Black-on-Black homicide will most often pertain to a killing of passion, a spur-of-the-moment episode, albeit an act intended to kill. This act will likely be triggered by a quarrel or dispute over money, or sex, or some third party.

The homicide incident has a 60/40 chance of occurring on the street in close proximity of an eating or drinking establishment. When it occurs in the home, it will happen in either the kitchen or the bedroom. If the homicide occurs in the kitchen, the male most likely will be killed, since most men who are killed in the home are killed by their wives in the kitchen. If the killing occurs in the bedroom, the male will likely be the killer, since most men kill their spouses in the bedroom. At any rate, it will be a homicide of passion, a spur-of-the-moment response, an unplanned act, void of premeditation, but nevertheless intended to kill, triggered by a quarrel, or dispute over lovers' rights, sex, money, or a third party. Both parties may have drunk some alcohol before the violent encounter.

Seasonally, the incident can happen in any month of the year but has higher chances of happening in December, around Christmas, or August or July, when the weather is warmest.

A female has a better chance of avoiding involvement in an act of homicide than the male, although being Black also reduces her life chances. Twenty per-

142

cent of the homicides involve women as victim-offender. Females usually kill males who are their mates. A female is more likely to be killed by a male of the same race than by another person of the same sex or of a different race. The gun will be the lethal instrument with a 60/40 chance of the act occurring in the home.

Black females are killed three to four times more frequently than White females, given to the fact that they are predominantly exposed to the geographic, spatial, and socio-economic factors previously described for the male. Like their White counterparts, Black women are usually killed by males of their own race.

Interracially, Black males have always been the main targets of interracial homicides, and Black females are more often victims of the violent offenses of White males than vice versa. Black females are more often victimized by Black males. On the other hand, White males are more victimized by Black females than White females are victimized by Black males.

There are a variety of view-points posited as to why Black homicides occur. Some theorists hold that Blacks are disproportionately represented in the homicide statistics because of their Southern roots. They are able to show that Southerners are more violent than Northerners. Others hold that homicide is a product of a culture of violence. Still others proclaim that criminal homicide results from differential association wherein the actors are influenced by significant others with whom they associate.

And then there is the dense population theory that purports to show that over-crowding is the instigating source of homicide. Clearly, none of these theories sufficiently answer the question of a disproportionate Black representation in homicide statistics.

We are disproportionately represented precisely because we are constrained from expressing our will to be in direct control of the course of our own destiny. The Black-on-Black homicide statistic is a barometer of our oppression here in America, and the ghetto-colony is the crucible.

We are disproportionately represented precisely because we are constrained from expressing our will to be in direct control of the course of our own destiny. The Black-on-Black homicide statistic is a barometer of our oppression here in America. It is a hallmark, an artifact, of our experience, and the ghetto-colony is the crucible wherein this death process takes place. It is the penitentiary wherein we are systematically deprived of an equal opportunity to take affirmative action against those who control the dynamics of our exclusion from the mainstream, where we increasingly are regarded as dispensable, useless, degraded, exploited and despised.

We live in a white-dominated system that, on the one hand, enforces a prohibition against our taking out aggression on the White people who frustrate and oppress us. On the other hand, it rewards, sanctions and legitimizes Black-on-Black aggression. Accordingly, some members of the Black community have discovered that it is safe and far less punishable to kill their cultural brothers and sisters who live in close and covenient proximity. Thus the status quo of their oppression remains unchanged, and history lives on.

Internationally, Frantz Fanon well recognized this insidious dynamic of oppression. The socioecopolitical context of Fanon's thesis on violence is contained in the historical European-African encounter out of which arose a structure of colonization, of caste, color, class and racial oppression. In the encounter with European settlers in Africa, strict colonial relationships were controlled by the gun, political coercion, economic exploitation, cultural degradation, and the violent inhumanization of the indigenous African. In confrontation with the settler, the oppressor, the natives are submissive. By contrast, within the colony, among cultural brothers, the aggressive acting-out is intense and easily triggered. It is a mechanism of defense.

This mechanism of denial affords the native the means to evade the inevitable encounter with the direct aggression of the colonizer. Until that which is denied is consciously acknowledged as a concrete reality needing psychological resolution or objective transformation, sublimation (behaving in a manner acceptable to the oppressor) is the means employed to give release to the aggrieved. But it always falls short of the imperative for complete ablution, i.e., cleansing of the soul.

Fanon maintained that all of these penultimate activities of aggression are always and relentlessly operative whenever the native is subconsciously aware of the dynamics of oppression. Moreover, the aggression and tension that lie at the surface of the native's skin are prerequisite to the ultimate overthrow of the oppressor. When the native becomes critically aware of the economic-politics of his existence, the "autodestructive" activities cease and ultimate freedom commences. At this junction, the interspecific or interspecies aggression described by Lorenz arises, now directed at those who occupy the seat of power. However, under this arrangement, homicide continues, for the gun is the instrument Fanon ordained for usage in changing the social order. But no longer is the target of aggression the intra-colonial native.

In other words, the colonial structure is constituted so as to make it easy, safe, and rewarding to exclusively exact violence on those in the domestic colony itself. The arrangement of spatial and political components of the colony render it more difficult, hazardous and punishable to counterattack the colonizer.

In this way, the high rate of intraghetto homicide prevails and serves the dual function of maintaining the status quo in the American colonial system while simultaneously upholding the value that Black life is worthless or not important.

This author's research on Black-on-Black homicide in New Orleans, involving Black public housing project residents, reveals that the Black low-income resident of New Orleans recognizes the colonial relationship of Black-on-Black homicide. Given an opportunity to specify why we kill each other, the Black community will designate drugs, the lack of money, and quarrels over money as the three main causes of Black-on-Black homicide. The syndicate and the government in turn were named as the agents responsible for the problems of drugs and money, respectively.

Unequivocally, the low-income Black community is aware of their colonial status, albeit a status unable to fully distort their perception of the facts and circumstances surrounding the homicides that occur in their immediate neighborhood.

From a theoretical perspective, within the confines of the ghetto-colony, Black-on-Black homicides occur on the spur of the moment amongst acquaintances who are easily influenced by each other and who, out of a sense of powerlessness and jealousy, acquiesce to killing a friend, relative or acquaintance or mate, with a gun. These acts are not condoned. Those who live in close proximity fear for their lives in the community Tragically, 42 percent of those surveyed believe that they cannot prevent homicides from occurring. This sense of personal impotence relegates the future to those who are the colonizers.

By the findings of my research emerges a picture of a tentacle of death wrapped around the Black Male. Dating back to the early 1900's, the Black male has loomed as the central figure in Black-on-Black homicides, as well as interracial homicides. When Black males kill Blacks, they largely kill males. When White men kill Blacks, it is also the male. When White women kill Blacks, once again it is the male. Eighty percent of all urban homicides, in fact, involve Black males as both victim and offender. If you are a Black male between the ages of 18 to 35, within the ghetto-colony, you are an endangered species, number one on the homicide list.

In an economic system founded on productivity, the most productive period of a man's life is between the ages of 18 and 35. Please observe that this is the same age bracket of those Black males most likely to be killed and the same bracket of those who kill.

In system theory, there is the concept entropy. Entropy is the stage where a unit of the system, void of its essential maintenance resource, i.e., energy, is deprived of the capacity to carry out its ascribed function. At this juncture the unit begins to disintegrate randomly and ultimately dies. During this death process, the disintegrating unit causes havoc as it becomes a hostile force, arbitrarily, capriciously and spontaneously bombarding other units, quite often causing damage and death to these units before ultimately succumbing itself.

I recognize this entropic process within the Black community. Without a clear sense of purpose, and lacking the essential resources of collective maintenance, young brothers and sisters are given over to havoc, turning into hostile forces in the community, arbitrarily, capriciously, and spontaneously displacing their anger and aggression upon other Black people, bringing damage and often death to those Black people who have a sense of purpose and function. In the end, however, the young culprits also risk death and destruction at the hands of the implacable foe.

All of this requires that we become critically aware of what is happening to us through us and through those who are the external foe. It requires that we risk challenging the White and Black foe who would dare kill us. Finally, it requires that we dare organize to perfect, to protect, to project what our ancestors struggled to preserve. We must emerge as radical, gallant warriors, armed with a will and a plan to protect our traditional ethos for life.

146

Crime and the Unemployed Black Male

by Erica E. Tollett

As a Black mother of an eleven-year-old daughter and a two-year-old son, I am extremely concerned about the number of Black males dying at the hands of each other. In Washington, D.C., where I live, the number of drug-related and senseless murders of Black males has become a gruesome countdown. The overwhelming majority of the 80 murders committed in the first three months of 1988 have been of Black males by Black males. The average citizen knows this body count because of the frequency and publicity given to these tragedies. These incidents have forced me to step back and explore the roots of the problem.

All too often the family histories of many of the victims, and their assailants, are similar: they are young males being raised by their single mother. I believe the key to this nationwide problem is the absence of employed Black male role models and the large percentage of households headed by females who are unable to fully provide for their sons, both economically and socially. These two issues must be aggressively addressed.

In this country, men have been historically defined by being employed. Therefore, when a man is unemployed, he can feel invisible, even emasculated. In the Black community, where the unemployment rate is the highest, this feeling is particularly present.

In February 1988, when the country's unempolyment rate fell to 5.7 percent, this was viewed as an economically healthy situation. The country's overall unemployment rate for Whites *fell* from 5.0 percent to 4.8 percent while it *grew* for Blacks from 12.2 percent to 12.6 percent. For Black males 20 years and over, the unemployment rate was 12.2 percent while for White men the rate was 5.0 percent. Clearly, a great number of Black men are unable to be providers, or even co-providers for their offspring.

Moreover, the sons have few role models on which to base appropriate behavior. Thus, they are searching for a way to feel powerful and respected. Many young Black males have chosen to find this by using their legal and illegal money to purchase guns, gold necklaces, oversized rings and Timberland boots. they don't see their fathers providing the necessary material things. They do see their mothers earning or doing the best they can, while at the same time they are mothered and depended upon to be the "man of the house" and contribute to the household monetarily. Many of their mothers are not doing very well economically. The unemployment rate for Black women 20 years old and over in February 1988 was 10.7 percent, compared to 4.6 percent for White women.

Compunding the problem is that a great many of these men do not live with their families. When men are employed. families have a better chance of forming and/or staying together. This has important consequences on the control over the sons. George Gilder, who has written much on the family, says that only men can successfully discipline boys. Of course, this is not always the case. Nathan Hare, a highly-regarded psychologist and sociologist who has co-authored with his wife, Julia, books on the Black family, points out that a parent does a better job of handling the same sex child. This has much merit, because traditionally fathers were the more strict disciplinarians in the family. It was not unusual for the father to look his strapping six foot son in the eye and indicate that he better do right. The mother, saying the identical words, is looked at differently, no matter how many fishing and baseball trips on which she takes him.

In community meetings, I often hear talk about parental responsibilities and the lack of them. There is criticism of those parents who avoid questioning their child's sudden wealth or expensive possessions. How can it be that police can confiscate over $3,000 and a .22-caliber automatic gun from a 14-year-old boy while he is in his own home?

I also hear people in the community assert that parents should be responsible for their children when they have babies. Evidently, this is an opinion that is not held by community people alone. Last year, the House of Representatives passed The Family Welfare Reform Act of 1987, which stipulates that unmarried minor parents be required to live with their parent(s) unless this is determined to be inappropriate. There also seems to be a consensus among many community-active people that there should be special drug abuse programs directed specifically at Black males. One can see that there is a local and federal concern for addressing parental responsibility and at least a local concern for targeting Black males for special consideration.

Officials and community leaders in Washington, as in probably other large urban areas, are debating, discussing and wringing their hands trying to find solutions to the problem of youth violence. Frequently, one hears that poverty and teen unemployment are major contributing factors to the problem. Poverty certainly does play a role because the employment problems for the parents of many of these teens is obviously in a crisis situation. Although youth employment programs have been embraced as a tactic to help guide "at-risk" youth, I believe greater emphasis should be placed on employment policies that enable parents, particularly fathers, to contribute to the welfare of the family.

Presently, employment and training issues are being debated as part of federal welfare reform. There is much discussion about requiring mothers receiving public assistance to work and mandating automatic child support payments from absent fathers. Much of this reform will impact on Black folk. Stopping the killing of Black youth in our low-income Black communities requires a change in attitude towards the family unit. It will mean not forgetting that men help make up the family and their roles are crucial to the well-being of boys. Policies must not only be focused on women.

William Julius Wilson tells us in his book, *The Truly Disadvantaged: The Inner City, the Underclass and Public Policy,* that the number of marriageable Black men is falling because of their high unemployment. If more Black men are employed, marriage will be a viable option and women will see they don't have to carry the weight of raising children by themselves.

Americans can generate jobs if there is the will to do so. Rebuilding the infrastructure of our cities or guaranteeing jobs for young adult males similar to the summer youth job program in Washington, D.C., are examples. Jobs for both parents can lead to more family stability and help bring back needed control over youths through their employed mothers and fathers.

Families of Imprisoned Black Men

by Alex Swan, Ph.D.

Based on my research on Black families and their experiences resulting from the imprisonment of the husband/father, this paper is in some respects a synopsis of information elaborated in my book, *Families of Black Prisoners.* Although mine was a critical study and a statistical examination of the lives of the families of Black prisoners, it also identified the psychological, social and economic crises black family members face before, during and after imprisonment. In the short space of this essay, let me present some of the more qualitative points of the study of prisoners and their families.

The Crisis of Imprisonment Family Dismemberment

The crisis of imprisonment produces a double crisis for the family—demoralization and dismemberment—especially when the prisoner is a father or a husband. Dismemberment is obvious since the family must adapt to the temporary or permanent loss of a very significant member. The absence from the family is caused by imprisonment with the probability, but not the certainty, of return by the member. In the meantime, the family must deal with the sense of shame and establishing a new relationship with the imprisoned person. This is not always necessary in some families because the absent member's input *prior* to imprisonment may have been such as to force many of their wives into working out a plan for their own survival. Nonethless, during the extended period between the initial arrest and imprisonment, the wife undergoes a series of shocks: *the initial arrest, the search for help in the form of legal help; search for fees; the need to secure money for bail; the loss of job,* and the *expenditure of time to assure release.*

151

Most wives try to help their partners immediately upon arrest because they care about what happens to them; because they sense their obligation as wives; and because their partners were good to them and in turn they want to show their gratitude. More importantly, however, the wives and their children need their partners at home, and they do everything to prevent their partners from going to prison. Even those partners who have to be reminded of their responsibility to the family are assisted.

After the conviction, the families maintained a high level of stability in family composition, and their residential status was not adversely affected by the imprisonment. However, the majority of families experienced pressures of inadequate income and many had to rely on their small welfare checks to help their financial situation. Some of the wives did not depend entirely upon the partner's income to take care of the family needs in the first place. These wives worked part-time or full-time to assist with the family's financial situation. Wives help their husbands whether or not their partners' acts were against, to assist, or on behalf of their families.

Upon the initial arrest, the majority of families sought to secure the release of the men to the extent that their available financial resources were expended. This was the case among some who did not experience much financial input from their men prior to the arrest. For many families, imprisonment was the removal of the possibility of financial and/or emotional input into the family scheme of life. The sense of hope that this would be their experience if the men were released was very operative. As long as the partners remained out of prison the families could hope for that input.

This period during the initial arrest is crucial because normal bills go unpaid and all resources, both financial and emotional, are channeled into the one goal of keeping the man from going to prison. In many cases, all of the available assets of the family are sacrificed to help the partner.

In many instances families come to the day when their partners are to be sentenced completely drained of both financial resources and emotional energy. It is from this initial and sometimes total expenditure of available assets that families find it difficult to recover.

Families also had to make adjustments in sexual needs and with the responsibility of caring for the children. In those families where the fathers spent more time with the children and the children knew that their fathers were in prison, the separation greatly affected the children. Often they were depressed, unhappy, and expressed their hatred of the situation. However, the financial situation of the families was the major problem faced by Black families of prisoners before and during imprisonment. Their financial problems grew worse after

152

imprisonment—even for those who did not experience financial problems before imprisonment. But those families where the prisoners' wives had a high school diploma and beyond and a higher occupation were managing fairly well financially

More than half of the help received by Black families of prisoners was from government agencies of which welfare accounted for the most. The relatives and friends were the major sources of emotional support. Help in child care, household chores, transportation, etc., was provided by the relatives of wives and their friends and neighbors. The immediate family members tried to cope with their financial and emotional problems first before they reached out for help from extended family members, friends, and agencies.

Generally, the information from officials (police, lawyers, and court officials) necessary for families to make a reasonable assessment of their situation was not available. This lack of information creates cognitive disabilities and confusion among families during the crisis period. It creates an inability to understand fully what is happening, how to evaluate the reality of the situation, how to anticipate, formulate and evaluate the possible outcome of the crisis. There were no prompt intervention services available to those families in the community at the point of each crisis. There was also a lack in the community in terms of resources to assist families to recover. Most families lived in poor, oppressed communities. There were no professional services to prepare the wives and children for the visitation or to assist them after the visitation. There was an absence of preparation for families, the community and the prisoner for successful reentry of the former inmates.

The restrictions placed on the activities and behavior of prisoners in terms of letter writing, phone calls, personal contact, etc., added stress to the family situations. Wives felt that the stress had potential for destroying family cohesiveness and adjustment. In this regard, families felt that they too experienced some degree of punishment, they who had commited no crime.

During visits by the families to the prison, partners attempted to keep before their wives and children their importance to the families. They asserted their fatherly and/or husbandly roles in conversation and consultation. The faraway, rural location of most state and federal prisons made planning of visits particularly anxiety-provoking.

Transportation for many did not exist. However, in most families the wives looked forward to the return of their partners and felt that they would someday "pick up the pieces" together and work to make a happy future for their families.

Review and Recommendations

Heretofore, few studies of prisoners' famiies have ever been made. This was due to several problems: 1) locating families, 2) difficulty in research design—i.e., establishing a control group and making before imprisonment measures of families, particularly.

In 1928 the first empirical study of prisoners' families was conducted by the U.S. Department of Labor. The subjects were from the state of Kentucky where the state government had requested the study because of a concern over Kentucky's rate of compensation for prison labor and its consequent effects on prisoners' families. The study resulted in an increased rate of compensation for prison labor in Kentucky, because it was found that many of the families, especially farm families, suffered financially to the point of scarcely being able to eke out an existence.

In the District of Columbia in 1938, another study of prisoners' families found that the majority of the families were unable to make a satisfactory economic or social adjustment subsequent to the incarceration of the family head.

In 1959, James Blackwell studied prisoners' families in the state of Washington. He found that favorable adjustment to the crisis caused by the loss of the incarcerated family head was positively related to a high level of family income, high level of education of the wife, and good marital adjustment.

Then, in 1964, a study of the effects of incarceration on the children of female offenders in the Los Angeles area found that 50 percent of the children had been separated from one or more of their siblings. Nearly half of the children had not seen their mother since her incarceration and more than a third had experienced at least one change of responsible adult after their mother was put in prison.

In 1965, two studies were conducted in England and Wales and the other in Australia. Both studies found money problems, loneliness and problems relating to children to be among the most frequently experienced hardsips of prisoners' wives.

Finally, in the 1970's a study was conducted in North Carolina by Gordon Waldo. Two were conducted by Ann Stanton and Stanley Brodsky [*When Mothers Go To Jail* (Lexington Books, D.C. Heath, 1980), and *Families and Friends of Men in Prison* (D.C. Heath, 1975) respectively].

Recommendations

There should be prompt intervention services for families at the point of each crisis period. Such intervention services should involve a community reach-out program that offers services especially at the point of arrest and at the time of sentencing. Inmate-family workshops should be encouraged in the jails during the period from arrest to sentencing to enhance family solidarity and reduce the possibility of recidivism.

Referrals should be systematically made from all agencies having contact with the husbands and families and should include probation officers, lawyers, clergymen, neighborhood centers, etc. These services, community based so that families might be served more quickly and easily, should vary and be relevant to the specific situation of each family.

Wives should be provided with a manageable cognitive grasp of the situation in order to strengthen their coping ability. Services in this regard should include information regarding husband's incarceration, prison visiting rules and regulations, transporation possibilities, availability of jobs, child care opportunities, legal aid and welfare possibilities.

Those wives who grieve and express anger as a result of the crisis situation should be counseled by those trained to do so. With this counseling should flow some discussion of how the wives and other family members may help the children with similar reactions of grief, shame, and anger.

Wives and children are sometimes depressed and frustrated, especially after visiting the prison. They should be prepared before and after visitation to deal with their feelings and emotions. The need to reassure them that their *family scheme of life* will continue to develop and be strengthened as they construct a new social support network over which they have some control is very important.

Final Comment

Organizing immediate financial assistance, preparing the children and wives for visitation, and information systems sufficient to keep the families informed during and covering the entire crisis period, helping the family, relatives and friends in the structuring of social support systems for coping purposes, these are all factors which must be realized if these families of prisoners are to continue their scheme of life. The realization of these services to the families will simply allow them to survive. What will enhance the progress of these families, however, is the restructuring of the political and economic arrangements of the social order which presently render them and their community insignificant and powerless.

Given the employement history, relative power position in the political economy of America, and the income status of these families, it will be difficult for them, upon the reentry and return of their husbands/fathers, to recover from this crisis situation in a community which has a colonial status devoid of the resources to give its members the opportunities and skills to recover, survive, and make progress.

PART IV:

SOLUTIONS

Solutions: A Complete Theory of the Black Family

by Nathan Hare, Ph.D.

We are prisoners of the mind, unwary captives of a white-dominated public mindset, (or perhaps more accurately a "rainbow", a "crossover," a "one-dimensional" frame of reference) pressing us down the "mainstream" in our frenzied search for inclusion and acceptance. It is a mindset manipulated daily and throughout the day by the most awesome, advanced and efficient media of communication and commercialization the world has so far known.

Guided by the accumulated techniques in the now gigantic armamentarium of the science of propaganda, of such modern devices as "subliminal seduction,"[1] with stubborn regularity, the machinery of communication assault our senses and our sensibilites by the hour with increasingly centralized "networks" of electronic and computerized ideas and impulses, including what black Harvard psychiatrist, Chester Pierce, calls "little white karate chops" on the receptive black psyche.

Even more deadly is the printed page, for it attracts the intellectual elite of whatever strata and demands that all thinkers and writers of ideas and opinions, no less than in music, "crossover" in essential tone and timbre, not to mention ideological slant, in the work that they produce, if they are to gain promotion and prevail. More than in the clothes we wear, the fashions in ideas and interpretations are designed for us, what we think and what we feel and what we think we ought to know, what is known, and what is to be known or regarded as really knowable, these rain down on us at somebody else's instigation.

To seriously resist this cacophonous distortion of what we will know and believe, merely to keep up and retain minimal clarity in the realm of so much as one single issue, requires a relentless skepticism, a continual if not compulsive vigil, what Price Cobbs and William Grier, in *Black Rage*[2] called "a healthy cultural paranoia," an endless searching and probing beneath the surface and behind the scenes.

Most people are not impelled, not nearly so driven enough, to do this, even in one small area of knowledge; nobody can do this in all, or even many, areas. We may have the capacity but not the time or interest. Thus we live and discourse, and sometimes act, as disorganized and too often disarrayed carrier pigeons, parrots, of distorted and inaccurate, piecemeal information, lacking true insight, even as "experts" and "authorities," into the too often limited fund of manipulated facts that we possess, culled as a general rule from white-directed sources, including the images of our heroes and the limits of our most cherished opinions and ideas.

At the same time, this very condition falsely persuades us to view each area of life as isolated from the rest. Thus politics is what rulers and leaders do; family, the domain of parenting and sex, is apart from politics; black male/female relationships, perhaps the most political thing of all in our time, if not in others, is regarded as not political, as something for the women. This year, for instance, one of the most politically conscious black movement organizations, the National Black United Front, an umbrella grouping of black movement intellectuals, at its annual convention held in Kansas City, scheduled workshops on major areas of institutional life, including such theoretical issues of political economy as "the land question" whose panelists were dominated by males. But only females were assigned to the panel on the family.

Europeanization: A Cultural Conga Dance. Within the context of a black male intellectual ambivalence, black families are left to drift toward, to follow in circular fashion, sequentially, the white female's whimsical theoretics, in turn helping the white world to pull the black male intellectual along, to inspire and cajole him, in circular fashion, to second black female mimicry of ephemeral white liberal feminist theoretics, to join in ideological concert, in snakedance fashion, the variegated agenda of white male orchestrated reproductive control. The white female inevitably winds up in the end following the white male, the black female following the white female, the black male ideologically following the black female (and the white male), all led around in the genocidal rhythms of a white-male-directed cultural conga dance. Such slippery conformity may sometimes be cloaked in blackness and Africanity. It also may even slide in on the underbelly of lipservice to the importance of the preservation of distinctive African and afrocentric culture.

158

In a time when the europeanization of the world has brought us to the place where we risk being the first species to self-destruct (in a hailstorm of nuclear fire and man-made brimstone), when one-fourth of all babies in America are born at the scapel-wielding hands of a surgeon; when surgery is the most popular form of birth control in a sex-crazed or sex-sublimated amoral society now undergoing a random clean-up craze of self-purification, even as it thrashes about for a barometer, if not a rudder, of values in a normless, transformed and transitional society; when barbells and sex-change operations are altering the very physiognomy of the genders, if not the species; when people increasingly cannot be heard, living in massified physical proximity and social and psychological isolation, with even hope-to-die lovers unable to talk harmoniously to each other, let alone to "communicate" or get the intimate, human "feedback" they long for, the "input" they desire within the multiplying but empty "modules" of their existence; when the ideal (and practice) of biological motherhood and parentage is being denigrated and diminished; when gene-splicing, genetic engineering, is gaining approval and even priority, and biomedical organisms threaten to escape and present new and unknown risks; the black intellectual class is silenced or preoccupied with the social acceptance and inclusion demanded by integrationist-minded "rainbow" civil rights on the one hand or nationalist-minded pursuits of simple racial recognition in the form of ancient glories on the other.

While the black race seeks social acceptance and directs social-work-style experimentations (or programs), white society changes what is *social*, the definition of a man, a woman, a mother, a father, a child, a human being. At a time when the *New York Times* reports "a link between the earth's gradual warming trend" and an anticipated drought which would be "catastrophic for the world's food supply,"[3] ; when it is admitted that "releasing carbon dioxide and other chemicals into the atmosphere is generally recognized as producing an effect in which the world's climate is warming up," producing a "greenhouse effect," and drought diminishing the world's food supply, the solution to the problem (and frequently the cause) is placed on the "growing population," we fall silent or join the fray, agreeing essentially, or at least in effect, sometimes openly that, "yes, there are too many niggers."

Having refused so much as to acknowledge the program of black family destruction which, as Moynihan admitted in 1965,[4] the white world had produced, the black intellectual class in 1985 came face-to-face with a family problem they could no longer deny. However, they now move with a straight fact to accept white solutions. Thus many of the solutions which black intellectuals present, no less than in the case of their white liberal mentors, are but unconscious adaptations to the demands of a post-industrial, white-dominated society, and accordingly will contribute to and intensify the very problems they seek to correct.

159

The Algedonic Effect. Because black intellectuals today do not see the connection of the family to the whole, the white world is able to manipulate the black family agenda, or a portion of that agenda, unbeknown to black intellectuals. We may call this the *algedonic* effect. As the *Harper Dictionary of Modern Thought* defines it, algedonic, a hybridization of the etymological words for pain and pleasure, refers to the fact that regulators within a system may operate apart from criteria that exist only in the metasystem. Algedonically, a metasystem may exercise control by "regulating outcomes" without "direct intervention."[6] "For example, a fail-safe device switches off an entire system because some output of the system has reached a level regarded as dangerous to the whole: it may take days to discover later [if ever] what actually went wrong." A case in point occurred in the late summer of 1988 in the city of New York when the electrical power systems were turned off in a number of large apartment buildings to prevent a blackout of the city as a whole.

White society similarly may manipulate the black family agenda, or a portion of that agenda, while black intellectuals remain unaware of its metagenesis or causes, camouflaged additionally by the black intellectual failure to keep clear the white/black dichotomy rather than overidentifying with the white liberal direction. Understandably recoiling against the most extreme proponents of white racism (historically but not exclusively promoted by conservatives), black intellectuals seem too often unaware that the value-setting and policy-making establishment is in fact liberal-moderate, despite the conservative political "swing" in recent years.

Indeed, not only did white liberals lead the dominant family ideology which emerged simultaneous with the rise of the Nixon-Reagan 1970s era of conservative political preeminence, the conservative mood or backlash in the country was fed in part by the punishingly destructive and even openly anti-family agendas pushed by white liberals as they presented a gender alternative to racial change and seized the reform initiative from blacks.

The Whiplash Effect. Yet in a *whiplash effect* arising out of the necessarily dualistic nature of white family sociopolitics, black intellectuals overidentify with white liberals and white liberal family thought. We here refer to a dualism beyond the preachment-practice dichotomy popularized by Nobel prizewinning Swedish economist, Gunnar Myrdal, in his 1940s *An American Dilemma,*[7] The whiplash effect grows out of the white power structure's inherent need to camouflage contrasting family agendas for whites and blacks. In whiplash fashion, white society is able to begin with the black program, then switch to the white agenda, while leaving the black intellectual class some years later following the initial agenda, the white one.

For instance, in the beginning of the rise of early 1970s white feminism, the typical black response was "the black woman has always had to work; she's trying to get *into* the house, not out of it, for a change."[8] However, now that the white woman is impelled to return to childbirth and family, the program of the black woman is increasingly directed toward the world of work. As white feminists are questioning and even changing many feminist focuses (Cf. Germaine Greer's *Sexual Destiny* and Betty Fredian's *The Second Stage*),[9] with white feminism moving increasingly toward essentially a fight for benefits associated with the very motherhood in the 1970s deemed inherently oppressive, black intellectuals are increasing their feminist adherence and advocacy; and this is true of black males and females, nationalist and assimilationist. At the present rate, it will in time emerge that white feminists will be fighting essentially for rights and privileges of motherhood and nurturance, while black feminists will be fighting for the career and manhood privileges white feminists will have ideologically left behind or dampened.

Let us pause, then, before taking up the issue of solutions, concretely, to direct our attention to prolegomena to a complete theory of the black family.

A Complete Theory of the Black Family in a Situation of Racial Subordination. First a platitude, though one almost unanimously forgotten by black intellectuals from 1969 to 1984: it is not possible to fully understand the condition and structure of the black family (or the family of any oppressed or subjugated group) without a proper assessment of the nature and impact of that oppression on the family, nor without correctly ascertaining the nature of the oppressor's family policies and family agenda, with reference to both the oppressed and the oppressor. The oppressor, at any given time, may wish to turn the oppressed *and* the oppressor away from childbirth and family, or toward childbirth and family, or one toward childbirth and family and the other away from childbirth and family.

However, because only women can give birth to children, the role of a minimal number of women in any society at any time is at least minimally tied to reproduction (for instance, there must be an estimated 2.1 children produced for every woman of childbearing age -- one for herself and one for the male and 0.1 for demographic measures -- just to keep the population stabilized, the size that it already is, as portions of the population continue inevitably to die off). Less would be required if there is in-migration of persons who will be accepted and assimilated into the group, as people redistribute themselves in search of unevenly distributed resources.

True, this reproductive role of women can be offset, variously and to some extent, by the needs of production. For instance, the crises and demands of war, or a scarce labor supply, when women may be needed more fervently in productive labor. Culture, including technological development, as well as demographic goals and the relative value placed on children in a given time and place, can also curb the feminine reproductive imperative. But there can be no permanent or total negation of this reproductive imperative, so long as women give birth to children and men do not.

When fewer children are needed or wanted in a group, women are turned away from childbirth and family; when more children are needed in a group, women are turned toward childbirth and family -- and this has been true in every land from the beginning of recorded history and throughout all anthropological literature.

Because eurocentric culture has been and remains considerably anti-nature (in many regards distorting nature in order to control it), social mobility or achieved affluence within it tends toward infertility, unless augmented by programmed or artificial means, while poverty (perhaps partly because the poor are not so assimilated into eurocentric culture) tends toward high fertility. Within a situation of oppression, therefore, at a certain point and variously, the oppressor inevitably arrives at a dual or two-pronged reproductive/family agenda: fewer children for the oppressed group -- lest through population pressure they become a "powder keg of social rebellion" -- but more childbirths within the oppressor's group; in contemporary society more white and middle class children, fewer black and poor children.

This agenda becomes necessary to maintain the status quo of oppression and the socioeconomic relationships of subjugation. Aside from the inauspicious impregnation of the female -- and this is no longer wholly necessary because of the test tube and sperm banks -- the social role of the male has appeared to be to protect the female while she reproduces.[10] In human terms, protection, especially in industrialized society, includes providing, socioeconomically. However, the oppressor's family agenda for the oppressed group will tend toward suppression of the role of both male and female within the subordinate group: the oppressor will (relatively speaking) seek to suppress the fertility of the female of the oppressed group, and the productivity or the social instrumentality of the oppressed male; that is to say, the social potency of the male and the reproductive generativity and sexual adjustment of the female.

Both strategies, turning the female away from family and the male away from his role as protector/provider for the family unit, distorts the family; and this will be true of the oppressed middle class as well as the oppressed poor, though the nature of the distortion will manifest itself differently. Such distortion will emerge even when the oppressor wishes to *increase* the fertility of the oppressed group -- e.g., when slaves were needed on the plantation, the master raped and bred slaves for auction and in the process invalidated and violated black family bonds and stability. Either way, the reproductive/family agenda of the oppressor will tend toward the distortion of the reproductive/sexual adjustment of the female of the oppressed group and the productive/social instrumentality of the male.

This of course can be offset to varying extent by the actions and resistance of the oppressed, including self-sustaining and antithetical cultural traits retained from their pre-oppressive condition, e.g., from the African past. However, to the extent that the oppressor's two-pronged (in the present case, black/white) reproductive/family agenda is invoked, to that extent is the family unit distorted and decimated and — except as it may be somewhat resisted by the culture (e.g. African carryovers, customs or values) and/or the social will of the oppressed — to that extent will there be decay of the oppressed family structure. For instance, the cultural resistance of traditional segments of Africa can delay but not completely prevent the process of family decay in Africa without direct political rejection and resistance to the white world's program of reproductive control. The program of population or reproductive control in Africa will, in tending toward distortion of the female's role in reproduction, bring decimation of the family unit, just as the economic decimation of the male's productive function, pulling him into shanty towns apart from his family, will tend to generate family decay. This is no doubt a part of the reason Daniel Moynihan could find such high and consistent correlations of black female marital decay (and fertitity rates) with unemployment rates of black males![11] Hence, the contemporary afrocentric desire to reclaim a pre-colonial African culture is commendable, but not sufficient to save the family.

Meanwhile, to attempt to explain the present African-American family condition as a simple derivative of the pre-colonial African family at a certain point may risk slandering the African family and our African ancestors for sociocultural effects in actuality produced by white oppression and our failure to effectively resist it. As in the case of the extended maternal family (where a young mother lives with or leaves her children in the home of her own mother), we are frequently observing a culture of necessity, not a culture of choice; a culture of adaptation, not a culture of resistance.

This is true in our family traits as in the food we eat, though our food will differ in many regards from the white diet or ''standard'' and may even retain certain African antecedents. This does not prove that our food or culinary or dietary culture derives from Africa. Nor is it necessary to pretend that we have no dietary problems (as in the case of the family *circa* 1969 to 1984) in order to prove that some food or culinary traits derive from Africa. Likewise, it is not necessary to exaggerate the quantity of such carryovers in order to foster the need to reclaim them.

Moreover, if the white imperialist's reproductive/family agenda (with its distortions of the productive/social instrumentality of the male and the family/reproductive schema of the female) is not defeated in Africa, there will be more decay of the family in Africa as in African-America.

With an understanding of the place of reproduction (weighted occasionally by crises and the fluctuating demands of production), no oppressed race or individual can claim for fifteen years with a straight face that there is no "pathology" or weakness in the oppressed family structure. Similarly, no scholar can fully understand the weakness within the black family apart from an assessment of the impact of oppression or/and the weight of the oppressor's reproductive/family agenda on the weaknesses which in actuality do appear.

Thus, it becomes always and easily and readily ascertainable as to whom the benefits will flow from such programs as maternity/paternity leave; and welfare reform and teenage pregnancy hype come more fully into view.

The reproductive/productive law of family change leaves us with two simple questions for assessing any family program or agenda presented to us (in terms of its underlying social meaning and the interests it will serve): 1) whose population, whose numbers, will it affect — and how and why; 2) who actually will get the money, or a disproportionate share of the material (and nonmaterial) benefits proposed. A third question we would do well to ask is what will be its social meaning, its effects on us as a people or society as a whole, in both its latent (or unintended) and manifest consequences.

We have already seen (in the "Introduction" to this volume) the sometimes contrasting and contadictory meaning of the foregoing dimensions in the case of child care, maternity/paternity leave, child tax breaks, the abortion/sterilization connection, the anachronistic black teenage pregnancy hype, and the still unfolding welfare reform. All these programs will involve disproportionate shifts of money and benefits to the white middle class or/and differentially endeavor to affect the population growth of the blacks and whites. At the same time, the manner in which the programs are designed will tend to further undermine and destroy the cohesion and coherence of the black family unit.

For instance, welfare reform as currently conceived, will tend to train and develop the socioeconomic potential of the females, leaving the black male role in the family even more dystonic. Women who are single and on welfare in the first place because of a shortage of socioeconomically viable males, will be encouraged to increase this disparity, as the males are left undeveloped. The relative significance of the reproductive component (not only in outright family planning

164

programs but also in the encouragement of the women to seek alternatives to motherhood and black male collaboration) is apparent in the fact that there will not be enough jobs to hire the redirected women. There were not enough acceptable and viable jobs for the men in the first place.

Instead, recipients will be compelled to perform involuntary community service or makework, itself demeaning, for instance clean-up details and other timekilling and unfulfilling endeavors. The community service idea is also a concession to white labor union opposition confronting the threat of lowered wages. Worst of all, perhaps, is the requirement that absent males take over some of the welfare financial load or face a routine lien on their checks. Poor black men do not have enough money for one family. (In fact this is often the source of a sometimes involuntary exit, as when their women grow dissatisfied with the male's slow economic capacity and boot him out). The "reform" stipulation giving authorities the right to garnish the absent male's check will not only compound this condition; in many cases it will provoke black males to work even less than they already did.

In essence, the new welfare reform will encourage and implement the *manhood* of the black *woman* and the *womanhood* of the black *man*. It will encourage the productive/social instrumentality of the female, while intensifying her sexual disparity and complicating further her reproductive/sexual adjustment. At the same time, in allowing black males to stay in the welfare home, it will contribute to the sexual/reproductive adjustment of the male while providing alternatives (including female economic independence) to the significance and viability of his productive/social instrumentality. This is the final hangup that Hegel might have had in mind when he wrote that the master cannot free the slave.[12]

Moreover, the slave cannot be a slave and a full human being at the same time. To that extent, the most irreversible fact is that a female slave cannot gain complete acceptance as a woman, no matter how this may be defined, any more than a male slave can be fully admitted to the male rites of passage in the patriarchal preserve.[13]

Just as the white oppressor cannot envision and implement a plan giving full reproductive/family independence and fulfillment to the black female; he/she cannot present full productive/social instrumentality to the oppressed black male. Such complete and natural freedoms would comprise the final stroke of the hammer of demolition to white social dominance and can never be permitted to flourish in a situation of racial oppression. The female slave can be permitted a conspicuous role in customary masculine duties and achievements and the male slave can be permitted conscpicuious sexual/reproductive and expressive excellence, indeed "sexual superiority," (including qualities more characteristic of the female, e.g.

dependency, feminine-type narcissism and sexual exhibitionism, relational/emotional concern and even preoccupation). But these do not generate — and tend ultimately to distort and diminish — overall adjustment in all heterosexual social reality. Again, this social fact may be tempered, but will not be denied, by the mere incorporation of African customs and symbolism into family life in the absence of a forthright move toward total socioeconomic freedom.

Minister Louis Farrakhan, of the Nation of Islam, has spoken of the way in which the black male has been stripped of the social meaning to his masculinity.[14] Blocked from the avenues to social potency and institutional manhood reinforcements controlled by the white patriarchy, the black male has achieved conspicuous sexual/physical masculinity, but not social/instrumental masculinity. This is at bottom the complaint of the black intellectuals who shortsightedly advocate that black males withdraw from athletics in order to increase their academic viability. Such intellectuals appear to forget that many black males, let alone black females, are flunking and dropping out of school, yet in most cases play no sports whatsoever. Some can't even dance, let alone sing. Rather than concentrating on solving the academic problems of the non-athletic majority, they would rather throw out the dishpan with the water and fall into the hands of the white world's wish to whiten athletics, to increase the dwindling proportion of white athletes in the sports arenas. This is what the NCAA raising of athletic standards and SAT score requirements (Proposition 48) was all about. Random addictive drug testing of athletes, while more philosophically tenable, will tend to serve the same whitening function. Thus a considerable portion of the athletic reforms backed by leading black intellectuals are essentially anti-black male in their consequence, though their advocates will be viewed as champions of black male elevation by black intellectuals.

However, black intellectuals correctly sense that the athletic focus is to some extent a sublimation of the black male's compensatory focus on *physical* masculinity and to that extent may be antithetical to the black male's overall *social* adjustment. It may be ironic that, despite the comparative physical development of males and females, the adjustment of the male pivots more on social challenges while the female's social adjustment is more related to the protection and management of her body: e.g., pregnancy prevention or management, child support, marital stability, maternal care, rape prevention and other safeguards against sexual exploitation and vulnerability. While her socialization demands attention to the protection of her body from external forces, including her mate, the most fundamental challenge to male socialization involves learning to protect others from himself (from delinquency, crime, violent impulses, marital and family irresponsibility) and himself from social and psychological self destruction and the external or institution decimation of his productive/protective performance.

166

The male inherits a social imperative to achieve social/instrumental/productive proficiency and responsibility (whether he likes it or not), including the commitment to the support and protection of the female and the family. For instance, only ten per cent of violent crimes are committed by females, and seventy per cent of the crimes committed by females are connected to some male. The protective imperative in the male/female bond, despite distortions and usurpation of the protective function by contemporary institutional arrangements, may be apparent in the fact that in the heterosexual embrace the male prefers to hold but the female prefers to be held.

In the absence of male protection (including protection from alien ideological assaults from the white unisexualized patriarchy), the black female is likewise immobilized and courted by the forces of division. Thus, at the very time when the white world is re-examining the basic tenets of unisexual feminism, increasingly redirected to demands for motherhood rights, the black intellectual embrace of feminism is on an upsweep. Yet, avowed black feminists have not fomented one unique demand and in general mistake conflicts or difficulties with males in heterosexual relations with feminism. While the white feminist complains that the white male is getting too much, many black feminists see sexism in the black male's failure to thrive in the market place — the antithesis of feminism. Yet this antithesis will lurk behind and give momentum to the feminist-inspired attacks on black males. Some attack black males for past sexist practices by the white male dominated establishment; for instance, the fact that black female novelists were not published as frequently as black male writers in the past.

In the end, what, the black woman wants from the black man is respect and dependability (honesty, love and trust); beyond that she wants him to provide for his family, once more the opposite of the demands of white feminists seeking the right to provide for themselves. From the white man, the black woman wants respect also, but on a less intimate plane; and it is there where her demands for equal job rights and equal pay dovetail with white feminists. Yet, unlike the white feminist, she must deal with racism (including the white feminist's racism), for she is black and woman and, in her dual or pivotal position, is generally aware of the possibility of being used against the race. The typical black woman, in any case, has no illusions about the bare privileges of work, something she has always had to do.

What the black woman has *not* had is the chance for full family rights, access to the full care and comfort of her children, adequate housing or even the right to a socioeconomically sufficient man, an adequate mate, an employed husband, instead of a black male shortage accruing from disproportionate black male frontline, down-in-the-trenches military service, mass imprisonment; patriarchal racism to which the black male, not the female, poses the primary threat;

hardtimes and psychosocial destruction. In that sense, she demands and needs black male equality. Thus, she may need to include in her armamentarium some advocacy for the black male, demanding a halt to the destruction of the black male, her man; it is in her own best interests to do so, if she is going to expect and understandably demand black male socioeconomic support as husbands and fathers.

The black woman's family rights include the right to discipline and direct the devlopment of her own children's minds. She may need childcare but she also may need the chance to care for her children. Even as a slave she could care for the children of the mistress, somebody else's children. She must not now become pseudoblack nannies to white "yuppie" children as technicians and paraprofessionals in childcare programs designed and directed by white professionals. White-based European-style fertility incentives now emerging cannot elevate the black woman collectively and suppress her fertility at the same time, whether she is on welfare or not.

In short, the black woman must be aware of the needs of reproduction and production as they impact upon her race, and it is productive rights for the black male and reproductive/family rights for herself which can most make the black race whole. In the absence of black clarity on the unisexual reproductive agenda, neglected black feminist issues (by black feminists themselves) increasingly are taken up, usurped (and distorted) by white feminists. For instance, "reproductive rights" are projected on the basis of individual "choice," the right of individual women of whatever hue to decide the particulars of their reproduction, though in fact these are more subject to societal influences than the choice of her fashions or whether whe will wear any clothes. Besides, black women are not oppressed as individuals and individual rights will not suffice to free them. Individual rights are already decreed by the U.S. Constitution. Even anti-sterilization, the issue for blacks and the poor now camouflaged by the middle class white disagreement over abortion, receives no collective play in the black feminist agenda. Indeed, while there is an anti-sterilization movement among whites on the continent of Europe, American feminists of whatever stripe have been slow to copy it. Circa 1970, the New York chapter of the National Organization of Women was drumming up a movement, but Planned Parenthood pulled their coattail.[15]

White feminists who, a few years ago, denied male/female differences and the special place of motherhood and nurturance in the reconceptualization of the woman,[16] now seek to exploit male/female differences such as the idea of special qualities of nurturance and even a special corner on the milk of human kindness, a relative disdain for war and violence, and so on, all of which only a few years ago were denied. However, this trend has not been developed into a program combining fermimine qualities with the male-oriented marketplace, let alone transforming it, beyond the trend toward part-time work and working from the home.

We may conclude, then, theat the most basic solution to the black or oppressed female's condition or adjustment as a group will be unavoidably in the reproductive/sexual realm, while the solution to the male's condition will be notably in the sphere of productive/social instrumentality. Programs aimed primarily at correcting the black woman's socioeconomic status (but not her marital and family/reproductive enhancement or adjustment) will not be sufficient for her overall adjustment any more than the promotion of reproductive/family adjustment such as sexual "responsiblity" and the dilligent use of condoms (honorable and desirable, even necessary, as that may be) will solve the male's socioeconomic or overall adjustment.

Strategy and Tactics. First, we must remember that a strategy is an approach to achieving a goal, while a tactic is an instance or a variation of a strategy. Hence, the first level of awareness is awareness of conditions, of the goal, of the problem; out of this grows the second level, awareness of solutions. It is folly to start on the wrong end of the scale, just as it is useless, if not ludicrous, to deny the existence of a problem as black intellectuals did almost unanimously from 1969 to 1984. Before you can address collectively a problem, there must first be the recognition and acknowledgement that a problem exists. This is the first and most essential solution: the recognition of a problem. Further, without proper knowledge of the problem, it is difficult to correctly discern its solution; and this is today the primary failure of the black intellectual class and its black family experts and authorities.

Secondly, it is important to bear in mind that solutions may and must be both individual and collective. However, because our problem is collective, the most efficacious solutions for us as a people will also be collective. Instead, not only is there currently a tendency to focus on individual tactics, as over against collective strategies and subsidiary tactics, many persons (such as misused, abused, and understandably embittered black middle-aged women) will frequently stand in a workship situation and insist that the group disdain the collective solution to focus exclusively on one person's individual dismay or maladjustment, something perhaps more appropriately taken up with the psychotherapist or the pastor.

A third dimension of solution-formation is the developmental-resistance dilemma, the famous Booker T. Washington-W.E.B.DuBois debate, the need for self-development on the one hand and resistance on the other. Resistance without self-development of our family unit will fail to benefit from battles won; family development without resistance to external forces of black family destruction (whether direct or indirect) will leave us and whatever we construct perennially at risk and in peril from the persistent onslaught of oppression.

As things now stand, the black intellectual class is relegated to directing social programs and social experiments for black development and amelioration, while white society defines and changes what is *social*.

This includes the norms and practices in the very process of socialization. Socialization is the key dimension of human perpetuity and intergenerational transmission, whatever that may be or entail, including children's possibilities of gaining a clear core to their personality and identity, to know what they want to become, to be able to become the person that they and their elders wish them to be. Aside from the removal of the restrictions and prohibitions of prejudice and discrimination (a primary task), the key obstacle to achievement is derailed or distorted motivation. Though motivation may be high, as reflected, for instance, by the latency or adolescent drug pusher, the key to achievement is motivation.

In our time, in the nadir of the socialization and motivation of black youth, when our children's minds are increasingly captured by alien concepts and practices, it is popular to repeat many scholarly rationalizations in preference to confronting the breakdown of socialization. These include "role models" (the notion that a child must have an adult example to emulate, though nothing is said of the motivation of the role models emulated by the role models in the first place or the necessity to wait on the emergence of role models before other role models can be generated in turn); "low self esteem" (another word for the now denigrated white liberal concept, "self hatred," in the collective sense, ignoring the possibility of compensatory performance or achievement if the individual or personal self concept is the one being called into question); even the simple need to study black history, honorable on other grounds as that may be (there is no available evidence that black historians are more adjusted than, say, black economists, or mathematicians, biologists, or even black theologians or ministers of the gospel); "eurocentric (versus afrocentric) cognitive learning styles," which while real enough, risks neglecting the affective component of learning (including intrapsychic motivation and socialization) and fails to account for the fact that continental Africans, being the most Afrocentric of all, should logically experience the most trouble with eurocentric learning but do not.

Meanwhile, the socialization and parental efficacy of Afroamerica is being continually undermined and denigrated with hardly a whimper from the black intelligentsia. The "kidnapping and incarceration" (forced removal from the home and foster placement), often on the basis of a phone call from a neighbor or ex-husband, of more and more black children in the multi-million dollar child abuse protection bonanza, disrupting parent-child relations and usurping the authority to discipline from parents and teachers on the part of the white-defined and directed agents of punishment and rehabilitation mounts. Indeed, the very idea of discipline is increasingly undermined, including the simple right to spank, which is gradually becoming the preserve or special privilege of affluent whites.[17]

Black parents, prohibited from disciplining their children, must later watch them brutalized and incarcerated by white police. Black inner city teachers, having lost the authority to truly discipline, must spend most of their time in the quest of an elusive discipline, so that very little of anything else goes on in too many inner city public classrooms.

It is necessary, then, for us to resist the denigration of parenting, the devaluation of biological parentage and the usurpation of parental influence and authority by the state and its governmental apparatus. There must be a return to effective discipline in the black repertoire of socialization, just as it is necessary to build black masculine responsibility in the many ways emerging now, such as the rites of passage, the Simba program being re-implemented today, kupenda (Swahii for "to love") black love groups[18], and many other efforts to find out what we lost in Africa that we can reclaim or/and reconstruct to serve us today, are to be encouraged.

Also commendable are the efforts of public school systems such as those in Portland, Oregon (with educational psychologists Asa Hilliard and Robert Green as chief consultants)[19] and New Orleans, Louisiana (spearheaded by Dwight McKenna, M.D., publisher of the *New Orleans Tribune* and the Total Communtiy Action Group), are devoting special attention to the improvement of the educational performance of black boys. The National Black United Front, under the impetous of Oba Tshaka and Conrad Worrill, are developing indigenous movements for educational reforms in local black communities across the country. Notable independent educational institutions long established include Haki Madhubuti's Institute of Positive Education in Chicago, the W.E.B. DuBois Learning Center in Kansas City, and Maulana Karenga's in Los Angeles. The Urban League and the NAACP have programs for excellence and special attention to the development of black boys. Principal George McKenna, in Los Angeles, and Joe Clark, in Newark, New Jersey, have demonstrated not only what discipline can do but also the way in which efforts at black correction can conflict with white liberal-moderate conceptualizaions, including even the American Civil Liberties Union, not to mention Boards of Education themselves.

Nation of Islam (Black muslim) and other neighborhood stomp-downs of drug pushers are courageous and admirable, to say the least, as are efforts, including Jesse Jackson's and Congressman Rangel's, to pressure the federal government to take a more forthright, appropriate and effective stand. For, although we will still have a black family problem, even without the drug epidemic, the drug problem complicates and demoralizes any other efforts. Black men's forums in Chicago, Los Angeles, Denver and Cincinnati, are cropping up as self-help peer groups devoted to black male understanding and responsibility.

Black fathers councils are being prepared and advocated by psychologist Lige Dailey, to promote the idea and the ideal of black fatherhood. Dr. Morris F.X. Jeff, of New Orleans, president of the black social workers, has sought to elevate and rescue the level of discourse and dialogue on the issue of teenage pregnancy out of the grasp of white liberal-moderate definitions. Dr. Cecilia Arrington, a Merritt College black studies pioneer, is among those noted across the country for their courses in black family and black male/female relationships. Joseph McMillan, of the University of Louisville, has stalwartly put on a black family conference since 1970; so has University of California, Davis, and Compton College and Long Beach State (on black children). Black colleges such as North Carolina A & T and Oklahoma's Langston University, and major white universities such as the University of Pennsylvania, the University of Illinois at Chicago and Princeton University, have infused the special study of black family/male-female relationships in curricular and/or extra-curricular programs and activities.

It is good that these and many other efforts are emerging, and these are limited only by our initiative and our imaginations. In the end, however, or at the same time, we must also remember that our requirements are two-pronged, to *build* and to *resist*. For instance, the issue of AIDs is slowly being manipulated, consciously or unconsciously, by white society into a black disease. While claiming that AIDS originated in Africa, white propagandists cannot deny the fact that most persons dying of AIDS, and therefore its early carriers, are, as of this writing, white gay males. Yet, this disease uniquely has been treated as a civil rights rather than a health issue. While the affluent and well educated white gay males have been learning to practice "safe sex," the black poor have acquired it predominantly from intravenous needles and infused it into the *hetero*sexual domain, including newborn babies. Drug addicts cannot be expected to shoulder the responsibility of safe needless, let alone safe sex. Yet, the establishment has on occasion tested the babies, or mothers, or military personnel, or prisoners, or blood banks (not to mention the testing of athletes for everything under the sun — in other words, testing the helpless — while refusing to test gays or even everybody's mother's uncle in the manner of tuberculosis. The home-based quarantine, which served us well in the heyday of tuberculosis, polio, and even measles, is now likened to the red herring of leprosy and the leper colonies to win public sympathy for this handsoff political stance on AIDS. We are witnessing the process of making a black disease.

Meanwhile, black intellectuals are hungup on disproving white notions of the chemical or germinal origins of AIDS, including speculations that it is manmade or a product of some imagined but unnamed conspiracy. The issue is not so much where AIDS came from as what will be done with it now that it is here. Nor will simple programs of AIDS education and the dissemination of condoms and needles be enough. This is merely one more indication of the way in which black solutions require black definitions and an independent race-specific impact on the generation of social policies, social definitions, social trends and the broad-based, normative social agendas.

This is a challenge which the black intellectual class is best positioned to address. However, they cannot do this by operating on a me-too, open-up-and-let-me-in approach to matters social, political and economic, seeing their interests as equal only to the duplication of white liberal desires.

On the contrary, a more efficient route to clarity in negotiating and assessing racist machinations and conceptualizations is the *fictive* approach. The fictive approach routinely regards anything which the white society (master, mistress, gay liberationist or whatnot) brings us as fiction until proven fact. If it is something we have not asked for, originated, so long as we are not free, our first response or tendency must be to reject it. This is especially so in the cultural or moral domain, let alone in the realm of liberation, lest we forever find ourselves embracing pseudoliberations, treading water or slipping backwards in our endeavor to reach the other side of the muddled but rising river of white domination.

We cannot do this, as Malcolm X for one observed, by simply struggling to integrate into a burning ship, aflame with diabolical forms of white neo-racism at the helm. We will fashion and build our own ship, so help us, but meanwhile, at the very least, we must open our eyes and, with our own independent and unique vision, begin once more ourselves to locate and point out the most brilliant and proper stars for the human race to steer by.

Contributors

Bamidele A. Agbasegbe, Ph.D., has done anthropological studies in the field sites of the South Carolina Sea Island, Haiti and Nigeria. His work reported here was produced during his affiliation with the Black Family Literature Review Project in the University of Michigan's Center for Afroamerican and African Studies.

Na'im Akbar, is immediate past president of the National Association of Black Psychologists. Author of such highly regarded workds as Chains and Images of Psychological Slavery, he is on the faculty of Florida State University.

Joanna Bowers, Ph.D., is on the faculty of the College of Human Learning and Development at Governors State University in Park Forest South, Illinois.

David R. Burgest, Ph.D., a colleague of Joanna Bowers in the College of Human Learning and Development (Governors State), has studied and taught in Africa.

Bebe Moore Campbell, author of *Successful Women, Angry Men*, has won the National Endowment for the Arts Literature Award.

John Henrik Clarke, professor emeritus of African and African-American history at Hunter College in New York, and formerly an editor of *Freedomways*, is an internationally respected and published scholar-activist.

Harold Cruse, author of the seminal book of the late 1960s, *The Crisis of the Negro Intellectual*, is on the faculty of the University of Michigan. His most recent book, *Plural But Equal*, is a compelling study of the effects of integration on African-Americans today.

Julia Hare, Ed.D., is on the national motivational lecture circuit with seminars, trainings and workshops on the black family/male-female relationships. She is co-author (with Nathan Hare) of *The Endangered Black Family* and *Bringing the Black Boy to Manhood*.

Nathan Hare, Ph.D., is author of *The Black Anglo Saxons* and many articles in psychology and sociology. With Harold Cruse, he has won the National Award from the National Council for Black Studies.

Jacquelyne Johnson Jackson, Ph.D., an eminent medical sociologist, is widely published on issues in black family, health and gerontology. She is on the faculty of Duke University's Department of Psychiatry.

Morris F.X. Jeff, Ph.D., is president of the National Association of Black Social Workers as well as Director of Social Services for the City of New Orleans.

Maulana Karenga, Ph.D., a major figure in the 1960s black consciousness movement and creator of Kwanzaa, is director of the Institute of Pan-African Studies and a faculty member of the University of California at Riverside.

Jawanza Kunjufu, Ph.D., a popular lecturer and workshop leader, is author of such books as *Countering the Conspiracy to Destroy Black Boys, Volumes I & II, Developing Positive Self-Images and Discipline in Black Children, Motivating Black Youth to Work, and Lessons in History.*

Haki Madhubuti, director of the Institute for Positive Education, is editor of *Black Books Bulletin* and publisher of Third World Press. Perhaps the most influential black poet to come out of the late 1960s, he is on the Chicago State University faculty.

The Honorable Gus Savage is a member of the U.S. House of Representatives. Congressman Savage represents the Second District of the State of Illinois and is active with the Congressional Black Caucus.

Joseph Scott, Ph.D., is a prominent black sociologist and chairman of the Department of Afroamerican Studies at the University of Washington. He was for many years the chairman of black studies at the University of Notre Dame.

Robert Staples, Ph.D., a widely published authority on the black family, is author of many articles and books, including *Black Masculinity, The World of the Singles* and *The Black Woman*. He is on the faculty of the University of California, San Francisco.

James Stewart, Ph.D., a promising young economist, is chairman of black studies at Pennyslvania State University. He has published many articles and has taught at the University of Notre Dame.

Alex Swan, Ph.D., a widely published sociologist of the black condition, including the book, *Families of Black Prisoners*, is Dean of the College of Liberal Arts at Houston's Texas Southern University.

Erica Tollett, a freelance writer, works for a social policy agency in Washington, D.C. She is the mother of two sons and the daughter of Kenneth Tollett, the eminent black educator.

Footnotes and References

Crisis in Black Sexual Politics   by Nathan Hare, Ph.D. and Julia Hare, Ed.D.

1. Weathers, Diane, *et.al.*, "A New Black Struggle," *Newsweek* (August 27, 1979), pp. 58-60.
2. Murray, Charles, *Losing Ground.* New York: Basic Book, 1984.
3. Hare, Nathan and Hare, Julia, "Strong Women, Emasculated Men ("The Debate: Black Families," Opinion Page), *USA Today,* (May 7, 1984), p. 10A.
4. Hare, Nathan, "Is the Black Middle Class Blowing It?" *Ebony* (Special Issue: "The New Black Middle Class," August, 1987.
5. Shapiro, Thomas, Population Control Politics: Women, Sterilization, and Reproductive Choice. Philadelphia: Temple University Press, 1985, passim.
6. Hare, Nathan and Hare, Julia, "Unisexualization: Blueprint for Genocide," *Black Male/Female Relationship,* No. 7 (Autumn, 1982), pp. 7-26.
7. Davis, Angela, "Racism, Birth Control and Reproductive Rights," in *Women, Race and Class.* New York: Random House, 1981 (Vintage Books Edition, 1983), pp. 202-221, and *passim.*
8. Ben Wattenberg, "The Birth Death," *U.S. News & World Report* (cover story, 1987).
9. "Parental Leave Gets Senate OK," San Francisco *Examiner,* (August 27, 1988), p. A-3.
10. Wilson, William Julius, *The Truly Disadvantaged: The Inner City, the Underclass and Public Policy.* Chicago: University of Chicago Press, 1987.
11. Rodgers, Harrell, Jr. *Poor Women, Poor Families: The Economic Plight of America's Female-Headed Households.* Amonk, New York: M.E. Sharpe, Inc., 1986.
12. Billingsley, Andrew. *Black Families in White America.* Englewood Cliffs, N.J.: Parentice-Hall, Inc., 1968.
13. Edelman, Marian Wright. *Families in Peril: An Agenda for Social Change.* Cambridge: Harvard University Press, 1987.
14. Linda Greenhouse, "Church-State Debate on Child-Care Bill," reprinted from the *New York Times,* in the *San Francisco Chronicle,* September 20, 1988), p. A23.
15. *Ibid.*
16. Kathleen Teltsch, "Foundations Expand Family Planning Aid Abroad," *New York Times,* (September 5, 1988), pp. 1, 7.
17. Frances Cress Welsing, M.D., "When Birth Is A Tragedy -- Black Teenage Reproduction." (undated, authors' files).
18. World Bank, "Slowing Population Growth," in *Population Change and Economic Development.* "Reprinted with adaptations from *World Development Report 1984,* of which it formed

Part II"), Wash., D.C.: International Bank for Reconstruction and Development/The World Bank. Published for the World Bank by Oxford University Press, New York etc., 1985, p. 73.

19. Hare, Nathan and Hare, Julia, "Teenage Pregnancy: Myth?", *The Final Call* (August 20, 1988).
20. "Racism,", Low, W. Augustus and Low, Virgil, eds. *Encyclopedia of Black America*. New York: Da Capo Press (A Subsidiary of Plenum Publishing Corporation, Reprinted by arrangement with McGraw-Hill, 1981, pp. 711-723.
21. Grant, Madison. *The Passing of the Great Race*. New York: C. Scribner, 1916.
22. Goddard, Lothrop. *The Rising Tide of Color*. New York: C. Scribner, 1920.
23. Hussein Abdilahi Bulhan. *Frantz Fanon and the Psychology of Oppression*. New York: Plenum Press, 1985. p. 8.
24. Hare, Nathan, "The Fads and Foibles of Black Radical Sociologists," *The Black Sociologist*, (journal of the Association of Black Sociologists, Circa 1975-77
25. Lasch, Christopher. *The Culture of Narcissism: American Life in an Age of diminishing Expectations*. New York: W.W. Norton & Co., 1978.
26. Hare, Nathan and Hare, Julia. *Bringing the Black Boy to Manhood: The Passage*. San Francisco: Black Think Tank, 1985.
27. Herskovitz, Melville, "Significance of West Africa for Negro Research," *Journal of Negro History*, 1936, pp. 15-30. Herskovitz, Merklville, Melville, "The Ancestry of the American Negro," *American Scholar (1938-39), pp. 84-94. Herksovitz, Melville. Myth of the Negro Past*. New York: Harper, 1941. Herksovitz, Melville. "Present Status and Needs of Afro-American Research," *Journal of Negro Histroy*, 36 (1851), pp. 123-47.
28. Nobles, Wade W. *Africanity and the Black Family: The Development of a Theoretical Model*. Oakland, California: The Institute for the Advanced Study of the Family, 1985.
29. Hale-Benson, Janice. *Black Children: Their Roots, Culture, and Learning Syles* Salt Lake City: Brigham Young University Press, 1982. Reissued by John Hopkins University Press, 1986, p. 10 and *passim*.
30. Patterson, Orlando, "Rethinking Black History," *African Report*, 17 (1972), pp. 29-31. This article also appeared in Harvard's campus newspaper about the same time, though no exact date is currently in our files.
31. Hare, Nathan, "What Black Intellectuals Misunderstand about the Black Family," *Black World*, 20 (March, 1976), pp. 4-14.
32. Nobles, *op. cit.*
33. Moynihan, Daniel P. *The Negro Family; The Case for National Action*. Washington, D.C.: Office of Policy Planning and Research, United States Department of Labor, March 1965.
34. Frazier, E. Franklin. *The Negro Family in the United States*. Chicago: The University of Chicago Press, 1939. See also his *The Negro Family in Chicago*, Chiago: The University of Chicago Press, 1932. Also, *The Negro in the United States*. New York: Macmillan, 1949.
35. DuBois, W.E.B. *The Negro American Family*. Atlanta: Atlanta University Press, 1908.
36. Gould, J. and Kolb, W., eds. *A Dictionary of the Social Sciences*. New York: The Free Press of Glencoe, 1964.
37. *Webster's New Collegiate Dictionary*. Based on Webster's New International Dictionary. Springfield, Massachusetts: Merriam Co.
38. Diop, Cheikh Anta. *The Cultural Unity of Black Africa* Chicago: Third World Press, 1978 (originally published by *Presence Africaine in Paris in 1959, under the title of L'United Cultuirelle De L'Afrique Noire.*
40. Farrakhan, Louis, *"The Color Purple"* (Audio-visual tape of a lecture on the book, The Color Purple, by Alice Walker, circa 1986).
41. Greer, Germaine. *Sex & Destiny: The Politics of Human Fertility*. New York: Harper Colophon Books, 1985. Freidan, Betty. *The Second Stage*. New York: Summit Books, 1981.

42. Goldberg, Steven. *The Inevitability of patriarchy: Why the Biological Difference between Men and Women Always Produces Male Domination.* New York: William Morrow & Co., 1973, *passim.*
43. Goldberg, Steven, "Anthropology and the Limits of Societal Variation," *ibid,* pp. 29-74; "Confusion and Fallacy in the Feminist Analysis," *ibid,* pp. 158-184, and *pasim.*
44. Van Sertima, Ivan, *op. cit., passim.*
45. Leary, Warren, "Panel Supports Research Uses of Fetal Tissue," *New York Times,* Spetember 16, 1988, pp. 1, 7.
46. Moynihan, *op. cit.*
47. Gibbs, Jewelle Taylor, ed. *Young, Black, and Male in America: An Endangered Species.* Dover, Massachusetts: Auburn House, 1988.
48. Gibbs, Jewelle Taylor, "Black Males Are Threatened," (cover arrtilce on a flyer distributed by Tayyib Islamic books & Things, Sharker Heights, Ohio, September, 1988.
49. Murray, *op. cit.*
50. Scott, Joseph and Steward, James, "The Institutional Decimation of the Black Male," *Western Journal of Black Studies*
51. Hare, Nathan and Hare, Julia. *The Endangered Black Family.* San Francisco: The Black Think Tank, 1984.
52. Skolnick, Arlene S. and Skolnick, Jerome, "Rethinking the Family," *Family in Transition.* Boston: Little, Brown and Co., 1971. See also Hare, Nathan, "Revolution Without a Revolution: The Psychosociology of Sex and Race," *The Black Scholar,* 9 (April, 1978), pp. 2-7.
53. Gibbs, Jewelle Taylor, *op. cit.,* pp. 97-128.
54. Larson, "Employment and Unemployment of Young Black Males," in Gibbs, Jewelle Taylor, ed., *op. cit.,* pp. 97-128.
55. Cruse, Harold, *The Crisis of the Black Intellectual.* New York: William Morrow & Co., 1967. Fanon, Frantz. *Black Skin, White Masks.* Tr. by Markmann, C.L. New York: Grove Press, 1967 (first published in the French, 1952). Frazier, E. Franklin, *Black Bourgeoisie. Glencoe, Illinois: Free Press, 1957.* Hare, Nathan. *The Black Anglo Saxons.* New York: Marzani and MUnsell, 1965 (reissued by Thunder and Ligtning Press, with Collier-Macmillan, 1970; scheduled to be released, Chicago: Third World Press, February, 1989).
56. Woodson, Carter G., *This Miseducation of the Negro,* Washington, D.C.: The Associated Publishers, 1933.

The Black Male   Female Connection   by Maulana Karenga, Ph.D.

1. Boggs, James and Grace Boggs. *Revolution and Evolution in the Twentieth Century,* New York: Monthly Review Press, 1973.
2. Toure, Sekou. *Towards Full Reafricanization.* Paris: Presence Africaine, 1959.
3. Wallace, Michelle. *Black Macho and the Myth of the Superwoman.* New York: Dial Press, 1979.
4. Shange, Ntozake. *For Colored Girls.* New York; Emerson Hill Company, 1977.
5. Karenga, Maulana. "On Wallace's Myth: Wading Thru Troubled Waters," in *The Black Scholar.* Vol. 10, No 8,9 (May/June, 1979) 36-39.
6. Jackson, Jacqueline. "But Where Are The Men," in Robert Staples(ed) *The Black Family: Essays and Studies.* Belmont, Ca.: Wadsworth Publishing Company, Inc., 1978, pp. 64-67
8. *Ibid.*
9. Karenga, Maulana. *Beyond Connections: Liberation i Lova and Struggle.* New Orleans: Ahidiana, 1978, 87-89.
   Madhubuti, Haqki. "Not Allowed To Be Lovers," *Black Books Bulletin,* Vol. 6, No. 4 (1980) 48-57, 71.
10. Karenga, Maulana. *op. cit,* p. 4.
11. Phillips, William. "Writing About Sex," *Partisan Review,* Vol. 34 (Fall, 1967) 552-563.
12. Karenga, *op. cit.,* 15

13. Nobles, Wade. "Africanity: Its Role In Black Families," in Robert Staples(ed) *The Black Family: Essays and Studies.* Belmont, Ca,: Wadsworth Publishing Company, Inc., 1978, pp. 19-25.

Note: Karenga, Maulana. Essays on Struggle: Position and analysis. San Diego: kawaida Publications, 1978b.

Black Men: Obsolete, Single and Dangerous   by Haki Madhubuti

1. Bogle, Donald. *Toms, Coons, Mulattoes, Mammies and Bucks,* New York: The Viking Press, Inc. 1973.
2. Day, Beth. *Sexual Life Between Blacks and Whites.* New York: Oxford World Publishing. 1972.
3. de Vise, Pierre. *62% of Black Births in Chicago are Illegitimate.* 79, 13.
4. Douglas, Grace *Rape: Taking by Force.* Rumbel. 1978.
5. *Children born to Unmarried Women.* Washington Post 5.4.78.
6. Freedman, Daniel G. *Human Socio-biology.* New York: The Free Press. 1979.
7. Gardner, John W. *Morale,* New W.W. Norton & Co., Inc. 1978.
8. Gibson, D. Parks, *70 Billion in the Black.* New York: Mac Millan, 1978.
9. Gilder, George. *Sexual Suicide.* New York: Quadrangle. 1973.
10. Goldberg, Steven. *The Inevitability of Patriarchy. New York: Morrow, 1974.*
11. *Hernton, C. Alvin, Sex and Racism* New York: Doubleday. 1965.
12. Kenyatta, Jomo, *Facing Mt. Kenya.* London: Secker & Warburg. 1938.
13. Lorenz, Konrad. *On Agression.* New York: Bantam. 1967.
14. Morin, Richard. *Profile of an: Under 30, Male Frustrated, Washington, D.C.* Washington Post, 1980.
15. Perkins, Eugene. *Home is a Dirty Street: The Malcolm X Doctrine.* Chicago: Ujamaa Distributors. 1968.
16. Scott, Joseph, School Age *Black Books Bulletin.* 1979. Polgygyny: A Futuristic Family Arrangement for African-Americans. *Black books Bulletin,* Summer, 1976.
17. Staples, robert. *The Black Woman in America.*Chicago- Nelson Hall. Introduction to Black Sociology. New York: McGraw Hill Gook. 1976. The Myth of Black Sexual Superiority: A Re-examination. The Black Scholar. April, 1978.
18. Stember, Charles Herbert. *Sexual Racism.* New York: Harper Colphon Books. 1976.
19. Storr, Anthony. *Human Destructiveness.* New York: Basic 1972.
20. Tiger, Lionel. *Omnigamy: The New Kinskip System. Psychology Today.* 1978.
21. J. Jackson, *"Where are the Black Men?"* The Black Scholar, Reprinted in *Ebony,* 1970

Erroneous Assumptions Black Men Make About Black Women
                    David R. Burgest, Ph.D., and Joanna Bower, Ph.D.

Barbour, Floyd(ed); *The Black Power Revolt:* Boston Porter Sargent, 1968.
Grier, William and Price Cobes; (Black Rage, New York: Basic books, 1968
Hare, Nathan, *The Black Anglo Saxons,* New York: Marzani and Munsell, 1965.
Herskovitz, Melville J.; *The Myth of the Negro Past,* Boston: Beacon Press, 1958.
Lifton, Robert J. (Ed); *The Women in American,* Cambridge: Houghton Mifflin Co., 1965.
Moynihan, Daniel; *The Negro Family: The Case for National Action,* Government Printing Office, March, 1965.
Myrdal, Gunnar; *An American Dilemma,* New York: Harper & Row, 1962.
Reuter, Edward B.; *Race Mixture,* New York: McGraw-Hill, 1931.

Men Who Play   Jacqueline Johnson Jackson, Ph.D.

1. Jackson, Jacqelyn Johnson, "Black women in a racist society." In Charles V. Willie, Bernard M Kramer and Bertram S Brown (eds). *Racism and Mental Health.* Pittsburg: University

180

of Pittsburg Press.

2. Jackson, Jacquelyne Johnson. "But where are the men?" *The Black Scholar.* December, 1971, pp. 30-41.

3. Moynihan, Daniel. *The Negro Family: The Case for National Action.* Government Printing Office, March, 1965.

Beauty and the Beast: The Role of Physical Attraction in the Black Community
by Robert Staples, Ph.D.

1. Regina Turner, The Ordeal of the ugly black Woman. *Balck Male/Female Relationships.* Number Six (Winter, 1982), pp. 21-29.

2. Helen fisher, Female Sex Appeal an Asset Even in Prehistoric Times. *Jet,* April 29, 1981, p.43.

3. Ellen Berscheid and Elaine Walser, Beauty and the Beast, *Psychology Today.* 6, 1971: 42-47.

4. Louis Villa, *The Sexuality of a Black American.* Oakland: Ashforn Press, 1982.

5. Pearl Stewart, Shades of Black. *Oakland Tribune.* May 13, 1979, p.18.

6. Dolly Katz, *High Blood Pressure Perils Dark Blacks, Light Whites.* Detroit Free Press, January 31, 1979, p. 15-A.

7. Horace Cayton and St. Clair Drake, *Black Metropolis.* New York, Harcourt Brace and Jovanovich, 1945.

8. Thomas Pettigrew, *et.al.,* Color Gradations and Attitudes among Middle Income Negroes. *American Sociological Review.* 31, 1966: 365-374.

9. E. Franklin Frazier, *The Black Bourgeoisie,* New York: Colier, 1957.

10. Trellie Jeffers, The Black Woman and the Black Middle Class. *The Black Scholar.* 4. 1973: 37-41.

12. Roper Organization, *The Virginia Slims American Women's Opinion* 3, 1974, p.20.

13. Ten Things Men Notice About Women. *Jet Magazine,* June 7, 1981, pp. 38-39.

14. Gilbert Kaats and Keith Davis, The Dynamics of Sexual Behavior of College Students. *Journal of Marriage and the Family,* 32, 1970, 390-399.

16. J. Richard Udry, the Importance of Being Beautiful: A Reexamination and Racial Comparison. *American Journal of Sociology,* 83, 1977, 154-160.

17. Quote in the *San Francisco Chronicle,* August 4, 1979, p. 31.

19. Sheila Banks, Success and Beauty: A Blessing or a Curse. *Ebony,* 33, 1978: 33-42.

20. Marla Zellerbach, The Good, The Bad, The Beautiful. *San Francisco Chronicle.* June 13, 1979, p.37.

21. Arthur J. Snider, Men, Women View Beauty Differently. *Tallahassee Democrat.* December 4, 1977, p.15E.

22. Clifford Kirkpatrik and John Cotton, Physical Attractiveness, Age and Marital Adjustment. *American Sociological Review.* 16, 1951: 81-86.

23. Jack Slater, Football Star's Wife Tells of Problems of Looking White. *Ebony.* 37, 1981: 110-116.

24. Roper Organization, *loc. cit.*

25. Ten Things women Notice About Men. *Jet Magazine.* May 31, 1982, p.52.

Woman-to-Woman Marriages in Africa and African-America
Bamidele Ade Agbasegbe, Ph.D.

1. Ye Ye A. F. Olade, "Many a Lost Tomorrow: A Sister Speaks from Afraics," *Black Male/Famale Relationships,* 1980, 2(1), p. 19-20.

2. Audre Lorde, "Scratching the Surface: Some Notes on Barriers to Women and Loving," *The Black Scholar,* 1978, 9(7), pp. 31-5.

3. *Ibid.*

4. *Ibid.,* p. 33.

5. Lorde, *op. cit.,* p. 33-4.

6. *Ibid.,* p. 34.

7. *Ibid.*
8. John S. Mbiti, *Love and Marriage in Africa.* London: Longman, 1983.
9. *Ibid.,* p. 35.
10. Lorde, *op. cit.,* p. 34.
11. *Ibid.,* p. 35.
12. Lorde, *op. cit.*
13. Woman-to-woman marriage is one of three types of phenomena that anthropologists working in Africa have genericly call "Woman Marriages," Bamidele Agbasegbe (1980a, 1980b, 1981) calls the other types Adjunctive marriage and posthumous marriage. In an adjunctive marriage an older married barren woman presents a bride-gift for a genetrix who (with the barren woman's husband) will procreate descendants that will be regarded as the lawful offspring of the infertile female. The gentrix is thus an adjunct or an annexation to an already existing marriage. In posthumous marriage, a woman in behalf of an heirless deceased kinsman (i.e., husband, son, father, brother) will contract a marriage in his name to a fertile female who (with the assistance of a genitor) will procreate lawful descrendants to the decesased man.

   The nuptial arrangements that anthropologists designate as *woman marriages* have been discussed in various contexts: (re)definition of marriage, descent, friendship, social context of aging, sex roles, gender identity, sexual stratification, and so forth. See e.g. Agbasegbe (1975, 1980a, 1980b, 1981); Bohannan (1949); Brian (1976); Herskovitz (1937); Huber (1968-1969); Krige (1974); Oboler (1980); O'Brien (1977), Sudarkasa (1980).
14. Charles Meerk, *The Northern Tribes of Nigeria,* 1925, Vol. 1. London: Oxford University Press.
15. Melville Herskovitz, "A Note on 'Woman Marriage' in Dahomey," *Africa,* 1937, 10 (3): pp. 335-41. *Dahomey: An Ancient West African Kingdom.* Vol. 1. New York: Augustine, 1938, pp. 318, 320.
16. G.P. Murdock, *et. al, An Outline of World Cultural Materials.* Behavior Science Outlines, 1961, Vol. 1, New Haven: Human Relations Files.
17. Anonymous, "When A Woman Weds a Woman," *African Progress,* 1949, 1 (3) pp. 22-4. E.E. Evens-Pritchard, *Some Aspects of Marriage and the Family Among the Nuer.* Livingstone: The Rhodes-Livingstone Institute, 1945. Max Gluckman, "Kingship and Marriage among the Lozi of Northern Rhodesia and the Zulu of Natal," in A.R. Radcliffe-Brown and D. Forde (eds.), *African Systems of Kinshipand Marriage.* London: Oxford University Press. 1950, pp. 184, 196. Melville Herskovitz, *op. cit.,* p. 335-341. Herksovitz. *op. cit.,* 1938, pp. 320-1. Eileen J. Krite, "Woman Marriage" with special reference to the Lovedu- Its Significance for the Definition of Marriage, *Africa,* 1974, 44 (1), pp. 11-37. Victor C. Uchendu, *The Igbo of Southeast Nigeria.* New York: Holt, Rinehart and Winston, 1965, p. 86.
18. Anonymous, *op. city.,* 1971, pp. 22-3.
19. *Ibid.,* p. 23.
20. *Ibid.,* p. 24.
21. *Ibid.*
22. Herskovitz, *op. cit.,* 1937, p. 338; Herkovitz, *op. cit.,* 1938, p. 320-1.
23. It is interesting to note that Herskovits, unlike Lorde, did not extend his pernicious notions regarding African homosexual woman-to-woman marriages to an analogy with female homosexuality among Afroamericans. Rather, in his book, *The Myth of the Negro Past,* Herskovitz (1941: 172) asserted that the cultural link or heritage of the "self-sufficient" female husband-father in West Africa manifest itself among "competent, self-sufficient" Afroamerican females who *choose* to have children while at the same time declining a marital relationship with a man.
24. No doubt there are some social scientists and laypersons who do not consider same sex unions in America as true marriages. Marriage, as used in this paper to refer to same sex unions among Afroamerican females, to a large measure rests on the emic conceptualization of the parties involved in the union (see Lucas, 1978).

25. Ethel Sawyer, "A Study of a Public Lesbian Community," Master's thesis, 1965. Washington Unviersity. (Cited in Martin S. Weinberg and Alan P. Bell. *Homosexuality. An Annotated Bibliography.* New York: Harper & Row, 1972.)
26. Bob Lucas, "Lesbian 'Wife' Seeks Court Aid to Make 'Husband' Pay," *Jet, 1978, 54 (17), pp. 46-8.*
27. *Ibid.* p. 48.
28. Audred Lorde, *op. cit.,* 1978, p. 29.

Additional References:
Bamidele A. Agbasegbe, "Is There Marriage between Women in Africa?", in J.S. Williams. *et. al.* &eds), *Sociological Research Symposium V.* Richmond, VA.' Virginia Commonwealth University, 1975, p. 202-7.

Bamidele A. Agbasegbe, "Posthumous Marriage sin Traditional African Soceities: A Re-examination, Unpublished manuscript. 1980.

Bamidele A. Agbasegbe, "Women Without Sons: Some Perspective on Aging Females, 'Woman Marriage': Toward a Typology of the Phenomena and a Reassessment of the Concept." Unpublished manuscript.

Laura Bohannan, "Dahomean Marriage: A Revaluation." *Africa,* 1949, 19 (4), pp. 273-87.

Robert Brian, "Female Husbands and Male Wives," *Friends and Lovers.* New York: Basic books, 1976, pp. 55-75, 268.

Evans Pritchard, *Kinship and Marriage among the Nuer.* London: Oxford University Press, 1951.

Hugo Huber, "Woman Marriage" in Some East African Societies.

Anthropos, 1968-69, 63/64 (5/6), pp. 745-52.

Dregina Oboler, "Is the Female Husband A Man? Woman/Woman Marriage among the Nandi of Kenya," *Ethnology,* 1980, 19(1).

Denise O'Brien, "Female Husbands in Southern Bantu Societies," in Alice Schlegel (ed.), *Sexual Statification: A Cross-Cultural View.* New York: Columbia University Press, 1977, p. 109-26.

Not Allowed To Be Friends And/Or Lovers   Jawanza Kunjuku, Ph.D.
1. *U.A. News,* Jan 22, 1979, p. 47.
2. *U.S. Statistical Abstract,* 1978, passim.
3. *Ibid.*
4. Diop, Cheikh Anta, *Cultural Unity of Black Africa.* Third World Press, 1978, Chicago, p. iii.
5. *Black Books Bulletin,* Vol, 6, No. 4, p. 61-65.

Conclusions and Solutions: A Complete Theory of the Black Family   Nathan Hare, Ph.D.
1. Wilson B Key, *Subliminal Seducation.* New York. New American Library, 1974.
2. William Grier, M.D. and Price Cobb, M.D. "Mental Illness and Treatment," *Black Rage.* New York: Basic Books.
3. 1968, pp. 154-180 *New York Times,* 1988.
4. Daniel Patrick Moynihan. *The Moynihan Report: The Case for National Action.* Office of Policy Planning and Research: U.S. Department of Labor, March, 1965.
5. Cf. Arlene S. Skolnick and Jerome H. Skolnick, "Rethinking the Family," *Family in Transition.* 1971.
6. Alan Bullock and Oliver Stallybrass, eds. *The Harper Dictionary of Modern Thought.* New York: Harper & Row, 1977, p. 16.
7. Gunnar Myrdal. *An American Dilemma.* New York: Harpers & Brothers, 1944.
8. Nathan and Julia Hare, "The Black Woman: 1970," *Transaction Vol. 8* (November-December), 1970, pp. 65-68.
9. Germaine Greer. *Sexual Destiny: The Politics of Human Fertility.* New York: Harper Colophon Books, 1984. Betty Friedan, *The Second Stage.* New York: Summit Books, 1981.

10. Fred Hapgood. *Why Males Exist: An Inquiry into the Evolution of Sex.* New York: New American Library, 1979.
11. Daniel Patrick Moynihan, *op. cit., passim.* See also the thoughtful book by Douglas Glassow, *The Black Underclass: Poverty, Unemployment and Entrepoven of Ghetto Youth.* New York: Random House, 1980.
12. Georg Wilheim Friedrich Hegel. Cf. his essay on the master and the slave.
13. *Ibid.*
14. Louis Farrakhan, video tape on "The Color Purple," *circa 1986.* This was an exceedingly profound and insightful lecture.
15. Thomas Shapiro. *Population Control Politics: Women, Sterilization, and Reproductive Choice.* Philadelphia: Temple University Press, 1985, p. 155.
16. Cf. Charlyn A. Harper-Bolton, "A Reconceptualization of the African-American Woman," *Black Male/Female Relationships,* Winter, 1982, pp. 32-42.
17. Kerby T. Alvy. *Black Parenting: Strategies for Training* New York: Irvington Publishers, 1987.
18. Nathan Hare and Julia Hare, "Black Love Groups (Kupenda) -- How It Works," Black Male/Female Relationships, Vol. 1. (November,1 979), pp. 21-24.
19. The Portland Public Schools' baseline manual for teachers, despite its primary focus on the historical component, is an excellent compendium and would make a good college black studies textbook or cupplement, rivaled only by Maulana Karenga's seminal *Introduction to Black Studies:* Los Angeles, California: Kawaida Publications, 1982. See Mathew W. Prophet, Superintendent, *African-American Baseline Essays.* Portland, Oregon: Portland Public Schools, 1987.

Sexual Anorexia   by Nathan Hare, Ph.D., and Julia Hare, Ed.D.
1. Nathan Hare, Ph.D., *Black Male/Female Relations,* Unpublished Ph.D. dissertation. Berkeley: California School of Professional Psychology, 1975.
2. Janice L. Green, "Temporary Celibacy," *Black Male/Female Relationships.* Year 2, #5, 1981. Audrey Chapman, *Mansharing* 1986.
3. Rollo May, *Love and Will.*
4. Ernie Smith, Ph.D., quoted in "What Makes a Man a Pimp?", *The Endangered* Black Family, San Francisco: Black Think Tank, 1984, pp. 69-76.